THE USBORNE ILLUSTRATED
DICTIONARY OF BIOLOGY

Corinne Stockley

Designed by Nerissa Davies

Scientific advisors:

Dr. Margaret Rostron and Dr. John Rostron

Illustrated by: Kuo Kang Chen
Ian Jackson, Chris Lyon, Sue Stitt, Jeremy Banks, Peter Bull,
Chris Shields, Eric Robson, Alan Harris, Gabrielle Smith,
Jayne Goin, Annabel Milne, Jeane Colville and Sue Walliker.

Contents

General

4	Living things and their environment
6	Within an ecosystem
8	Life and life cycles
10	The structure of living things
12	Cell division

Plants

14	Vascular plants
16	Stems and roots
18	Inside an older plant
20	Leaves
22	Types of leaf
23	Plant sensitivity
24	Plant fluid transportation
26	Plant food production
28	Flowers
30	Reproduction in a flowering plant
31	Types of flower
32	Seeds and germination
34	Fruit/Vegetative reproduction

Animals

36	The body structure of animals
38	Animal body coverings
40	Animal movement
42	Animal feeding
44	Animal respiration
45	Animal excretion
46	Animal senses and communication
48	Animal reproduction and development

Humans

50	The skeleton
52	Joints and bone
54	Muscles
56	Teeth
58	Blood
60	The circulatory system
62	The heart
64	Tissue fluid and the lymphatic system
66	The digestive system
68	Glands
70	The respiratory system
72	The urinary system
74	The central nervous system
76	The units of the nervous system
78	Nerves and nervous pathways
82	The skin
84	The eyes
86	The ears
88	The reproductive system
90	Development and reproduction

General

92	Types of reproduction
94	Cell division for reproduction
96	Genetics and heredity
99	Fluid movement
100	Food and how it is used
102	Metabolism
104	Energy for life
105	Homeostasis
106	Hormones
108	Digestive juices and enzymes
109	Vitamins and their uses
110	Plant classification
112	Animal classification
114	Informal group terms
115	Index

First published in 1986 Usborne Publishing Ltd, 20 Garrick Street, London WC2E 9BJ, England.

Copyright © 1986 Usborne Publishing Ltd.

The name Usborne and the device ⬚ are Trade Marks of Usborne Publishing Ltd.

Printed in Great Britain

About this book

Biology is the study of living things. It can be divided into two major areas of study – botany (the study of plant life) and zoology (the study of animal life). This book also divides the subject up, using five main colour-coded sections.

Yellow section / A general introduction to all living things.

Blue section / Botany section – definitions relating to plants.

Green section / First zoology section – specific terms relating to various different animals.

Red section / Second zoology section – terms related to human biology

(the study of humans as living things). In many cases, its terms also apply to animals in the same group as humans, (i.e. the vertebrates – see page 113).

Black and white section / Terms in this section relate to all the different types of living thing. It includes charts and tables directly linked to subjects earlier in the book, the formal classification charts and a page of informal group terms.

How to use this book

This book can be used as a dictionary, or as a revision handbook. The definitions are arranged thematically, that is, all the words to do with the same subject are grouped together, in most cases on two facing pages. These subjects are listed as contents on page 2. The index on pages 115-128 forms the dictionary reference section. It is an alphabetical list of all the individual definitions in the book, giving page numbers for both main entries and supplementary entries. See page 115 for more about the use of the index.

Key to use of the book

1. Every main definition is preceded by a dot, and the entry word is printed in bold type, e.g.:

   • **Cytoplasm**.

2. Any singulars or plurals (which are not simply the addition of a letter s) follow straight after an entry, e.g.:

   • **Stomata** (sing. **stoma**).

3. Any synonyms of the word also follow immediately, e.g.:

   • **Cnidoblasts** or **thread cells**.
   (only one synonym)

   • **Red blood cells**. Also called **red corpuscles** or **erythrocytes**.
   (more than one synonym)

4. Many other words are also printed in bold. These are either defined where they appear, or the bold type is a sign that their own definitions can be found elsewhere on the same two pages.

5. If a word is in bold type and has an asterisk (*), it is defined elsewhere in the book and is in the footnote at the bottom of the page.

6. This is a typical footnote:

*Integuments**, 30 (**Ovules**); **Nucleus**, 10; **Stigma**, **Style**, 29.

a) The word **integuments** can be found inside the text of the main definition entry **Ovules** on page 30.

b) **Nuclei*** (the plural) may have been what appeared in the text, rather than **nucleus***. The singular is given since this is the entry word on page 10.

Living things and their environment

The world can be divided into a number of different regions, each with its own characteristic plants and animals. All the plants and animals have become adapted to their own surroundings, or **environment** (see **adaptive radiation**, page 9), and their lives are interwoven in a complex web of interdependence. The environment is influenced by many different factors, e.g. temperature, water and light (**climatic factors**), the physical and chemical properties of the soil (**edaphic factors**) and the activities of the living things (**biotic factors**). The study of the relationships between plants, animals and the environment is called **ecology**.

●**Biosphere.** The layer of the earth (including the oceans and the atmosphere) which is inhabited by living things, bounded (above) by the upper atmosphere and (below) by the first layers of uninhabited rock.

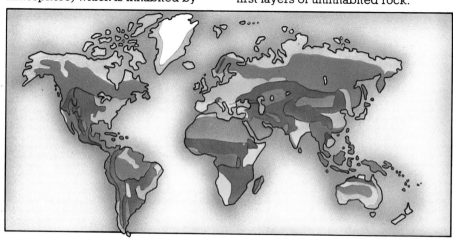

Key to biomes

Tundra. Very cold and windy. Commonest plants: **lichens*** and small shrubs. Animals include musk ox.

Coniferous forest. Low temperatures all year. Dominant plants: **conifers***, e.g. spruce. Commonest large animals: deer.

Deciduous forest. Summers warm, winters cold. Dominant plants: **deciduous*** trees, e.g. beech. Many animals, e.g. foxes.

Tropical forest. High temperatures all year, heavy rainfall. Great variety of plants and animals, e.g. exotic birds.

Grassland / savannah. Main plants: grasses, but savannah (with more rainfall) also has trees. Typical animals: giraffe.

Desert. High temperatures (cold at night), very low rainfall. Dominant plants: cacti. Animals include camels, scorpions.

Other areas

Scrubland (**maquis**)   Ice   Mountains

●**Biomes.** The main ecological regions into which the land surface can be divided. Each has its own characteristic seasons, day length, rainfall pattern and maximum and minimum temperatures. The major biomes are **tundra, coniferous forest, deciduous forest, tropical forest, temperate grassland, savannah** (tropical grassland) and **desert**. Most are named after the dominant vegetation, since this determines all other living things found there. Each is a giant **habitat** (**macrohabitat**).

* **Conifers**, 111; **Deciduous**, 8; **Lichens**, 114 (**Symbionts**)

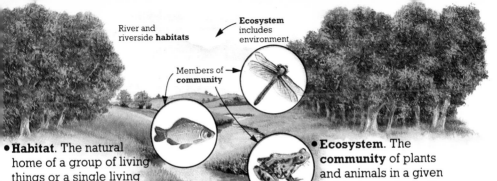

River and riverside **habitats**

Ecosystem includes environment

Members of **community**

- **Habitat**. The natural home of a group of living things or a single living thing. Small habitats can be found within large habitats, e.g. a river in the **deciduous forest biome**. Very small specialized habitats are called **microhabitats**, e.g. a rotting tree.

- **Community**. The group of plants and animals found in one **habitat**. They all interact with each other and their environment.

- **Ecosystem**. The **community** of plants and animals in a given **habitat**, together with their environment. An ecosystem is a self-contained unit, i.e. the plants and animals interact to produce all the material they need (see also pages 6-7).

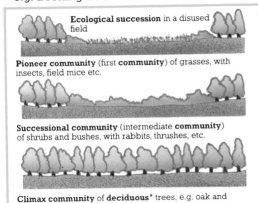

Ecological succession in a disused field

Pioneer community (first **community**) of grasses, with insects, field mice etc.

Successional community (intermediate **community**) of shrubs and bushes, with rabbits, thrushes, etc.

Climax community of **deciduous*** trees, e.g. oak and beech, with foxes, badgers, warblers, etc.

- **Ecological succession**. A process which occurs whenever a new area of land is colonized, e.g. a forest floor after a fire, a farm field which is left uncultivated or a demolition site which remains unused. Over the years, different types of plants (and the animals which go with them) will succeed each other, until a **climax community** is arrived at. This is a very stable **community**, one which will survive without change as long as the same conditions prevail (e.g. the climate).

- **Ecological niche**. The place held in an **ecosystem** by a plant or animal, e.g. what it eats and where it lives. **Gause's principle** states that no two species can occupy the same niche at the same time (if they tried, one species would die out or be driven off). For example, both the curlew and the grey plover can be found (in the winter months) living around the estuaries of Britain, and eating small creatures such as worms and snails. However, they actually occupy different niches. Curlews wade in the shallows, probing the river bed for food with their long beaks. Grey plovers, by contrast, wait on the shore and pick their food off the surface (their beaks are too short for probing). Hence both birds survive in the same general area.

Curlew probing below water (long, curved beak)

Grey plover picking from surface (short beak)

* Deciduous, 8.

5

Within an ecosystem

An **ecosystem** consists of a group (**community***) of animals and plants which interact with each other and with their environment to produce a self-contained ecological unit.

- **Food web.** The complex network of **food chains** in an ecosystem. Each food chain is a linked series of living things, each of which is the food for the next in line. Plants make their food from non-living matter by **photosynthesis*** (they are **autotrophic**) and are always the first members of a chain. Animals cannot make their own food (they are **heterotrophic**) and so rely on the food-making activities of plants.

Simple **food web** ▼

Humans

Foxes

Partridges

Thrushes

Moles

Rabbits

Snails

Caterpillars

Earthworms

Vegetation

Generalized **food chain**, showing **trophic levels**

| **Producers** – green plants, which make their own food. **Trophic level T1.** | **Primary consumers** or **first order consumers** – **herbivores** (plant-eating animals), e.g. rabbits. Energy-giving material obtained directly from **producers**. **Trophic level T2.** | **Secondary consumers** or **second order consumers** – **carnivores** (flesh-eating animals), e.g. foxes, when they eat herbivores. Energy-giving material obtained from bodies of **primary consumers**. **Trophic level T3.** | **Tertiary consumers** or **third order consumers** – carnivores, e.g. foxes, when they eat smaller carnivores. Energy-giving material is obtained by most indirect method – from bodies of secondary consumers, i.e. animals which ate **producers**. **Trophic level T4.** |

Notes:

1) **Omnivores**, e.g. humans, eat plant and animal matter. They are thus placed on trophic level T2 at some times and on T3 (or T4) at others.

2) Many carnivores, e.g. foxes, will eat both herbivores and smaller carnivores. They are thus on trophic level T3 at some times and on T4 at others.

- **Trophic level** or **energy level**. The level at which living things are positioned within a **food chain** (see **food web**). At each successive level, a great deal of the energy-giving food matter is lost. For example, a cow will break down well over half of the grass it eats (to provide energy). Hence only a small part of the original energy-giving

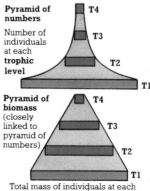

Pyramid of numbers

Number of individuals at each trophic level

T4
T3
T2
T1

Pyramid of biomass (closely linked to pyramid of numbers)

T4
T3
T2
T1

Total mass of individuals at each level (decrease is less extreme than above, since animals at higher levels tend to be larger).

material can be obtained from eating the cow (the part it used to build its own new tissue). This loss of energy means that the higher the trophic level, the fewer the number of animals, since they must eat progressively larger amounts of food to obtain enough energy. This principle is called the **pyramid of numbers**.

* **Community**, 5; **Photosynthesis**, 26.

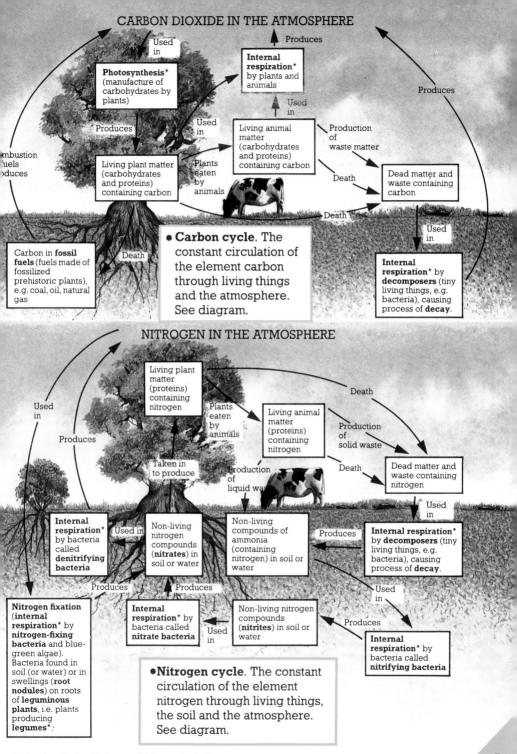

CARBON DIOXIDE IN THE ATMOSPHERE

Used in

Produces

Photosynthesis*
(manufacture of
carbohydrates by
plants)

**Internal
respiration***
by plants and
animals

Produces

Used in

Produces

Used in

Used in

Living animal
matter
(carbohydrates
and proteins)
containing carbon

Production
of
waste matter

Combustion
fuels
produces

Living plant matter
(carbohydrates
and proteins)
containing carbon

Plants
eaten
by
animals

Dead matter and
waste containing
carbon

Death

Death

Carbon in **fossil
fuels** (fuels made of
fossilized
prehistoric plants),
e.g. coal, oil, natural
gas

Death

Death

Used
in

● **Carbon cycle**. The
constant circulation of
the element carbon
through living things
and the atmosphere.
See diagram.

**Internal
respiration*** by
decomposers (tiny
living things, e.g.
bacteria), causing
process of **decay**.

NITROGEN IN THE ATMOSPHERE

Used
in

Produces

Death

Living plant
matter
(proteins)
containing
nitrogen

Plants
eaten
by
animals

Living animal
matter
(proteins)
containing
nitrogen

Production
of
solid waste

Death

Taken in
to produce

Production
of
liquid waste

Dead matter and
waste containing
nitrogen

Death

Used
in

**Internal
respiration***
by bacteria
called
**denitrifying
bacteria**

Used in

Non-living
nitrogen
compounds
(**nitrates**) in
soil or water

Non-living
compounds of
ammonia
(containing
nitrogen) in soil or
water

Produces

Internal respiration*
by **decomposers** (tiny
living things, e.g.
bacteria), causing
process of **decay**.

Produces

Produces

Used
in

Nitrogen fixation
(**internal
respiration*** by
**nitrogen-fixing
bacteria** and blue-
green algae).
Bacteria found in
soil (or water) or in
swellings (**root
nodules**) on roots
of **leguminous
plants**, i.e. plants
producing
legumes*.

**Internal
respiration*** by
bacteria called
nitrate bacteria

Used
in

Non-living nitrogen
compounds
(**nitrites**) in soil or
water

Produces

**Internal
respiration*** by
bacteria called
nitrifying bacteria

●**Nitrogen cycle**. The constant
circulation of the element
nitrogen through living things,
the soil and the atmosphere.
See diagram.

---

* **Internal respiration**, 104; **Legume**, 34; **Photosynthesis**, 26.

7

Life and life cycles

All living things show the same basic **characteristics of life**. These are respiration, feeding, growth, sensitivity (irritability), movement, excretion and reproduction. The **life cycle** of a plant or animal is the progression from its formation to its death, with all the changes this entails (in some cases, these are drastic – see **metamorphosis**, page 49). Below are some terms used to group plants and animals together according to their life cycle, or to describe characteristics of certain life cycles.

- **Perennials.** Plants which live for many years. **Herbaceous perennials**, e.g. delphiniums, lose all the parts above ground at the end of each growing season, and grow new shoots at the start of the next. **Woody perennials**, e.g. trees, produce new growth (**secondary tissue***) each year from permanent stems.

- **Biennials.** Plants which live for two years, e.g. carrots. In the first year they grow and store up food. In the second they produce flowers and seeds, and then die.

- **Annuals.** Plants which live for one year, e.g. marigolds. In this time they grow from seed, produce flowers and seeds, and then die.

- **Herbaceous.** A term describing plants which do not develop **secondary tissue*** above the ground, i.e. they are "like a herb", as distinct from shrubs and trees (**woody perennials**).

Delphinium

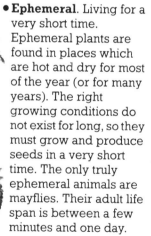

Carrot

Marigold

Phlox

- **Deciduous.** A term describing **perennials** whose leaves lose their **chlorophyll*** and fall off at the end of each growing season, e.g. beeches.

- **Evergreen.** A term describing **perennials** which do not shed their leaves at the end of a growing season, e.g. firs.

- **Ephemeral.** Living for a very short time. Ephemeral plants are found in places which are hot and dry for most of the year (or for many years). The right growing conditions do not exist for long, so they must grow and produce seeds in a very short time. The only truly ephemeral animals are mayflies. Their adult life span is between a few minutes and one day.

- **Anadromous.** A term describing fish which live in the sea but swim upriver to breed, e.g. salmon. This is a form of **migration**, and the opposite is **catadromous** (going from river to sea).

Beech

Fir

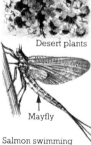

Desert plants

Mayfly

Salmon swimming upriver to sea

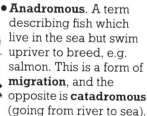

* Chlorophyll, 27 (**Pigments**); Secondary tissue, 18.

Migrating geese

Bee sting

Thorns on rose stalks

- **Migration.** Travelling seasonally from one region to another. This normally involves leaving an area in winter to find food elsewhere, and returning in the spring to breed. Migration is part of the life cycle of many animals, especially birds.

Dormouse in hibernation

- **Dormancy.** A period, or periods, of suspended activity which is a natural part of the life cycle of many plants and animals. Dormancy in plants occurs when conditions are unfavourable for growth (normally in winter). In animals, dormancy usually occurs because of food scarcity, and is either called **hibernation** or **aestivation**. Hibernation is dormancy in the winter (typical of many animals, e.g. some **mammals***), and aestivation is dormancy in drought conditions (occurs mainly in insects).

Life styles

The world has a vast diversity of living things, each one with its own style of life. This situation is a result of **adaptive radiation**. The living things can be grouped together according to shared characteristics, either by formal classification, based mainly on their structural similarities (see charts, pages 110-113) or by more informal groupings, based on general life styles (see list, page 114).

- **Adaptive radiation** or **evolutionary adaptation**. The gradual process which has produced many different forms of living thing from one prehistoric starting point. Each has become **specialized**, i.e. has evolved the best form to cope with its environment, e.g. streamlined shapes for swimming and flying.

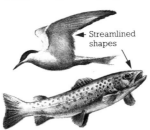

Streamlined shapes

Many living things have also developed **protective adaptations** – protective measures such as thorns or poison

stings. All adaptations become established in successive generations because those creatures with them are the most likely to survive long enough to breed (and perpetuate the adaptation). This is the basis of Darwin's theory of **natural selection**, (also called **Darwinism**), first expounded in the mid-nineteenth century.

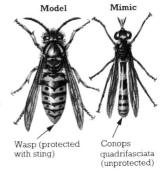

Model   Mimic

Wasp (protected with sting)   Conops quadrifasciata (unprotected)

- **Mimicry.** A special type of adaptation, in which a plant or animal (the **mimic**) has developed a resemblance to another plant or animal (the **model**). This is used especially for protection (e.g. many unprotected insects have adopted the colouring of those with stings), but also for other reasons (bee orchids are mimics for reproduction purposes – see page 31).

* **Mammals,** 113.

9

The structure of living things

A living thing capable of a separate existence is called an **organism**. All organisms are made up of **cells** – the basic units of life, which carry out all the vital chemical processes. The simplest organisms have just one cell (they are **unicellular** or **acellular**), but very complex ones, e.g. humans, have thousands or even millions. They are **multicellular** and their cells are of many different types, each type specially adapted for its own particular job. Groups of cells of the same type (together with non-living material) make up the different **tissues** of the organism, e.g. muscle tissue. Several different types of tissue together form an **organ**, e.g. a stomach, and a number of organs together form a **system**, e.g. a digestive system.

The parts of a cell

Despite the fact that cells can look very different, they are all made up of the same basic parts. Each of these parts has a specific role to play.

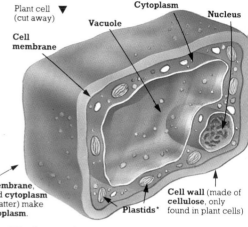

Plant cell ▼
(cut away)

Cytoplasm

Nucleus

Vacuole

Cell membrane

Cell wall (made of cellulose, only found in plant cells)

Plastids*

- **Cell membrane.** Also called the **plasma membrane** or **plasmalemma**. The outer skin of a cell. It is **semipermeable***, i.e. selective about which substances it allows through.

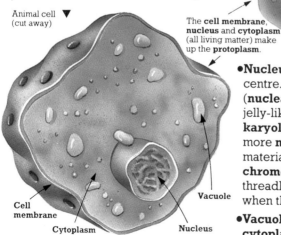

Animal cell ▼
(cut away)

The **cell membrane**, **nucleus** and **cytoplasm** (all living matter) make up the **protoplasm**.

Cell membrane

Cytoplasm

Vacuole

Nucleus

- **Cytoplasm.** The material where all the chemical reactions vital to life occur (see **organelles**). It generally has a more jelly-like outer layer and a more liquid inner one (see **ectoplasm** and **endoplasm** – picture, page 40).

- **Nucleus** (pl. **nuclei**). The cell's control centre. Its double-layered outer skin (**nuclear membrane**) encloses a jelly-like fluid (**nucleoplasm** or **karyolymph**), which contains one or more **nucleoli*** and the genetic material **DNA***. This is held in **chromosomes*** – bodies which form a threadlike mass called **chromatin** when the cell is not dividing.

- **Vacuoles.** Fluid-filled sacs in the cytoplasm. They are small and temporary in animal cells, and either remove substances (see **Golgi complex**) or contain fluid brought in (see **pinocytosis**, page 99). Most plant cells have one large, permanent vacuole, filled with **cell sap** (dissolved minerals and sugars).

* Chromosomes, 96; DNA, 96 (Nucleic acids); Nucleoli, Plastids, 12; Semipermeable, 99.

Organelles

The **organelles** are tiny bodies in the **cytoplasm**. Each type (listed below and on page 12) has a vital role to play in the chemical reactions within the cell.

Animal cell (showing the **organelles** in the **cytoplasm**)

Centriole

Vacuole

Cell membrane

Endoplasmic reticulum (smooth ER)

Mitochondrion

Nucleolus

Endoplasmic reticulum (rough ER)

Nucleus (double membrane cut away). **Nucleoplasm** and **chromosomes** not shown.

The **mitochondria**, **centriole** and **nucleolus** are defined overleaf.

•**Ribosomes**. Tiny round particles (most are attached to the **endoplasmic reticulum**). They are involved in building up proteins from amino acids (see page 100). "Coded" information (held by the **DNA** in the **nucleus**) is sent to the ribosomes in strands of a substance called **messenger RNA (mRNA)**. These pass on the "codes" so that the ribosomes join the amino acids in the correct way to produce the right proteins. **RNA*** is present in at least two other forms in the cells. The ribosomes are made of **ribosomal RNA** (see **nucleoli***) and molecules of **transfer RNA (tRNA)** "carry" the amino acids to the ribosomes.

•**Lysosomes**. Round sacs containing powerful **enzymes***. They take in foreign bodies, e.g. bacteria, to be destroyed by the enzymes. Their outer skins do not usually let the enzymes out into the cell (to break down its contents), but if the cell becomes damaged the skins disappear and the cell digests itself.

•**Golgi complex**. Also called a **Golgi apparatus**, **Golgi body** or **dictyosome**. A special area of **smooth ER**. It collects and distributes the substances made in the cell (e.g. proteins and waste from chemical reactions). The substances fill the sacs, which gradually swell up at their outside edges until pieces "pinch off". These pieces (**vacuoles**) then travel out of the cell via the **cytoplasm** and **cell membrane**.

•**Endoplasmic reticulum** or **ER**. A complex system of flat sacs, folding inwards from the **cell membrane** and joining up with the **nuclear membrane** (see **nucleus**). It provides a large surface area for reactions or fluid storage, and a passageway for fluids passing through. ER with **ribosomes** on its surface is **rough ER**. ER with no ribosomes is **smooth ER**.

* **Enzymes**, 103; **Nucleoli**, 12; **RNA**, 96 (**Nucleic acids**).

Organelles (continued)

- **Centrioles.** Two bodies just outside the **nucleus*** in animal cells. Each lies in a dense area of **cytoplasm*** (**centrosome**) and is made up of two tiny cylinders, forming a T-shape. Each cylinder is made up of nine sets of three tiny tubes (**microtubules**). Centrioles are vital to **cell division**.

Centriole

Microtubule

- **Mitochondria** (sing. **mitochondrion**) or **chondriosomes**. Rod-shaped bodies with a double layer of outer skin. The inner layer forms a series of folds (**cristae**, sing. **crista**), providing a large surface area for the vital chemical reactions which go on inside the mitochondria (called the "powerhouses" of a cell). They are the places where simple substances taken into the cell are broken down to provide energy. For more about this, see **aerobic respiration**, page 104.

Mitochondrion

Cristae

- **Nucleoli** (sing. **nucleolus**). One or more small, round bodies in the **nucleus***. They produce the component parts of the **ribosomes*** (made of **ribosomal RNA**), which are then transported out of the nucleus and assembled in the **cytoplasm***.

Nucleolus

- **Plastids.** Tiny bodies in plant cell **cytoplasm***. Some (**leucoplasts**) store starch, oil or proteins. Others – **chloroplasts*** – contain **chlorophyll*** (used in making food).

Plastid (chloroplast*)

Cell division

Cell division is the splitting up of one cell (the **parent cell**) into two identical **daughter cells**. There are two types of cell division, both involving the division of the **nucleus*** (**karyokinesis**) followed by the division of the **cytoplasm*** (**cytokinesis**). The first type of cell division (**binary fission**) is described on these two pages. It produces new cells for growth and also to replace the millions of cells which die each day (from damage, disease or simply because they are "worn out"). It is also the means of **asexual reproduction*** in many single-celled organisms. The second, special type of cell division produces the **gametes*** (sex cells) which will come together to form a new living thing. For more about this, see pages 94-95.

- **Mitosis.** The division of the **nucleus*** when a plant or animal cell divides for growth or repair (**binary fission**). It ensures that the two new nuclei (**daughter nuclei**) are each given the same number of **chromosomes*** (the bodies which carry the "coded" hereditary information). Each receives the same number as were in the original nucleus, called the **diploid number**. Every living thing has its own characteristic diploid number, i.e. all its cells (with the exception of the **gametes***) contain the same, specific number of chromosomes, grouped in identical pairs called **homologous chromosomes**. Humans have 46 chromosomes, in 23 pairs. Although mitosis is a continuous process, it can be divided for convenience sake into four phases. Before mitosis, however, there is always an **interphase**.

* Asexual reproduction, 92; Chlorophyll, 27 (Pigments); Chloroplasts, 27; Chromosomes, 96; Cytoplasm, 10; Gametes, 93; Nucleus, 10; Ribosomes, 11.

● **Interphase**. The periods between cell divisions. Interphases are very active periods, during which the cells are not only carrying out all the processes needed for life, but are also preparing material to produce "copies" of all their components (so both new cells formed after division will have all they need). Just before **mitosis** begins, the **chromatin*** threads in the **nucleus*** also duplicate, so that, after coiling up, each **chromosome*** will consist of two **chromatids** (see **prophase**).

Phases of **mitosis** (only two **chromosomes*** shown – humans have 46)

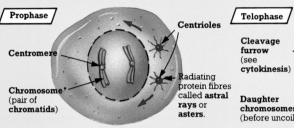

Prophase

Centrioles

Centromere

Chromosome*
(pair of
chromatids)

Radiating
protein fibres
called **astral
rays** or
asters.

The threads of **chromatin*** in the **nucleus*** coil up to form **chromosomes*** and the **nuclear membrane*** disappears. Each has already duplicated to form two identical coils (**chromatids**), joined by a small sphere (**centromere**). The two **centrioles** move to opposite poles of the cell.

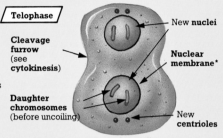

Telophase

Cleavage
furrow
(see
cytokinesis)

New **nuclei**

Nuclear
membrane*

Daughter
chromosomes
(before uncoiling)

New
centrioles

The **spindle fibres** and **astral rays** disappear and a new **nuclear membrane*** forms around each group of **daughter chromosomes**. This creates two new **nuclei*** (**daughter nuclei**), inside which the chromosomes uncoil to once again form a threadlike mass (**chromatin***). The **centrioles** also duplicate, so that a pair will be found in each new cell (after **cytokinesis**).

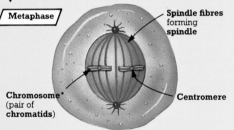

Metaphase

Spindle fibres
forming
spindle

Chromosome*
(pair of
chromatids)

Centromere

The **centrioles** (at opposite poles) project protein fibres called **spindle fibres** which join together and form a sphere, or **spindle**. The **chromosomes*** (paired **chromatids**) move towards its equator and become attached by their **centromeres** to the spindle fibres.
▼

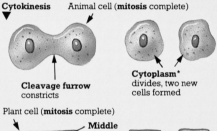

Cytokinesis   Animal cell (**mitosis** complete)

Cytoplasm*
divides, two new
cells formed

Cleavage furrow
constricts

Plant cell (**mitosis** complete)

Middle
lamella
formed,
new **cell
walls***
built up
along it

Cytoplasm* divides.

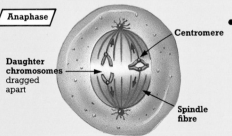

Anaphase

Centromere

Daughter
chromosomes
dragged
apart

Spindle
fibre

The **centromeres** duplicate and the two **chromatids** from each pair (now called **daughter chromosomes**) move to opposite poles of the **spindle**, seemingly "dragged" there by the contracting **spindle fibres**.

● **Cytokinesis**. The division of the **cytoplasm*** of a cell, which forms two new cells around the new **nuclei*** created by **mitosis** (or **meiosis***). In animal cells, a **cleavage furrow** forms around the cell's equator and then constricts as a ring until it cuts completely through the cell. In plant cells, a dividing line called the **middle lamella** forms down the centre of the cell, and a new **cell wall*** is built up along each side of it.

* Cell wall, 10; Chromatin, 10 (**Nucleus**); Chromosomes, 96; Cytoplasm, 10; Meiosis, 94; Nuclear membrane, 10 (**Nucleus**).

Vascular plants

With the exception of simple plants such as algae and fungi (see classification chart, pages 110-111), all plants are **vascular plants**. That is, they all have a complex system of special fluid-carrying tissue called **vascular tissue**. For more about how the fluids travel within the vascular tissue, see pages 24-25. All vascular plants are classified within the **Division Tracheophyta** (see page 111).

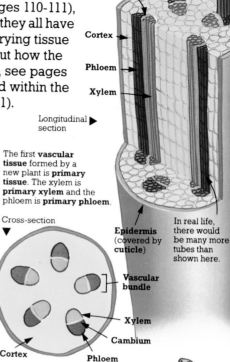

Young stem, or young part of a stem.▼

Cambium

Cortex

Phloem

Xylem

Vascular bundle

Longitudinal section ▶

The first **vascular tissue** formed by a new plant is **primary tissue**. The xylem is **primary xylem** and the phloem is **primary phloem**.

Cross-section ▼

Epidermis (covered by **cuticle**)

Vascular bundle

Xylem

Cambium

Cortex

Phloem

In real life, there would be many more tubes than shown here.

- **Vascular tissue**. Special tissue which runs throughout a **vascular plant**, carrying fluids and helping to support the plant. In young stems, it is normally arranged in separate units called **vascular bundles**; in older stems these join up to form a central core (**vascular cylinder***). In young roots, the arrangement of the tissue is slightly different, but a central core is also formed later. For more about the vascular tissue in older plants, see page 18. The vascular tissue is of two different types – **xylem** and **phloem**. They are separated by a layer of tissue called the **cambium**.

Constituents of vascular tissue

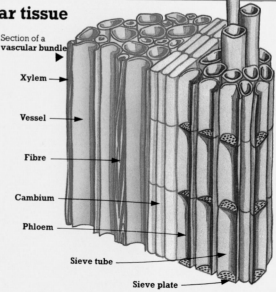

Section of a **vascular bundle** ▶

Xylem →

Vessel →

Fibre →

Cambium →

Phloem →

Sieve tube →

Sieve plate →

- **Xylem**. A tissue which carries water up through a plant. It is made up of **vessels**, with long thin cells (**fibres**) providing support between them. In older stems, the central xylem dies away and its vessels become filled in, forming **heartwood***.

- **Phloem**. A tissue which distributes the food made in the leaves to all parts of the plant. It consists of **sieve tubes**, with special **companion cells** running beside them and other cells packed around them for support. The companion cells are thought to transport fluids.

* Heartwood, 19; **Vascular cylinder**, 18.

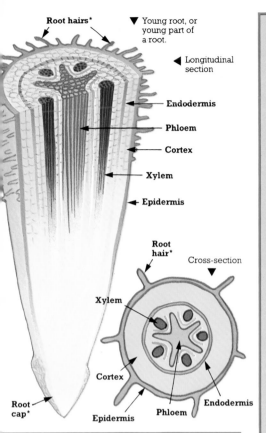

Root hairs*

▼ Young root, or young part of a root.

◀ Longitudinal section

Endodermis

Phloem

Cortex

Xylem

◀ Epidermis

Root hair*

Cross-section ▼

Xylem

Cortex

Root cap*

Epidermis

Phloem

Endodermis

- **Vessels** or **tracheae** (sing. **trachea**). Long tubes in the **xylem** which carry water. Their walls are strengthened with a hard substance called **lignin**. They consist of chains of cells whose walls and **protoplasm*** have died.

- **Sieve tubes**. Long columns of cells in the **phloem**. Their **nuclei*** and **protoplasm*** have been lost but their interconnecting walls have remained. These are called **sieve plates** and have tiny holes in them to allow substances to pass through.

- **Cambium**. A layer of narrow, thin-walled cells between the **xylem** on the inside and the **phloem** on the outside. The cells are able to divide, making more xylem and phloem. Such an area of cells is called a **meristem***.

Other tissues in vascular plants

- **Epidermis**. A thin surface layer of tissue around all parts of a plant. In some areas, especially the leaves, it has many tiny holes, called **stomata***. In older stems, the epidermis is replaced by **phellem***. In older roots, it is first replaced by **exodermis*** and then by phellem.

- **Cuticle**. A thin outer layer of a waxy substance called **cutin**, produced by the **epidermis** above ground. It prevents too much water being lost.

- **Cortex**. A layer of tissue just inside the **epidermis** of stems and roots. It consists mainly of **parenchyma**, a type of tissue with large cells and many air spaces. In some plants there is also some **collenchyma**, a type of supporting tissue with long thick-walled cells. The cortex tends to get compressed and replaced by other tissues as a plant gets older.

- **Endodermis**. The innermost layer of root **cortex**. It contains special **passage cells**. Fluids which have seeped in between the cortex cells, instead of through them, are directed by the passage cells into the central area of **vascular tissue**.

- **Pith** or **medulla**. A central area of tissue found in stems, but not usually in roots. It is generally only called pith once the stem has developed a **vascular cylinder***. It is made up of **parenchyma**, like the **cortex**, and is sometimes used to store food.

* **Exodermis**, 17 (**Piliferous layer**); **Meristem**, 16; **Nucleus**, 10; **Phellem**, 19; **Protoplasm**, 10; **Root cap**, **Root hairs**, 17; **Stomata**, 21; **Vascular cylinder**, 18.

Stems and roots

The **stem** and **roots** of a plant are its main supporting structures, as well as being important in transporting fluids (see pages 14-15 and 24-25). Their various parts are listed here. For more about the development of the stem and roots as a plant gets older, see pages 18-19.

- **Meristem**. Any area from which new growth arises. The cells of a meristem are able to divide, producing new cells. A meristem found at the tip of the root (the **growing point**) or the stem (part of a **terminal bud**) is known as an **apical meristem**.

Parts of a root

- **Growing point**. An area just behind a root tip where the cells divide to produce new growth.

- **Zone of elongation**. The area of new cells produced by the **growing point**, and located just behind it. The cells stretch lengthwise as they take in water, since their **cell walls*** are not yet hard. This elongation pushes the root tip further down into the soil.

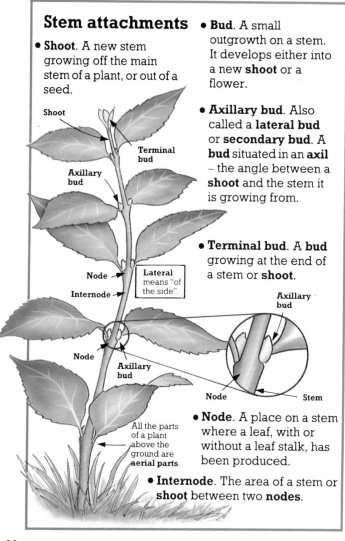

Stem attachments

- **Shoot**. A new stem growing off the main stem of a plant, or out of a seed.

Shoot

Terminal bud

Axillary bud

Node

Internode

Lateral means "of the side".

Node

Axillary bud

Node

All the parts of a plant above the ground are aerial parts.

- **Bud**. A small outgrowth on a stem. It develops either into a new **shoot** or a flower.

- **Axillary bud**. Also called a **lateral bud** or **secondary bud**. A **bud** situated in an **axil** – the angle between a **shoot** and the stem it is growing from.

- **Terminal bud**. A bud growing at the end of a stem or **shoot**.

Axillary bud

Node   Stem

- **Node**. A place on a stem where a leaf, with or without a leaf stalk, has been produced.

- **Internode**. The area of a stem or **shoot** between two **nodes**.

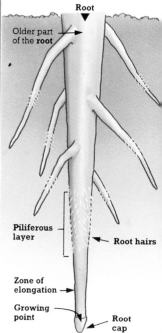

Root

Older part of the **root**

Piliferous layer

Root hairs

Zone of elongation

Growing point

Root cap

* Cell wall, 10.

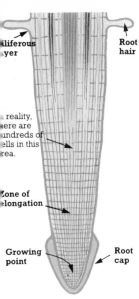

iliferous
ayer

Root
hair

reality,
ere are
undreds of
ells in this
rea.

Zone of
elongation

Growing
point

Root
cap

- **Piliferous layer.** The youngest area of the **epidermis***, or outer skin, of a root. It is the area which produces **root hairs**. It is found just behind the **zone of elongation**. As the walls of the elongating cells harden, the outermost cells become the piliferous layer. The older piliferous layer (higher up the root) is slowly worn away, to be replaced by a layer of hardened cells called the **exodermis** (the outermost layer of the **cortex***).

- **Root hairs.** Long outgrowths from the cells of the **piliferous layer**. They take in water and minerals.

- **Root cap.** A layer of cells which protects the root tip as it grows down.

Types of root

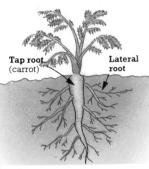

Tap root
(carrot)

Lateral
root

- **Tap root.** A first root, or **primary root**, which is larger than the small roots, called **lateral roots** or **secondary roots**, which grow out of it. Many vegetables are swollen tap roots.

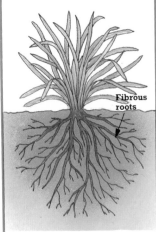

Fibrous
roots

- **Fibrous roots.** A system of fibrous roots is made up of a large number of equal-sized roots, all producing smaller **lateral roots**. The first root is not prominent, as it is in a **tap root** system.

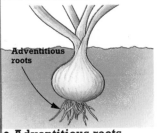

Adventitious
roots

- **Adventitious roots.** Roots which grow directly from a stem. They grow out of **bulbs*** (which are special stems), or from gardeners' cuttings.

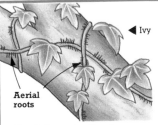

◀ Ivy

Aerial
roots

- **Aerial roots.** Roots which grow from stems and do not grow into the ground. They can be used for climbing, e.g. in an ivy. Many absorb moisture from the air.

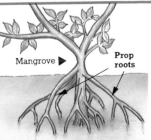

Mangrove ▶

Prop
roots

- **Prop roots.** Special types of **aerial root**. They grow out from a stem and then down into the ground, which may be under water. They support a heavy plant, e.g. a mangrove.

Inside an older plant

A plant which lives for many years, such as a tree, forms **secondary tissue** as it gets older. This consists of new layers of tissue to supplement the original tissue, or **primary tissue***. New supportive and fluid-carrying **vascular tissue*** is formed towards the centre of the plant and new protective tissue is produced around the outside. The production of the new vascular tissue is called **secondary thickening**, and results in what is known as a **woody plant**.

Secondary thickening in a stem

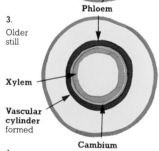

1.
Young stem

Xylem*

Phloem*

Vascular bundle*

Cambium*

2.
Slightly older

Xylem

Cambium joins up.

Phloem

3.
Older still

Xylem

Vascular cylinder formed

Cambium

4.
After another year

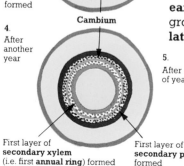

First layer of secondary xylem (i.e. first **annual ring**) formed

First layer of secondary phloem formed

New central tissue

- **Vascular cylinder.** A vascular cylinder develops as the first step of **secondary thickening** in stems. More **cambium*** forms between the **vascular bundles***, and this then gives rise to more **xylem*** and **phloem***, forming a continuous cylinder.

- **Secondary thickening.** The year-by-year production of more fluid-carrying **vascular tissue*** in plants which live for many years, resulting in a gradual increase in the diameter of the stem and roots. Each year, new layers of **xylem*** (**secondary xylem**) and **phloem*** (**secondary phloem**) are produced by the dividing cells of the **cambium*** between them. In stems this happens slightly differently than in roots, but the result throughout the plant is an ever-enlarging core of vascular tissue (which slowly "squeezes out" the **pith*** in stems). Most of this core is xylem, now also known as **wood**. The area of phloem does not widen much at all, because the xylem pushing outwards wears it away.

- **Annual rings.** The concentric circles which can be seen in a cross-section of an older plant. Each ring is one year's new growth of **xylem***, and has two separate areas – the soft **spring wood** (or **early wood**), produced in the early part of the growing season, and the harder **summer wood** (or **late wood**), produced later on.

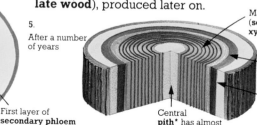

5.
After a number of years

Many **annual rings** (secondary xylem)

Cambium

Secondary phloem

Central pith* has almost disappeared.

* **Cambium**, 15; **Phloem**, 14; **Pith**, 15; **Primary tissue**, 14; **Vascular bundles**, 14 (**Vascular tissue**); **Xylem**, 14

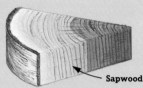

Heartwood

- **Heartwood.** The oldest, central part of the **xylem*** in an older plant. The **vessels*** are filled in and no longer carry fluids, but they still provide support.

Sapwood

- **Sapwood.** The outer area of **xylem*** in an older plant, whose **vessels*** still carry fluids. It also supports the tree and holds food reserves.

New outer tissue

As well as new **vascular tissue***, an older plant also forms extra areas of tissue around its outside to help protect it. These are called **phelloderm**, **phellogen** and **phellem** respectively (working from the inside). The three areas together are known as the **periderm**.

- **Phellogen** or **cork cambium.** A cell layer which arises towards the outside of the stem and roots of older plants. It is a **meristem***, i.e. an area of cells which keep on dividing. It produces two new layers – **phelloderm** and **phellem**.

- **Phelloderm.** A new cell layer produced by **phellogen** on its inside. It supplements the **cortex*** and is sometimes called **secondary cortex**.

- **Phellem** or **cork.** A new cell layer produced by **phellogen** on its outside. The cells undergo **suberization**, i.e. become impregnated with a waxy substance called **suberin**. This makes the outer layer waterproof. The phellem cells slowly die and replace the previous outer cell layer (**epidermis*** in stems and **exodermis*** in roots). Dead phellem cells are called **bark**.

Tree (many years old) — **Annual rings**

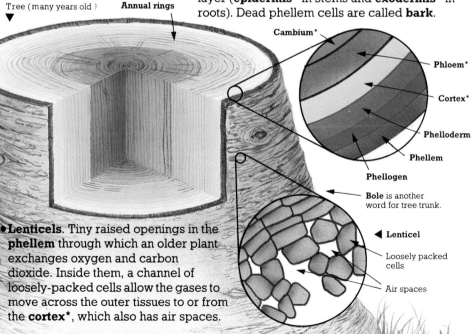

Cambium*

Phloem*

Cortex*

Phelloderm

Phellem

Phellogen

Bole is another word for tree trunk.

◀ Lenticel

Loosely packed cells

Air spaces

- **Lenticels.** Tiny raised openings in the **phellem** through which an older plant exchanges oxygen and carbon dioxide. Inside them, a channel of loosely-packed cells allow the gases to move across the outer tissues to or from the **cortex***, which also has air spaces.

---

* **Cambium, Cortex, Epidermis,** 15; **Exodermis,** 17 (**Piliferous layer**); **Phloem,** 14; **Meristem,** 16; **Vascular tissue,** 14; **Vessels,** 15; **Xylem,** 14.

Leaves

The **leaves** of a plant, known collectively as its **foliage**, are specially adapted to manufacture food. They do this by a special process called **photosynthesis**. For more about this, see pages 26-27. There are many different shapes and sizes of leaves, but only two different types. **Simple leaves** consist of one single leaf blade, or **lamina**, and **compound leaves** are made up of a number of small leaf blades called **leaflets**, all growing from the same leaf stalk. There is a chart showing some of the different leaf shapes on page 22.

Inside a leaf

•**Veins**. Long strips of **vascular tissue*** inside a leaf, supplying it with water and minerals and removing the food made inside it. Some leaves have long parallel veins, e.g. those of grasses, but most have a central vein inside a **midrib** (an extension of the leaf stalk), with many smaller branching veins.

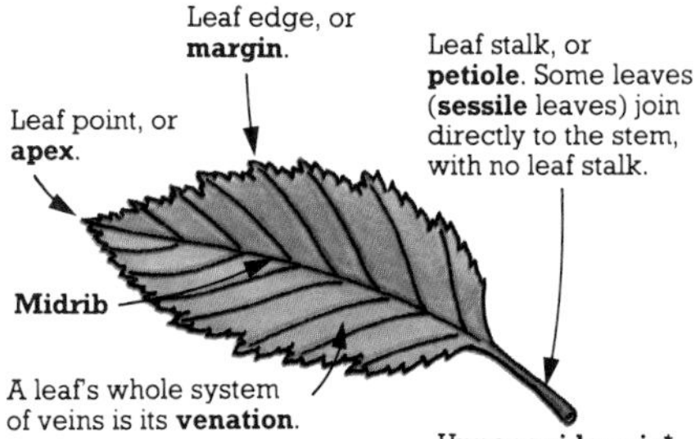

Leaf edge, or **margin**.

Leaf point, or **apex**.

Leaf stalk, or **petiole**. Some leaves (**sessile** leaves) join directly to the stem, with no leaf stalk.

Midrib

A leaf's whole system of veins is its **venation**.

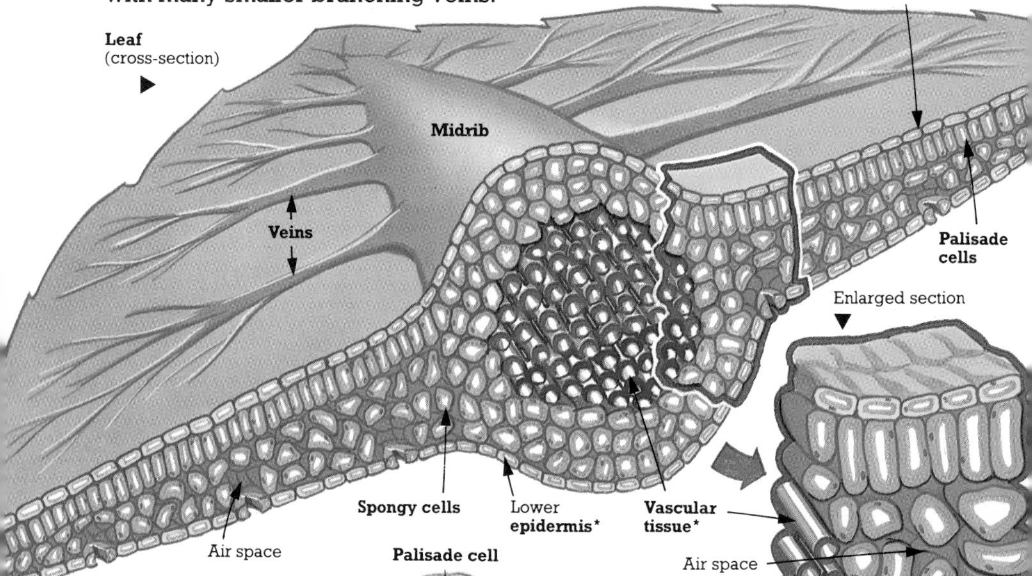

Upper **epidermis***

Leaf (cross-section)
▶

Midrib

Veins

Palisade cells

Enlarged section
▼

Spongy cells   Lower **epidermis***

Air space   **Palisade cell**

Vascular tissue*

Air space

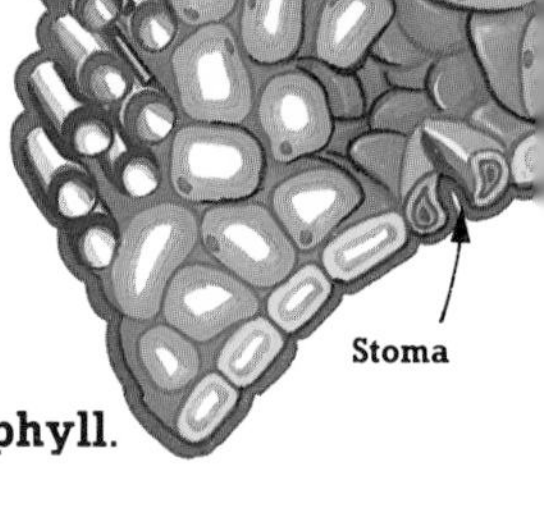

Stoma

•**Palisade layer**. A cell layer just below the upper surface of a leaf. It is made up of regular, oblong-shaped **palisade cells**. These contain many **chloroplasts***.

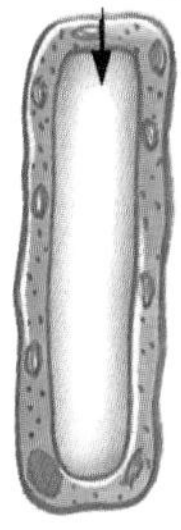

•**Spongy layer**. A layer of irregular-shaped **spongy cells** and air spaces where gases circulate. The spongy and palisade layers together are the **mesophyll**.

* Chloroplasts, 27; Epidermis, 15; Vascular tissue, 14.

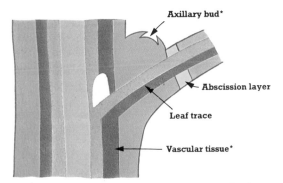

Axillary bud*

Abscission layer

Leaf trace

Vascular tissue*

- **Leaf trace**. An area of **vascular tissue*** which branches off that of a stem to become the central **vein** of a leaf.

- **Abscission layer**. A layer of cells at the base of a leaf stalk which separates from the rest of the plant at a certain time of year (stimulated by a **hormone*** called **abscisic acid**). This makes the leaf fall off, forming a **leaf scar** on the stem.

- **Stomata** (sing. **stoma**). Tiny openings in the **epidermis*** (outer skin), through which the exchange of water (**transpiration***) and gases takes place. They are mainly found on the underside of leaves.

- **Guard cells**. Pairs of crescent-shaped cells. The members of each pair are found on either side of a **stoma**, which they open and close by changing shape. This controls water and gas exchange. They are the only surface cells with **chloroplasts***.

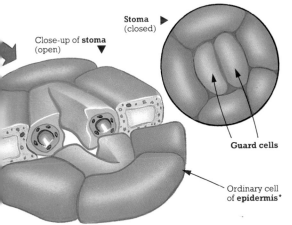

Close-up of **stoma** (open)

Stoma (closed)

Guard cells

Ordinary cell of **epidermis***

Special leaves

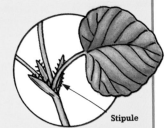

Stipule

- **Stipule**. A small stalkless leaf at the base of a leaf stalk in many plants.

Bract

- **Bract**. A leaf at the base of a flower stalk in many plants.

Tendril

- **Tendril**. A special threadlike leaf (or stem) which either twines round or sticks to a support.

Spine

- **Spine**. A specially modified leaf of a cactus. It has a reduced surface area to avoid losing much water.

Types of compound leaf

Shown here are some types of **compound leaf** (leaves made up of **leaflets***), as well as some common leaf arrangements and leaf edges, or **margins**. The pictures are not to scale.

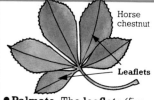

Horse chestnut

Leaflets

- **Palmate**. The **leaflets** (five or more) radiate from one common point.

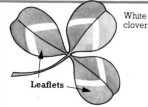

White clover

Leaflets

- **Trifoliate**. Three **leaflets** grow from the same point.

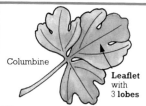

Columbine

Leaflet with 3 lobes

- **Ternate**. Special type of **trifoliate** leaf. Each **leaflet** has three **lobes**.

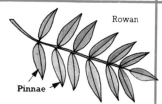

Rowan

Pinnae

- **Pinnate**. The **leaflets**, or **pinnae** (sing. **pinna**), are in **opposite** pairs.

Fern

This end is **tripinnate**

This end is **bipinnate**

- **Bipinnate / tripinnate**. A **pinnate** leaf with pinnate **leaflets**.

Leaf arrangements

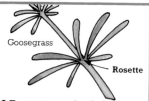

Orpine

Spiral of leaves

- **Spiral**. Leaves growing out from points forming a spiral around the stem.

Box

Opposite pairs

- **Opposite**. Leaf pairs whose members grow from opposite stem sides.

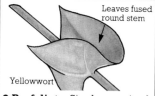

Purple loosestrife

Pairs at right angles

- **Decussate**. **Opposite** pairs, each pair at right angles to the one before.

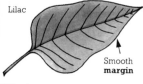

Goosegrass

Rosette

- **Rosette** or **whorl**. A circle of leaves growing from one point.

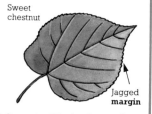

Primrose

Basal rosette

- **Basal rosette**. A **rosette** growing at the base of a stem.

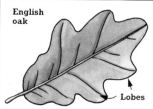

Leaves fused round stem

Yellowwort

- **Perfoliate**. Single or paired leaves whose bases are fused around the stem.

Leaf margins

Lilac

Smooth margin

- **Entire**. The leaf **margin** has no indentations of any kind.

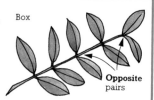

Sweet chestnut

Jagged margin

- **Serrate**. The leaf **margin** has tiny jagged "teeth". May also be **lobed**.

English oak

Lobes

- **Lobed**. The leaf **margin** forms sections, or **lobes**. May also be **serrate**.

* Leaflets, 20.

Plant sensitivity

Plants have no nervous system, but they do still show **sensitivity**, i.e. they react to certain forms of stimulation. They do this by moving specific parts or by growing. This is called **tropism**. **Positive tropism** is movement or growth towards the stimulus and **negative tropism** is movement or growth away from it.

- **Phototropism.** Response to light. When the light is sunlight, the response is called **heliotropism.** Most leaves and stems show this by curving around to grow towards the light.

Globe flower

Stems curve round to face light

- **Haptotropism** or **thigmotropism.** Response to touch or contact. For example, the sticky hairs of a sundew plant curl around an insect when it comes into contact with them.

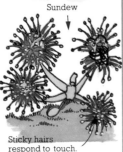

Sundew

Sticky hairs respond to touch.

- **Hydrotropism.** Response to water. For example, some roots may grow out sideways if there is more water in that direction.

- **Geotropism.** Response to the pull of gravity. This is shown by all roots, i.e. they all grow down through the soil.

Roots grow towards water

Roots grow down in response to gravity

- **Growth hormones** or **growth regulators.** Substances which promote and regulate plant growth. They are produced in **meristems*** (areas where

- **Photoperiodism.** The response of plants to the length of day or night (**photoperiods**), especially with regard to the production of flowers. It depends on a number of things, e.g. the plant's age and the temperature of its environment. **Short-day plants** only produce flowers if the length of the day is shorter than a certain length (called its **critical length**), **long-day plants** only if it is longer. It is thought that a

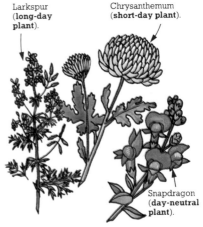

Larkspur (**long-day plant**).

Chrysanthemum (**short-day plant**).

Snapdragon (**day-neutral plant**).

"message" to produce flowers is carried to the relevant area by a **hormone***, produced in the leaves when conditions are right. This hormone has been called **florigen**. Some plants are **day-neutral plants**, i.e. their flowering does not depend on the length of day.

cells are constantly dividing). **Auxins, cytokinins** and **gibberellins** are types of growth hormone.

Plant fluid transportation

The transportation of fluids in a plant is called **translocation**. The fluids travel within the **vascular tissue***, made up of **xylem*** and **phloem***. The xylem carries water (with dissolved minerals) from the roots to the leaves. The phloem carries food from the leaves to areas where it is needed.

- **Transpiration**. The loss of water by evaporation, mainly through tiny holes called **stomata*** on the undersides of leaves.

- **Transpiration stream**. A constant chain of events inside a plant. As the outer leaf cells lose water by **transpiration**, the concentration of minerals and sugars in their **vacuoles*** becomes higher than that of the cells further in. Water then passes outwards by **osmosis***, causing more water to be "pulled" up through the tubes of the **xylem*** in the stem and roots (helped by **capillary action**). The roots then take in more water.

- **Capillary action**. The way that fluids travel up narrow tubes. The molecules of the fluid are "pulled" upwards by the attraction between them and the molecules of the tube walls.

- **Root pressure**. A pressure which builds up in the roots of some plants. In all plants, water travels in from the soil and on through the layers of root cells by **osmosis***. In plants which develop root pressure, the pressure of this water movement is enough to force the water some way up into the tubes of the **xylem***. It is then "pulled" on upwards by the **transpiration stream**. In other plants, the movement of water through root cells is all due to the "pull" of the transpiration stream.

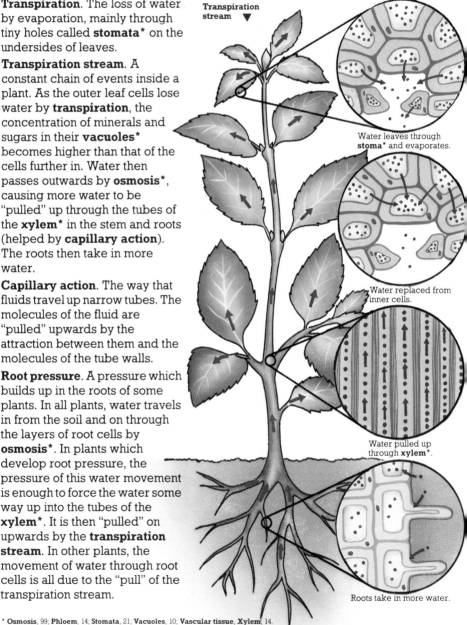

Transpiration stream ▼

Water leaves through **stoma*** and evaporates.

Water replaced from inner cells.

Water pulled up through **xylem***.

Roots take in more water.

* Osmosis, 99; Phloem, 14; Stomata, 21; Vacuoles, 10; Vascular tissue, Xylem, 14.

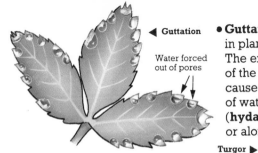

◀ **Guttation**

Water forced out of pores

- **Guttation**. A phenomenon occurring in plants which show **root pressure**. The extra pressure, added to the "pull" of the **transpiration stream**, may cause drops of water to be forced out of water-secreting areas of cells (**hydathodes**) via tiny pores at the tips or along the edges of the leaves.

Turgor ▶

Healthy plant

- **Turgor**. The state of the cells in a healthy plant. Each cell can take in no more water (it is **turgid**). Water has passed by **osmosis*** into the **cell sap*** (dissolved minerals and sugars) in its large central **vacuole***, and the vacuole has pushed as far out as it can go. It can go no further because its outward pressure (**turgor pressure**) is equalled by the opposing force of the rigid **cell wall*** (**wall pressure**). Such cells enable a plant to stand firm and upright.

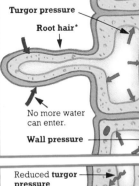

Root cells

Vacuole* containing cell sap*

Turgor pressure

Root hair*

No more water can enter.

Wall pressure

Wilting ▶

Wilting plant

- **Wilting**. A state of drooping, found in a plant subjected to certain conditions, such as excess heat. The plant is losing more water (by **transpiration**) than it can take in, and the **turgor pressure** (see **turgor**) of its cell **vacuoles*** drops. The cells become limp and can no longer support the plant, so it will droop.

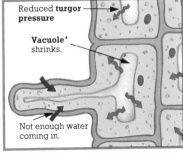

Reduced **turgor pressure**

Vacuole* shrinks.

Not enough water coming in.

Plasmolysis ▶

Dying plant

- **Plasmolysis**. An extreme state in a plant, which may cause it to die. Such a plant is losing a large amount of water, often not only by **transpiration** in excess heat (see **wilting**), but also by **osmosis*** into very dry soil or soil with a very high concentration of minerals. The **vacuoles*** of the plant cells then shrink so much that they pull the **cytoplasm*** away from the **cell walls***.

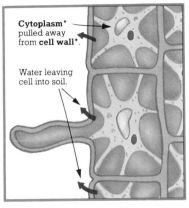

Cytoplasm* pulled away from cell wall*.

Water leaving cell into soil.

---

* Cell sap, 10 (Vacuoles); Cell wall, Cytoplasm, 10; Osmosis, 99; Root hairs, 17.

Plant food production

Most plants have the ability to make the food they need for growth and energy (unlike animals, which must take it in). The manufacturing process by which they make their complex food substances from other, simpler substances is called **photosynthesis**.

• **Photosynthesis**. The series of chemical reactions by which green plants make their food, occurring mainly in the **palisade cells*** in the leaves. Carbon dioxide is combined with water and minerals (containing nitrogen and sulphur), using energy absorbed from sunlight by **chloroplasts**. This produces oxygen as well as the plant's food. ▶

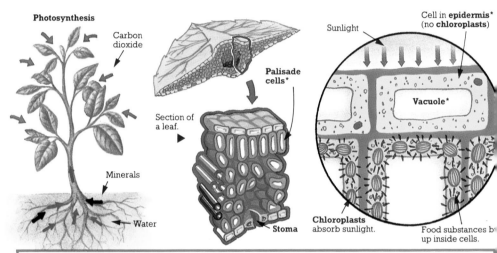

Photosynthesis

Carbon dioxide

Palisade cells*

Section of a leaf. ▶

Minerals

Water

Stoma

Sunlight

Cell in **epidermis*** (no **chloroplasts**)

Vacuole*

Chloroplasts absorb sunlight.

Food substances bup inside cells.

• **Compensation points**. Two points in a 24-hour period (normally around dawn and around dusk) when the two processes of **photosynthesis** and **internal respiration*** (see top of next page) are exactly balanced.

Photosynthesis is producing just the right amounts of carbohydrates and oxygen for internal respiration, and this is producing just the right amounts of carbon dioxide and water for photosynthesis.

1. Around dawn (**compensation point**)

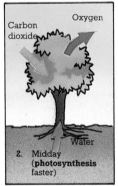

Carbon dioxide

Oxygen

Water

2. Midday (**photosynthesis** faster)

3. Around dusk (**compensation point**)

Carbon dioxide

Oxygen

Water

4. Midnight (no **photosynthesis**)

* Epidermis, 15; Internal respiration, 104; Palisade cells, 20 (Palisade layer); Vacuoles, 10.

The process of photosynthesis works in co-ordination with that of **internal respiration***, the breakdown of food for energy. Photosynthesis produces oxygen and carbohydrates (needed by internal respiration) and internal respiration produces carbon dioxide and water (needed by photosynthesis). At most times,

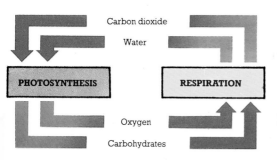

one of the two processes is occurring at a faster rate than the other. This means that excess amounts of its products are being produced, and not enough of the substances it needs are being made in the plant. In this case, extra amounts must be taken in and excess amounts given off or stored (see pictures 2 and 4 on the opposite page).

• **Chloroplasts**. Tiny bodies in plant cells (mainly in the leaves) which contain a green **pigment** called **chlorophyll**. This absorbs the sun's light energy and uses it to "power" **photosynthesis**. Chloroplasts can move around inside a cell, according to light intensity and direction. See also page 12.

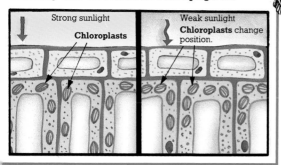

Strong sunlight
Chloroplasts

Weak sunlight
Chloroplasts change position.

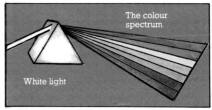

The colour spectrum

White light

• **Pigments**. Substances which absorb light. White light is actually made up of a spectrum of many different colours. Each pigment absorbs some colours and reflects others.

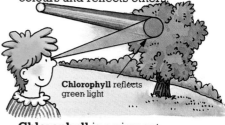

Chlorophyll reflects green light

Chlorophyll is a pigment found in all leaves. It absorbs blue, violet and red light, and reflects green light. This is why leaves look green. Other pigments, such as

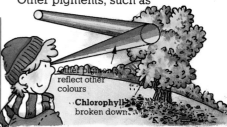

Other pigments reflect other colours

Chlorophyll broken down.

xanthophyll, **carotene** and **tannin** are also present in leaves. They reflect light in the orange, yellow and red part of the spectrum, but are masked by chlorophyll during the growing season. In the autumn, the chlorophyll breaks down, and so the autumn colours of the leaves appear.

* Internal respiration, 104.

Flowers

The **flowers** of a plant contain its organs of **reproduction** (producing new life – see also page 30). In **hermaphrodite** plants, e.g. the buttercup and poppy below, each flower has both male and female organs. **Monoecious** plants, e.g. maize, have two types of flower on one plant – **staminate** flowers, which have just male organs, and **pistillate** flowers, which have just female organs. **Dioecious** plants, e.g. the holly, have staminate flowers on one plant and pistillate flowers on a separate plant.

- **Receptacle.** The expanded tip of the flower stalk, or **peduncle**, from which the flower grows.

- **Petals.** The delicate, usually brightly coloured structures around the reproductive organs. They are often scented (to attract insects) and are known collectively as the **corolla**.

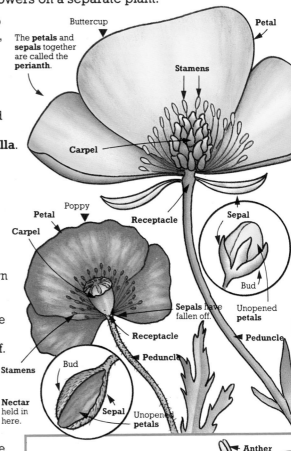

Buttercup

The **petals** and **sepals** together are called the **perianth**.

Petal

Stamens

Carpel

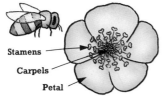

Stamens
Carpels
Petal

- **Sepals.** The small, leaf-like structures around a bud, known collectively as the **calyx**. In some flowers, e.g. buttercups, they remain as a ring around the opened **petals**; in others, e.g. poppies, they wither and fall off.

Poppy

Petal
Carpel
Receptacle
Sepal
Bud
Sepals have fallen off.
Unopened petals
Receptacle
Peduncle
Peduncle

Petal
Nectary
Stamens
Bud
Nectar held in here.
Sepal
Unopened petals

- **Nectaries.** Areas of cells at the base of the **petals** which produce a sugary liquid called **nectar**. This attracts insects needed for **pollination***. It is thought that the dark lines down many petals are there to direct an insect to the nectar, and they are known as **honey guides**.

The male organs

- **Stamens.** The male reproductive organs. Each has a thin stalk, or **filament**, with an **anther** at the tip. Each anther is made up of **pollen sacs**, which contain grains of **pollen***.

Anther
Stamen
Filament

* Pollen, Pollination, 30.

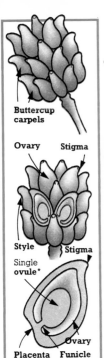

Buttercup carpels

Ovary Stigma

Style Stigma

Single ovule*

Placenta Funicle

Ovary

Poppy carpel

Stigma

Ovary

Stigma

Many ovules Ovary

The female organs

- **Carpel** or **pistil**. A female reproductive organ, consisting of an **ovary**, **stigma** and **style**. Some flowers have only one carpel, others have several clustered together.

- **Ovaries**. Female reproductive structures. Each is the main part of a **carpel** and contains one or more tiny bodies called **ovules***, each of which contains a female sex cell. An ovule is fixed by a stalk (**funicle**) to an area of the ovary's inside wall called the **placenta**. The stalk is attached to the ovule at a point called a **chalaza**.

- **Stigma**. The uppermost part of a **carpel**, with a sticky surface to which grains of **pollen*** become attached during **pollination***.

- **Style**. The part of a **carpel** which joins the **stigma** to the **ovary**. Many flowers have an obvious style, e.g. daffodils, but in others it is very short (e.g. buttercups) or almost non-existent (e.g. poppies).

- **Gynaecium**. The whole female reproductive structure, made up of one or more **carpels**.

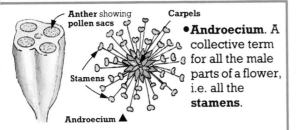

Anther showing pollen sacs

Carpels

Stamens

Androecium ▲

- **Androecium**. A collective term for all the male parts of a flower, i.e. all the **stamens**.

How the parts are arranged

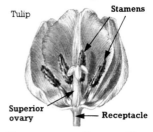

Tulip

Stamens

Superior ovary

Receptacle

- **Hypogynous flower**. The carpel (or carpels) sit on top of the **receptacle**; all the other parts grow out from around its base. The position of the carpel is described as **superior**.

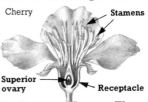

Cherry

Stamens

Superior ovary

Receptacle

- **Perigynous flower**. The carpel (or carpels) rest in a cup-shaped **receptacle**; all the other parts grow out from around its rim. The position of the carpel is described as **superior**.

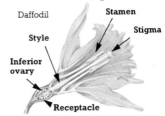

Daffodil

Stamen

Stigma

Style

Inferior ovary

Receptacle

- **Epigynous flower**. The flower parts grow from the top of a **receptacle** which completely encloses the **ovary** (or ovaries), but not the **stigma** and style. The position of the ovary is described as **inferior**.

---

* Ovules, Pollen, Pollination, 30.

Reproduction in a flowering plant

Reproduction is the creation of new life. All flowering plants reproduce by **sexual reproduction***, when a male **gamete*** (sex cell) joins with a female gamete. In flowering plants, the male gametes (strictly speaking only **male nuclei***) are held in **pollen** and the female gametes in **ovules**.

●**Pollen.** Tiny grains formed by the **stamens*** (male parts) of flowers. Each grain is a special cell which has two **nuclei***. When a pollen grain lands on an **ovary*** (female body), one nucleus (the **generative nucleus**) splits in half, forming two **male nuclei** (reproductive bodies – see introduction).

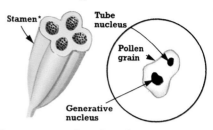

●**Ovules.** The tiny structures inside a flower's female body, or **ovary***. They become seeds after **fertilization**. Each consists of an oval cell (the **embryo sac**), surrounded by layers of tissue called **integuments**, except at one point where there is a tiny hole (**micropyle**). Before fertilization, the embryo sac **nucleus*** undergoes several divisions (looked at in more detail on page 95 – under **gamete production, female**). This results in a number of new cells (some of which become part of the seed's food store) and two naked nuclei which fuse together. One of the new cells is the female **gamete*** (sex cell), or **egg cell**.

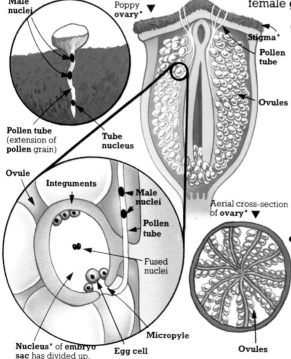

●**Pollination.** The process by which a grain of **pollen** transfers its **male nuclei** (see **pollen**) into the **ovary*** of a flower. The grain lands on the **stigma***, and forms a **pollen tube**, under the control of the **tube nucleus** (the one which did not divide – see **pollen**). The tube grows down through the ovary tissue and enters an **ovule** via its **micropyle**. The two male nuclei then travel along it.

●**Fertilization.** After pollination, one **male nucleus** (see **pollen**) fuses with the **egg cell** in the **ovule** to form a **zygote*** (the first cell of a new plant). The other joins with the two fused female nuclei to form a cell which develops into the **endosperm***.

 * Endosperm, 33; Male nuclei, 93 (Gametes); Nucleus, 10; Ovaries, 29; Sexual reproduction, 92; Stamens, 28; Stigma, 29; Zygote, 93.

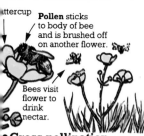

...ttercup **Pollen** sticks to body of bee and is brushed off on another flower.

Bees visit flower to drink nectar.

- **Cross pollination.** The **pollination** of one plant by **pollen** grains from another plant of the same type (if the grains land on a different type of plant, they do not develop further, i.e. they do not produce **pollen tubes**). The pollen may be carried by the wind, or by insects which drink the **nectar***.

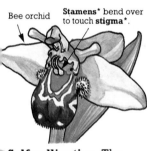

Bee orchid

Stamens* bend over to touch **stigma***.

- **Self pollination.** The **pollination** of a plant by its own **pollen** grains. For example, a bee orchid tries to attract male Eucera bees (for **cross pollination**) by looking and smelling like a female bee. But if it is not visited, its **stamens*** (male parts) bend over and transfer pollen to the **stigma*** of its **ovary*** (female body).

Types and arrangements of flowers

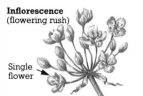

Inflorescence (flowering rush)

Single flower

- **Inflorescence.** A group of flowers or **flowerheads** growing from one point.

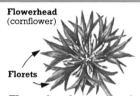

Flowerhead (cornflower)

Florets

- **Flowerhead** or **composite flower.** A cluster of tiny flowers, or **florets**.

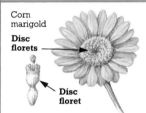

Corn marigold

Disc florets

Disc floret

- **Disc florets. Florets** whose petals are all the same size.

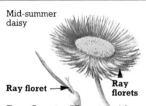

Mid-summer daisy

Ray floret

Ray florets

- **Ray florets. Florets** with one long petal.

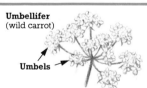

Umbellifer (wild carrot)

Umbels

- **Umbellifer.** An **inflorescence** with umbrella-shaped **flowerheads** (**umbels**).

Bell flower (nettle-leaved bellflower)

- **Bell flower.** Also called a **tubular** or **campanulate flower.** Its petals are joined to make a bell shape.

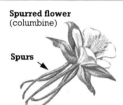

Spurred flower (columbine)

Spurs

- **Spurred flower.** A flower with one or more petals extended backwards to form **spurs**.

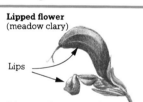

Lipped flower (meadow clary)

Lips

- **Lipped flower.** A flower with two "lips" – an upper and lower one. The upper one often has a hood.

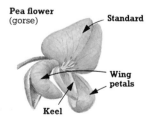

Pea flower (gorse)

Standard

Wing petals

Keel

- **Pea flower.** A flower with an upper petal (the **standard**), two side petals (**wing petals**) and two lower petals forming the **keel** (which encloses the reproductive parts).

* **Nectar**, 28 (**Nectaries**); **Ovaries**, 29; **Stamens**, 28; **Stigma**, 29.

Seeds and germination

After **fertilization*** in a flowering plant, an **ovule*** develops into a **seed**. This contains an **embryo**, i.e. a new developing plant, and a store of food. The **ovary*** ripens into a fruit, carrying the seed or seeds. There is a chart of different fruits on page 34.

●**Dispersal** or **dissemination**. The shedding of ripe seeds from the fruit of a parent plant. This happens in one of two main ways, depending on whether a fruit is **dehiscent** or **indehiscent**.

●**Dehiscent**. A word describing a fruit from which the seeds are expelled before the fruit itself disintegrates. For

Poppy capsule

Seeds are shaken out.

example, a poppy capsule has holes in, and the seeds are shaken out by the wind. Other fruit, e.g. broom pods,

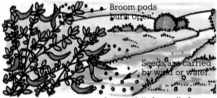

Broom pods burst open.

Seeds are carried by wind or water.

open spontaneously and "shoot" the seeds out. In all cases, the seeds may then be carried by wind, water or other means.

Indehiscent. A word describing a fruit which becomes detached from the plant and disintegrates to free the

Dandelion "parachutes"

Sycamore "keys"

seeds. For example, the "keys" of sycamores or the "parachutes" of dandelions are carried by the air, and hooked burrs catch on animal fur. The

Blackbird eats berries.

fruit then rot away in the ground to expose the seeds. Edible fruit may be eaten by animals, which then expel the seeds in their droppings.

Germination

When conditions are right, a seed will **germinate**. The **plumule** and **radicle** emerge from the seed coat, and begin to grow into the new plant, or **seedling**.

● **Hypogeal**. A type of **germination**, e.g. in pea plants, in which the **cotyledons** remain below the ground within the **testa**, and the **plumule** is the only part to come above the ground.

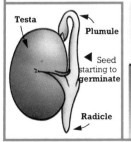

Testa

Plumule

Seed starting to germinate

Radicle

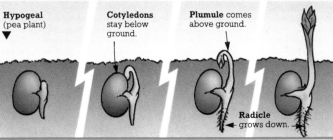

Hypogeal (pea plant)

Cotyledons stay below ground.

Plumule comes above ground.

Radicle grows down.

* Fertilization, 30; Ovaries, 29; Ovules, 30.

Parts of a seed

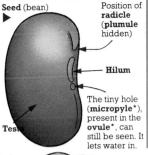

Seed (bean) ▶
Position of **radicle** (**plumule** hidden)
Hilum
The tiny hole (**micropyle***), present in the **ovule***, can still be seen. It lets water in.
Testa

- **Hilum**. A mark on a seed, showing where the **ovule*** was attached to the **ovary***.

- **Testa**. The seed coat. It develops from the **integuments***.

- **Plumule**. The first bud, or **primary bud**, formed inside a seed. It will develop into the first shoot of the new plant.

- **Radicle**. The first root, or **primary root**, of a new plant. It is formed inside a seed.

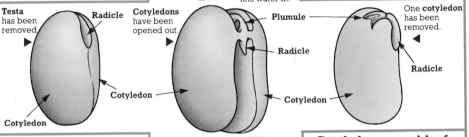

Testa has been removed.
Radicle
Cotyledon
Cotyledon

Cotyledons have been opened out. ▶
Plumule
Radicle
Cotyledon

One **cotyledon** has been removed.
Radicle

- **Endosperm**. A layer of tissue inside a seed which surrounds the developing plant and gives it nourishment. In some plants, e.g. pea, the **cotyledons** absorb and store all the endosperm before the seed is ripe, in others, e.g. grasses, it is not fully absorbed until after the seed **germinates**.

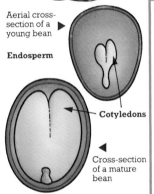

Aerial cross-section of a young bean ▶
Endosperm
Cotyledons
◀ Cross-section of a mature bean

- **Cotyledon** or **seed-leaf**. A simple leaf which forms part of the developing plant. In some seeds, e.g. bean seeds, it absorbs and stores all the food from the **endosperm**. **Monocotyledons** are plants with one cotyledon, e.g. grasses, in **dicotyledons**, e.g. peas, there are two.

- **Epigeal**. A type of **germination**, e.g. in tomato plants, in which the **cotyledons** appear above the ground, below the first leaves – the true leaves.

- **Coleoptile**. The first leaf of many **monocotyledons** (see **cotyledon**). It protects the first bud and the first leaves emerge from it.

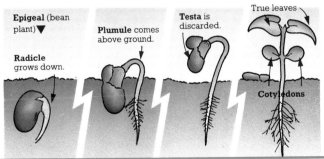

Epigeal (bean plant) ▼
Radicle grows down.
Plumule comes above ground.
Testa is discarded.
True leaves
Cotyledons

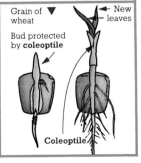

Grain of wheat ▼
New leaves
Bud protected by **coleoptile**
Coleoptile

Fruit

A **fruit** contains the seeds of a plant. **True fruit** develop purely from the **ovary***, false fruit from the **receptacle*** as well (e.g. a strawberry). The outer wall of a fruit is called the **pericarp**. In some fruit, it is divided into an outer skin, or **epicarp**, a fleshy part, or **mesocarp**, and an inner layer, or **endocarp**. Listed below are the main types of fruit.

- **Legume** or **pod**. A fruit with seeds attached to its inside wall. It splits along its length to open. E.g. a pea.

Pea **pod**   Seeds

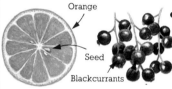
Orange
Seed
Blackcurrants

- **Berry**. A fleshy fruit which contains many seeds, e.g. an orange or a blackcurrant.

- **Nut**. A dry fruit with a hard shell, which only contains one seed, e.g. a hazelnut or a walnut.

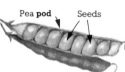
Hazelnut
Shell
Seed

Grains of wheat

- **Grain**. Also called a **caryopsis** or **kernel**. A small fruit whose wall has fused with the seed coat, e.g. wheat.

- **Achene**. A small, dry fruit, with only one seed, e.g. a sycamore or buttercup fruit. A "winged" achene like a sycamore fruit is a **samara** or **key fruit**.

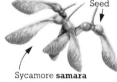
Seed
Sycamore **samara**

Plum   Seed or "stone"

- **Drupe**. A fleshy fruit with a hard seed in the centre, often known as a "stone", e.g. a plum.

- **Pome**. A fruit with a thick, fleshy, outer layer and a core, with the seeds enclosed in a capsule, e.g. an apple. Pomes are examples of **false fruits** (see introduction).

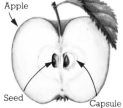
Apple
Seed   Capsule

Vegetative reproduction

As well as producing seeds, some plants have developed a special type of **asexual reproduction***, called **vegetative reproduction** or **vegetative propagation**, in which one part of the plant is able to develop unaided into a new plant.

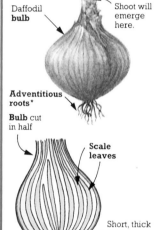
Daffodil **bulb**
Shoot will emerge here.
Adventitious roots*
Bulb cut in half
Scale leaves
Short, thick stem

- **Bulb**. A short, thick stem surrounded by scaly leaves (**scale leaves**) which contain stored food material. It is formed underground by an old, dying plant, and represents the first, resting, stage of a new plant, which will emerge as a shoot at the start of the next season. E.g. a daffodil bulb.

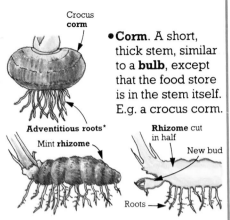

Crocus **corm**

Adventitious roots*

Mint **rhizome**

Rhizome cut in half

New bud

Roots

- **Corm**. A short, thick stem, similar to a **bulb**, except that the food store is in the stem itself. E.g. a crocus corm.

- **Rhizome**. A thick stem, which has scaly leaves and grows horizontally underground. It produces roots along its length and also buds from which new shoots grow. Many grasses produce rhizomes, as well as other plants, e.g. ferns and irises.

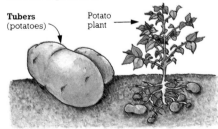

Older strawberry plant

New plant

Stolon

- **Stolon** or **runner**. A stem which grows out horizontally near the base of some plants, e.g. the strawberry. The stolon puts down roots from points at intervals along this stem, and new plants grow at these points.

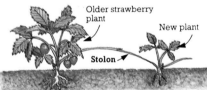

Tubers (potatoes)

Potato plant

- **Tuber**. A short, swollen, underground stem which contains stored food material and produces buds from which new plants will grow, e.g. a potato.

Artificial propagation

Artificial propagation is the commercial process, in agriculture and market gardening, which makes use of **vegetative reproduction**. The fact that new plants need not always grow from seeds means that many more plants can be produced commercially than would occur naturally.

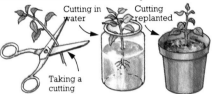

Cutting in water

Cutting replanted

Taking a cutting

- **Cutting**. A process in which a piece of a plant stem (the cutting) is removed from its parent plant and planted in soil, where it grows into a new plant. In some cases, it is first left in water for a while to develop roots.

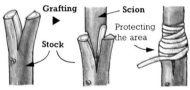

Grafting

Scion

Protecting the area

Stock

- **Grafting**. The process of removing a piece of a plant stem and re-attaching it elsewhere. This could be to a different part of the same plant (**autografting**), to another plant of the same species (**homografting**), or to a plant of a different species (**heterografting**). The piece removed is called the **scion**, and that to which it is attached is known as the **stock**.

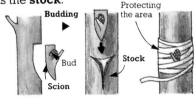

Budding

Protecting the area

Bud

Stock

Scion

- **Budding**. A type of **grafting** where a bud and its adjacent stem are the parts grafted.

* Adventitious roots, 17.

The body structure of animals

Animals exist in a great variety of forms, from single-celled organisms to complex ones made of thousands of cells. The way they are **classified***, or divided into groups, depends to a large extent on how complex their bodies are. The two terms **higher animal** and **lower animal** are often used in this context. The higher an animal is, the more complex its internal organs are. In general, the distinguishing features of higher animals are **segmentation**, body cavities and some kind of skeleton.

● **Segmentation**. The division of a body into separate areas, or **segments**, a step up in complexity from a simple undivided body. Generally, the more complex the animal, the less obvious its segments are. The most primitive form

Metameric segmentation in an earthworm ▼

Metamere

of segmentation is **metameric segmentation**, or **metamerism**. The segments (**metameres**) are very similar, if not identical. Each contains more or less identical parts of the main internal systems, which join up through the internal walls separating the segments. Such segmentation is found in most worms, for example, and in

myriapods*. More complex segmentation is less obvious. In insects, for example, the body has three main parts – the head, **thorax** (upper body region) and **abdomen** (lower body region). Each of these is in fact a group of segments, called a **tagma** (pl. **tagmata**), but the segments are not divided by internal walls. They are simply visible as external markings.

Dragonfly ▼   Head

Appendage (leg)

Segments can be seen as markings.   **Thorax**

Abdomen

● **Appendage**. A subordinate body part, i.e. one which projects from the body such as an arm, leg, fin or wing.

Arrangement of the parts

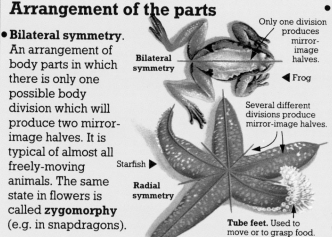

● **Bilateral symmetry**. An arrangement of body parts in which there is only one possible body division which will produce two mirror-image halves. It is typical of almost all freely-moving animals. The same state in flowers is called **zygomorphy** (e.g. in snapdragons).

Bilateral symmetry

Only one division produces mirror-image halves.

◀ Frog

Several different divisions produce mirror-image halves.

Starfish ▶

Radial symmetry

Tube feet. Used to move or to grasp food.

● **Radial symmetry**. A radiating arrangement of body parts around a central axis, e.g. in starfish. In such cases, there are two or more possible body divisions (sometimes in different planes) which will produce two mirror-image halves. The same state in flowers is called **actinomorphy** (e.g. in buttercups).

* **Classification**, 110; **Myriapods**, 113 (Note 5).

Body cavities

Almost all many-celled animals have a main fluid-filled body cavity, or **perivisceral cavity**, to cushion the body organs (very complex animals, e.g. humans, may have other smaller cavities as well). Its exact nature varies, but in most animals it is either a **coelom** or a **haemocoel**. In soft-bodied animals it is vital in movement, providing an incompressible "bag" for their muscles to work against. Such a system is called a **hydrostatic skeleton**.

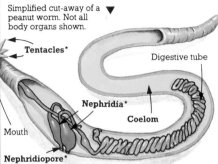

Simplified cut-away of a peanut worm. Not all body organs shown. ▼

Tentacles*

Digestive tube

Nephridia*

Coelom

Mouth

Nephridiopore*

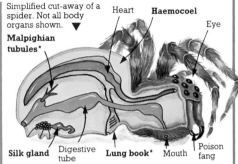

Simplified cut-away of a spider. Not all body organs shown. ▼

Heart   Haemocoel

Eye

Malpighian tubules*

Silk gland   Digestive tube   Lung book*   Mouth   Poison fang

- **Coelom.** The main body cavity (**perivisceral cavity**) of higher worms, **echinoderms***, e.g. starfish, and **vertebrates***, e.g. birds. It is fluid-filled to cushion the organs and is bounded by the **peritoneum**, a thin membrane which lines the body wall. In lower animals, e.g. many worms, the coelom assists in excretion. Their excretory organs, called **nephridia***, project into the coelom and remove fluid waste which has seeped into it. In higher animals, other more complex organs deal with these functions.

- **Haemocoel.** The fluid-filled main body cavity (**perivisceral cavity**) of **arthropods***, e.g. insects, and **molluscs***, e.g. snails. In molluscs, it is more of a spongy meshwork of tissue than a true cavity. Unlike a **coelom**, a haemocoel contains blood. It is an expanded part of the blood system, through which blood is circulated. In some animals, the haemocoel plays a part in excretion. In insects, for instance, water and fluid waste seep into it, and are then taken up by the **Malpighian tubules*** projecting into it.

- **Mantle cavity.** A body cavity in shelled **molluscs***, e.g. snails. It lies between the **mantle** (a fold of skin lining the shell) and the rest of the body. Digestive and excretory waste is passed into it, for removal from the body. In water-living molluscs, it also holds the **gills***; in land-living snails, it acts as a lung.

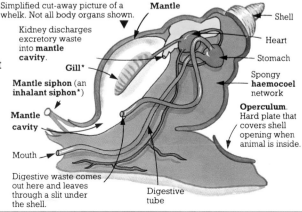

Simplified cut-away picture of a whelk. Not all body organs shown. ▼

Kidney discharges excretory waste into **mantle cavity**.

Mantle

Shell

Heart

Stomach

Gill*

Mantle siphon (an inhalant siphon*)

Spongy **haemocoel** network

Operculum. Hard plate that covers shell opening when animal is inside.

Mantle cavity

Mouth

Digestive waste comes out here and leaves through a slit under the shell.

Digestive tube

* Arthropods, 112; Echinoderms, 113; Gills, 44; Inhalant siphon, 44 (Siphon); Lung books, 44; Malpighian tubules, 45; Molluscs, 112; Nephridiopore, 45 (Nephridia); Tentacles, 47; Vertebrates, 113 (Craniata).

Animal body coverings

All animal bodies have an enclosing outer layer, or "skin", normally with a further covering of some kind. In many cases, the skin is multi-layered, like human skin (see pages 82-83), and in most higher animals its covering is soft, e.g. hair, fur or feathers. Hard coverings, e.g. shells, are found in many lower animals and may form their only supporting framework, if they have no internal skeleton (**endoskeleton**). In such cases, the covering is called an **exoskeleton**. Some of the main body coverings are listed here.

- **Cuticle.** A non-living, waterproof, outer layer in many animals, secreted by the skin. In most soft-bodied animals it hardens to form a supportive outer skeleton, or **exoskeleton**, e.g. the shells of crabs and the tough outer "coat" of insects. The term cuticle is in fact most often used to describe an insect "coat". This consists of a sugar-based substance (**chitin**) and a tough protein (**sclerotin**). It is often made up of **sclerites** – separate pieces joined by flexible, narrow areas. In other animals, e.g. earthworms, the cuticle remains a soft waxy covering.

Earwig ▼

Cuticle (sclerites)

The term **cuticle** is sometimes used to mean the **stratum corneum*** in humans.

- **Scales.** There are two different types of scales. Those of bony fish (Class **Osteichthyes***), e.g. carp, are small, often bony plates lying within the skin. Those covering the limbs or whole bodies of many **reptiles*** (e.g. the legs of turtles) are thickened areas of skin.

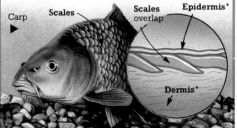

Carp ▶

Scales

Scales overlap

Epidermis*

Dermis*

- **Carapace.** The shield-like shell of a crab, tortoise or turtle. In tortoises and turtles, it consists of bony plates fused together under a horny skin, but in crabs, it is a hardened **cuticle**.

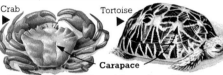

Crab ▶   Tortoise ▶

Carapace

- **Denticles** or **placoid scales.** Sharp backward-pointing plates, covering the bodies of cartilaginous fish (Class **Elasmobranchiomorphi***), e.g. rays. They are similar to teeth, and stick out from the skin, unlike **scales**.

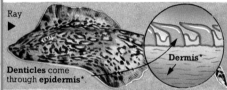

Ray ▶

Dermis*

Denticles come through epidermis*.

- **Elytra** (sing. **elytron**). The front pair of wings of beetles and some bugs. They are modified to form a tough cover for the back pair of wings, used for flying.

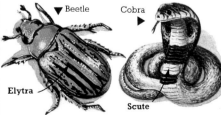

▼ Beetle   Cobra ▶

Elytra

Scute

- **Scuta** (sing. **scute** or **scutum**). Any large, hard, external plate, especially those on the underside of a snake, used in movement.

* Dermis, 82; Elasmobranchiomorphi, 113; Epidermis, 82; Osteichthyes, Reptiles, 113; Stratum corneum, 82.

Feathers

The insulating waterproof layer of a bird's body is made up of **feathers**, together known as its **plumage**. Each feather is a light structure made of a fibrous, horny substance called **keratin**. Each has a central **shaft** (or **rachis**) with thin filaments called **barbs**. The barbs of all **contour feathers**, i.e. all the feathers except the **down feathers**, have tiny filaments called **barbules**. Like body hairs, feathers have nerve endings attached to them, as well as muscles which can fluff them up to conserve heat (see **hair erector muscles**, page 82).

Northern parula warbler ▼

Uropygium. Contains **uropygial gland**, which secretes an oily fluid used in preening.

Rectrices (sing. **rectrix**). Tail feathers, controlling changes of direction in flight.

Mandibles. Upper and lower beak parts.

The feathers of the back, shoulders and wings are sometimes called the **mantle**.

Coverts. Feathers covering bases of wing and tail feathers.

Primaries (furthest from the body). Make up end section of wing (**pinion**).

Secondaries (nearer the body).

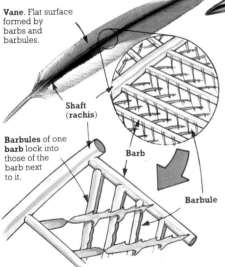

Vane. Flat surface formed by barbs and barbules.

Shaft (rachis)

Barbules of one **barb** lock into those of the barb next to it.

Barb

Barbule

Scutella (sing. **scutellum**). Small scales on birds' legs.

Down feather

- **Remiges** (sing. **remix**) or **flight feathers**. Those feathers of a bird's wings which are used in flight, consisting of the long, strong **primary feathers**, or **primaries**, and the shorter **secondary feathers**, or **secondaries**.

- **Down feathers** or **plumules**. The fluffy, temporary feathers of all young birds, which have flexible **barbs**, but no true **barbules**. The adults of some types of bird keep some down feathers as an insulating layer close to the skin.

- **Feather follicles**. Tiny pits in a bird's skin. Each one has a feather in it, just like a hair in a **hair follicle***. The cells at the base of the follicle grow up and out to form a feather, and then die away, becoming hard and tough.

Animal movement

Most animals are capable of movement from place to place (**locomotion**) at least at some stage of their life (plants can only move individual parts – see **tropism**). The moving parts of animals vary greatly. Many animals have a system of bones and muscles similar to humans (see pages 50-55). Listed here are some of the parts involved in moving animals.

Movement of simple animals

● **Cilia** (sing. **cilium**). Tiny "hairs" on the outer body surfaces of many small organisms. They flick back and forth to produce movement. Cilia are also found lining the internal passages of more complex animals, e.g. human air passages (they trap foreign particles).

● **Flagella** (sing. **flagellum**). Any long, fine body threads, especially the one or more which project from the surface of many single-celled organisms. These lash backwards and forwards to produce movement. Organisms with flagella are **flagellate**.

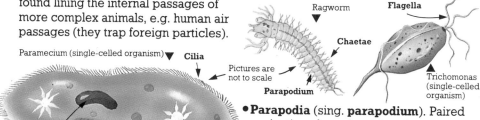

Ragworm ▼   Flagella

Chaetae

Parapodium

Trichomonas (single-celled organism)

Pictures are not to scale

● **Parapodia** (sing. **parapodium**). Paired projections from the sides of many aquatic worms, used to move them along. Each one ends in a bunch of bristles, or **chaetae** (sing. **chaeta**), which may also cover the body in some cases.

Paramecium (single-celled organism) ▼   Cilia

Food in sac called **food vacuole**.   Cilia inside channel called **oral groove** waft food particles inwards.   Contractile vacuole*

● **Pseudopodium** (pl. **pseudopodia**). An extension ("false foot") of the cell matter, or **cytoplasm***, of a single-celled organism. Such extensions are formed either in order for the organism to move or to enable it to engulf a food particle. The latter process is called **phagocytosis**.

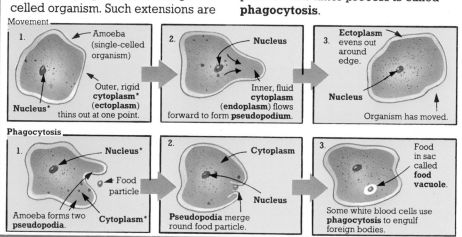

Movement

1. Amoeba (single-celled organism)
Nucleus*
Outer, rigid **cytoplasm*** (**ectoplasm**) thins out at one point.

2. Nucleus
Inner, fluid **cytoplasm*** (**endoplasm**) flows forward to form **pseudopodium**.

3. **Ectoplasm** evens out around edge.
Nucleus
Organism has moved.

Phagocytosis

1. Nucleus*
Food particle
Amoeba forms two **pseudopodia**.   **Cytoplasm***

2. Cytoplasm
Nucleus
Pseudopodia merge round food particle.

3. Food in sac called **food vacuole**.
Some white blood cells use **phagocytosis** to engulf foreign bodies.

Swimmers

- **Fins**. Special projections from the body of a fish, which are used as stabilisers and to change direction. They are supported by **rays** – rods of bone or **cartilage*** (depending on the Class of fish – see page 113) radiating out inside them. Fish have two sets of fins, called **median** and **paired fins**.

Trout ▼

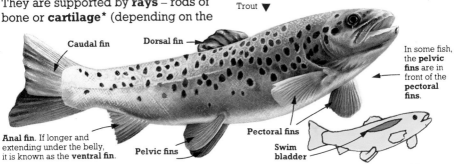

Caudal fin

Dorsal fin →

In some fish, the **pelvic fins** are in front of the **pectoral fins**.

Anal fin. If longer and extending under the belly, it is known as the **ventral fin**.

Pelvic fins

Pectoral fins

Swim bladder

- **Median fins**. The **fins** which run in a line down the centre of the back and the belly. In some fish, e.g. eels, they form one long continuous median fin, but in most they are divided into the **dorsal**, **caudal** (tail) and **anal** (or **ventral**) **fins**. The dorsal fin and the anal fin control changes of direction from side to side. The caudal fin helps to propel the fish through the water.

- **Paired fins**. The **fins** of a fish which stick out from its sides in two pairs: the **pectoral fins** and the **pelvic fins**. They control movement up or down.

- **Swim bladder** or **air bladder**. A long air-filled pouch inside most bony fish (Class **Osteichthyes***). The fish alters the amount of air inside the bladder depending on the depth at which it is swimming. This keeps the density of the fish the same as that of the water, so it will not sink if it stops swimming.

> **Median** or **medial** means "lying on the dividing line between the right and left sides"
>
> **Dorsal** means "of the back or top surface"
>
> **Caudal** means "of the tail or hind part"; **caudate** means "having a tail"
>
> **Ventral** means "of the front or lower surface"

Flyers

- **Pectoralis muscles**. Two large, paired chest muscles, found in many **mammals***, but especially highly developed in birds. Each wing has one **pectoralis major** and one **pectoralis minor**, attached at one end to the **keel**, a large extension of the breastbone. The muscles contract alternately to move the wings.

Keel

Pectoralis minor (pulls wing up)

Bastard wing or alula. Short **digit*** with a few feathers. Helps to deal with air turbulence.

Pectoralis major (pulls wing down)

Breastbone, or sternum

Coracoid bones

Walkers

- **Unguligrade**. Walking on hooves at the tips of the toes, e.g. horses.

- **Digitigrade**. Walking on the underside of the toes, e.g. dogs and cats.

- **Plantigrade**. Walking on the underside of the whole foot, e.g. man.

* Cartilage, 53; Digit, 51 (Phalanges); Mammals, Osteichthyes, 113.

Animal feeding

Different animals take in their food in many different ways, and with many different body parts. Some also have special internal mechanisms for dealing with the food (others have human-like **digestive systems** – see pages 66-67). Listed here are some of the main animal body parts involved in feeding and digestion.

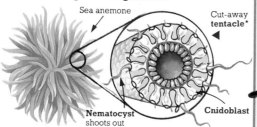

Sea anemone

Cut-away tentacle*

Nematocyst shoots out

Cnidoblast

- **Cnidoblasts** or **thread cells**. Special cells found in large numbers on the **tentacles*** of **coelenterates***, e.g. sea anemones, used for seizing food. Each one contains a **nematocyst** – a long thread coiled inside a tiny sac. When a tentacle touches something, the threads shoot out to stick to it or sting it.

Mouse skull ▶

Diastema

- **Diastema** (pl. **diastemata**). A gap between the front and back teeth of many plant-eaters. It is especially important in rodents, e.g. mice. They can draw their cheeks in through the gaps, so they do not swallow substances they may be gnawing.

- **Carnassial teeth**. The specially adapted second upper **premolar*** and first lower **molar*** of hunters, used for shearing flesh and cracking bones.

- **Radula**. The horny "tongue" of many **molluscs***, e.g. snails. It is covered by tiny teeth, which rasp off food.

Arthropod mouth parts

The mouths of **arthropods***, e.g. insects, are made up of a number of different parts. Depending on the animal's feeding method, these may look very different. The basic mouthparts, found in all insects, are the **mandibles**, **maxillae** (sing. **maxilla**), **labrum** and **labium**. The first two are also found in many other arthropods, e.g. crabs and centipedes (some of these other arthropods have two pairs of maxillae).

The **maxillae** of butterflies, moths and similar insects fit together to make a long sucking tube, or **proboscis**.

The **labium** of houseflies is an extended pad-like sucking organ.

Grooves called **pseudotracheae** (sing. **pseudotrachea**)

- **Filter-feeding**. The "sieving" of food from water, shown by many aquatic animals. Barnacles, for instance, sieve out microscopic organisms, or **plankton***, with bristly limbs called **cirri** (sing. **cirrus**). Some whales use frayed plates of horny **whalebone**, or **baleen**, hanging down from the top jaw. They sieve out small shrimp-like animals called **krill**.

Barnacle ▶

Krill   Cirrus   Plankton*

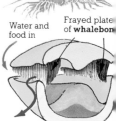

Water and food in

Frayed plate of whalebone

Water out

* Arthropods, Coelenterates, 112; Molars, 57; Molluscs, 112; Plankton, 114; Premolars, 57; Tentacles, 47.

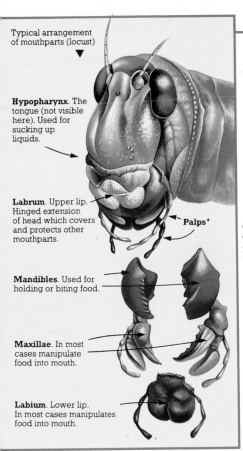

Typical arrangement
of mouthparts (locust)
▼

Hypopharynx. The
tongue (not visible
here). Used for
sucking up
liquids.

Labrum. Upper lip.
Hinged extension
of head which covers
and protects other
mouthparts.

Palps*

Mandibles. Used for
holding or biting food.

Maxillae. In most
cases manipulate
food into mouth.

Labium. Lower lip.
In most cases manipulates
food into mouth.

Digestive structures

- **Crop**. A thin-walled pouch, part of the gullet (**oesophagus***) in birds; also a similar structure in some worms, e.g. earthworms, and some insects, e.g. grasshoppers. Food is stored in the crop before it goes into the **gizzard**.

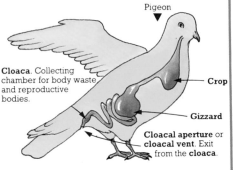

Pigeon
▼

Cloaca. Collecting
chamber for body waste
and reproductive
bodies.

Crop

Gizzard

Cloacal aperture or
cloacal vent. Exit
from the **cloaca**.

- **Gizzard**. A thick muscular-walled pouch at the base of the gullet (**oesophagus***) in those animals which have **crops**. These animals have no teeth, instead food is ground up in the gizzard. Birds swallow pieces of gravel to act as grindstones; in other animals, the muscular walls of the gizzard do the job, or hard tooth-like structures attached to these walls.

- **Rumen**. The large first chamber of the complex "stomach" of some plant-eating **mammals***, e.g. cows, into which food passes unchewed. It contains bacteria which can break down **cellulose***. Other animals pass this substance as waste, but these animals cannot afford to do this, as it makes up the bulk of their food (grass). The partially-digested food, which has also been processed in the second chamber, or **reticulum**, is then regurgitated to be chewed, and is known as the **cud**. When it is swallowed again it bypasses the first two chambers and is processed further in the third and fourth chambers – the **omasum** and the **abomasum** (the true stomach).

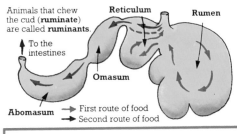

Animals that chew
the cud (**ruminate**)
are called **ruminants**.

Reticulum

Rumen

↑ To the
intestines

Omasum

Abomasum

→ First route of food
→ Second route of food

- **Caecum**. Any blind-ended sac inside the body, especially one forming part of a digestive system. In many animals, e.g. rabbits, it is the site of an important stage of digestion (involving bacterial breakdown of **cellulose*** – see **rumen**). In others, e.g. humans (see **large intestine***), it is redundant.

Animal respiration

The complex process of **respiration** consists of a number of stages (see introduction, page 70). Basically, oxygen is taken in and used by body cells in the breakdown of food, and carbon dioxide is expelled from the cells and the body. Below are some of the main animal respiratory organs.

- **Spiracle**. Any body opening through which oxygen and carbon dioxide are exchanged (e.g. a whale's blowhole). The term is used especially for any of the tiny holes (also called **stigmata**, sing. **stigma**) found in many **arthropods***, e.g. insects.

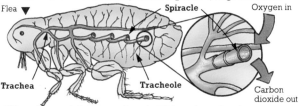

Flea ▼   Spiracle   Oxygen in

Trachea   Tracheole   Carbon dioxide out

- **Tracheae** (sing. **trachea**). Thin tubes leading in from the **spiracles** of **arthropods***, e.g. all insects and the most advanced spiders. They form an inner network, often branching into narrower tubes called **tracheoles**. Oxygen from the air passes through the tube walls to the body cells. Carbon dioxide leaves via the same route.

- **Lung books** or **book lungs**. Paired breathing organs found in scorpions (which have four pairs) and some (less advanced) spiders (which have one or two). Each one has many blood-filled tissue plates, arranged like book pages. Oxygen comes in through slits (**spiracles**), one by each lung book, and is absorbed into the blood. Carbon dioxide passes out the same way.

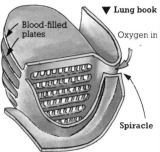

▼ Lung book

Blood-filled plates   Oxygen in

Spiracle

Gills

Gills or **branchiae** (sing. **branchia**), are the breathing organs of most aquatic animals, containing many blood vessels. Oxygen is absorbed into the blood from the water passing over the gills. Carbon dioxide passes out the other way. There are two types of gills – **internal** and **external**.

Breathing with **gills**

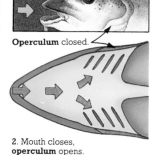

1. Water comes in through mouth.

Operculum closed.

2. Mouth closes, **operculum** opens.

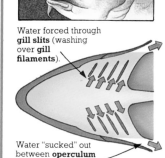

Water forced through **gill slits** (washing over **gill filaments**).

Water "sucked" out between **operculum** and body wall.

- **Siphon**. A tube carrying water to (**inhalant siphon**) or from (**exhalant siphon**) the **gills** of many lower aquatic animals, e.g. whelks (see picture, page 37). The exhalant siphon of **cephalopods*** (e.g. octopuses) is called the **hyponome***.

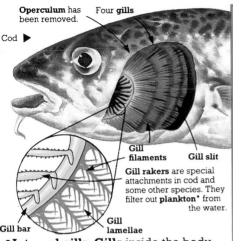

Operculum has been removed.   Four **gills**

Cod ▶

Gill **filaments**   Gill slit

Gill rakers are special attachments in cod and some other species. They filter out **plankton*** from the water.

Gill bar   Gill lamellae

- **Internal gills**. **Gills** inside the body, found in various forms in all fish, most **molluscs***, e.g. limpets, and most **crustaceans***, e.g. crabs. Most fish have four pairs of gills, with channels between them called **gill slits**. In more advanced fish, e.g. cod, they are covered by a flap called the **operculum**. In more primitive fish, e.g. sharks, they end in narrow openings in the skin on the side of the head. Each gill consists of a curved rod, the **gill bar** or **gill arch**, with many fine **gill filaments**, and even finer **gill lamellae** (sing. **lamella**) radiating from it. These all contain blood vessels.

- **External gills**. **Gills** on the outside of the body, found in the young stages of most fish and **amphibians***, some older amphibians and the young aquatic stages of many insects (e.g. caddisfly **larvae*** and mayfly **nymphs***). Their exact form depends on the type of animal, but in many cases they are "frilly" outgrowths from the head, e.g. in young tadpoles or axolotls (types of salamander).

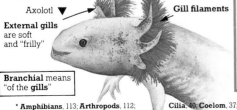

Axolotl ▼   Gill filaments

External gills are soft and "frilly"

Branchial means "of the **gills**"

Animal excretion

Excretion – the expulsion of waste fluid – is vital to life. It gets rid of harmful substances and is also vital to the maintenance of a balanced level of body fluids (see **homeostasis**, page 105).

- **Contractile vacuoles**. Tiny sacs used for water-regulation in single-celled freshwater organisms. Excess water enters a vacuole via several canals arranged around it. When fully expanded, it then contracts and bursts, shooting the water out through the outer membrane.

Paramecium ▼   Vacuole bursts
Contractile vacuole

Canals

- **Nephridia** (sing. **nephridium**). Waste-collecting tubes in many worms and the **larvae*** of many **molluscs***, e.g. slugs. In higher worms they collect from the **coelom*** (see picture, page 37). Lower worms and mollusc larvae have more primitive **protonephridia**. The waste fluid enters these via hollow **flame cells** (**solenocytes**), which contain hair-like **cilia***. In both a nephridium and a protonephridium, the waste leaves through a tiny hole, or **nephridiopore**.

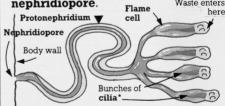

Flame cell   Waste enters here
Protonephridium ▼
Nephridiopore
Body wall
Bunches of **cilia***

- **Malpighian tubules**. Long tubes found in many **arthropods***, e.g. insects. They carry dissolved waste from the main body cavity (**haemocoel***) into the rear of the gut. See picture, page 37.

Animal senses and communication

All animals show some **sensitivity** (**irritability**), i.e. response to external stimuli such as light and sound vibrations. Humans have a high overall level of sensory development, but individual senses in other animals may be even better developed, e.g. the acute vision of hawks. Listed here are some of the main animal sense organs (and their parts). Their responding parts send "messages" (nervous impulses) to the brain (or more primitive nerve centre), which initiates the response.

Hearing and balance

- **Lateral lines**. Two water-filled tubes lying along each side of the body, just under the skin. They are found in all fish and those **amphibians*** which spend most of their time in water, e.g. some toads. They enable the animals to detect water currents and pressure changes, and they use this information to find their way about.

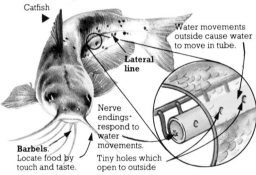

Catfish ▶

Water movements outside cause water to move in tube.

Lateral line

Nerve endings· respond to water movements.

Barbels. Locate food by touch and taste.

Tiny holes which open to outside

- **Tympanal organs** or **tympani** (sing. **tympanum**). Sound detectors found on the lower body or legs in some insects, e.g. crickets, and on the head in some **amphibians***, e.g. frogs. Each is an air sac covered by a thin layer of tissue. Sensitive fibres in the organs respond to high frequency sound vibrations.

- **Statocysts**. Tiny organs of balance, found in many aquatic **invertebrates***, e.g. jellyfish. Each is a sac with tiny particles called **statoliths** inside, e.g. sand grains. When the animal moves, the grains move, stimulating sensitive cells which set off responses.

Touch, smell and taste

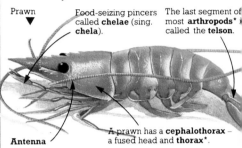

Prawn ▼

Food-seizing pincers called **chelae** (sing. **chela**).

The last segment of most **arthropods*** called the **telson**.

Antenna

A prawn has a **cephalothorax** – a fused head and **thorax***.

- **Antennae** (sing. **antenna**). Whip-like jointed sense organs on the heads of insects, **myriapods*** (centipedes and millipedes) and **crustaceans***, e.g. prawns. Insects and myriapods have one pair, crustaceans have two. They respond to touch, temperature changes and chemicals (giving "smell" or "taste"). Some crustaceans also use them for swimming or to attach themselves to objects or other animals.

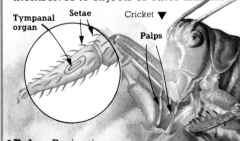

Tympanal organ

Setae

Cricket ▼

Palps

- **Palps**. Projections of the mouthparts of **arthropods***, e.g. insects. They respond to chemicals (giving "smell" or "taste"). The term is also given to various touch-sensitive organs.

* Amphibians, 113; Arthropods, Crustaceans, 112; Invertebrates, 113 (Note 8); Myriapods, 113 (Note 5); Thorax, 36 (Segmentation).

Communication

- **Pheromone.** Any chemical made by an animal that causes responses in other members of the species, e.g. sexual attractants produced by many insects.

- **Syrinx** (pl. **syringes**). The vocal organ of birds, similar to the **larynx***, but found at the base of the windpipe.

- **Vibrissae** (sing. **vibrissa**) or **whiskers.** Stiff hairs standing out from the faces of many **mammals***, e.g. cats, round the nose. They are sensitive to touch.

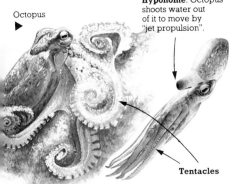

Octopus ▶

Hyponome. Octopus shoots water out of it to move by "jet propulsion".

Tentacles

- **Tentacles.** Long, flexible body parts, found in many **molluscs***, e.g. octopuses, and **coelenterates***, e.g. jellyfish. In most cases they are used for grasping food or feeling, though the shorter of the two pairs found in land snails and slugs have eyes on the end.

The cricket family **stridulate**, i.e. rub body parts together to make a shrill noise (often used to attract a mate). Crickets use their wing edges.

- **Setae** (sing. **seta**). Bristles produced by the skin of many **invertebrates***, e.g. insects. Nerves at their bases respond to movements of air or vibrations.

Sight

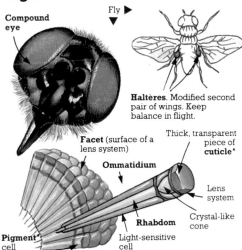

Compound eye

Fly ▶ ▼

Haltères. Modified second pair of wings. Keep balance in flight.

Facet (surface of a lens system)

Ommatidium

Thick, transparent piece of **cuticle***

Lens system

Rhabdom

Crystal-like cone

Pigment cell

Light-sensitive cell

- **Compound eyes.** The special eyes of many insects and some other **arthropods***, e.g. crabs. Each consists of hundreds of separate visual units called **ommatidia** (sing. **ommatidium**). Each of these has an outer lens system which "bends", or refracts, light onto a **rhabdom**, a transparent rod

Compound eye view of a flower (**mosaic image**)

surrounded by light-responsive cells.

After receiving information from all the ommatidia (each has a slightly different angle of vision and may record different light intensity or colour), the brain assembles a complete **mosaic image**. This is enough for the animal's needs, but not as well defined as the image produced by the human eye.

---

* Arthropods, 112; Coelenterates, 112; Cuticle, 38; Invertebrates, 113 (Note 8); Larynx, 70; Mammals, 113; Molluscs, 112; Pigments, 27.   **47**

Animal reproduction

Reproduction is the creation of new life. Most animals reproduce by **sexual reproduction***, the joining of a female sex cell, called an **ovum**, with a male sex cell, or **sperm**. Below are the main terms associated with the reproductive processes of animals.

Harvest mouse ▶

•**Viviparous**. A term describing animals such as humans, in which both the joining of the male and female sex cells (**fertilization**) and the development of the **embryo*** occur inside the female's body (the fertilization is **internal fertilization**), and the baby is born live.

Snake hatching from egg

•**Oviparous**. A term describing animals in which the development of the **embryo*** occurs inside an **egg** which has been laid by the mother. In some cases, e.g. in birds, the male and female sex cells join inside the female's body (**internal fertilization**) and the egg already contains the embryo when laid. In other cases, e.g. in many fish, the many eggs each just contain an **ovum** (female sex cell) when laid, and the male then deposits **sperm** (male sex cells) over them (**external fertilization**).

•**Eggs**. There are two main types of egg. **Cleidoic eggs** are produced by most egg-laying animals which live on land, e.g. birds and most **reptiles***, and also by a few aquatic animals, e.g. sharks. Such an egg largely isolates the **embryo*** from its surroundings, allowing only gases to pass through its tough shell (waste matter is stored). It contains enough food (**yolk**) for the complete development of the embryo, and the animal emerges as a tiny version of the adult. The other type of egg, produced by most aquatic animals, e.g. most fish, has a soft outer membrane, through which water and waste matter (as well as gases) can pass. The emerging young are not fully developed.

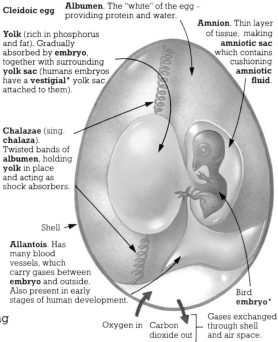

Cleidoic egg

Albumen. The "white" of the egg – providing protein and water.

Yolk (rich in phosphorus and fat). Gradually absorbed by **embryo**, together with surrounding **yolk sac** (humans embryos have a **vestigial*** yolk sac attached to them).

Amnion. Thin layer of tissue, making **amniotic sac** which contains cushioning **amniotic fluid**.

Chalazae (sing. **chalaza**). Twisted bands of **albumen**, holding **yolk** in place and acting as shock absorbers.

Shell →

Allantois. Has many blood vessels, which carry gases between **embryo** and outside. Also present in early stages of human development.

Bird **embryo***

Oxygen in   Carbon dioxide out

Gases exchanged through shell and air space.

* Embryo, 93; Reptiles, 113; Sexual reproduction, 92; Vestigial, 67 (**Appendix**).

- **Oviduct.** Any tube in females through which either **eggs** or **ova** (female sex cells) are discharged. In humans, the **Fallopian tubes***, **uterus*** and **vagina*** form the oviduct.

- **Ovipositor.** An organ extending from the back end of many female insects, through which **eggs** are laid. In many cases, it is long and sharp, and is used to pierce plant or animal tissues before laying.

- **Spermatheca.** A sac for storing **sperm** (male sex cells) in the female of many **invertebrates***, e.g. insects, and some lower **vertebrates***, e.g. newts. The female receives the sperm and stores them until her **ova** (sex cells) are ready to join with them (**fertilization**). Some **hermaphrodite** animals (animals with both male and female organs), e.g. earthworms, have spermathecae. They "swap" sperm when they mate.

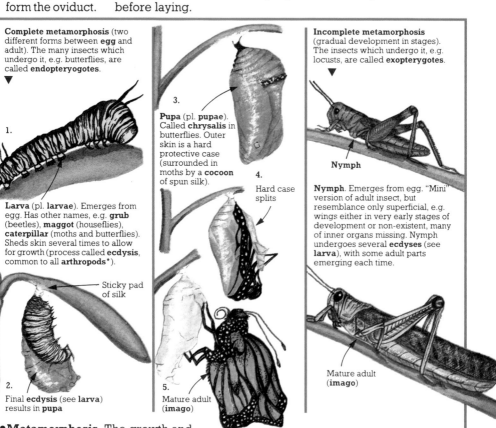

Complete metamorphosis (two different forms between **egg** and adult). The many insects which undergo it, e.g. butterflies, are called **endopteryogotes**.

1.

Larva (pl. **larvae**). Emerges from egg. Has other names, e.g. **grub** (beetles), **maggot** (houseflies), **caterpillar** (moths and butterflies). Sheds skin several times to allow for growth (process called **ecdysis**, common to all **arthropods***).

Sticky pad of silk

2.
Final **ecdysis** (see **larva**) results in **pupa**

3.
Pupa (pl. **pupae**). Called **chrysalis** in butterflies. Outer skin is a hard protective case (surrounded in moths by a **cocoon** of spun silk).

4.
Hard case splits

5.
Mature adult (**imago**)

Incomplete metamorphosis (gradual development in stages). The insects which undergo it, e.g. locusts, are called **exopterygotes**.

Nymph

Nymph. Emerges from egg. "Mini" version of adult insect, but resemblance only superficial, e.g. wings either in very early stages of development or non-existent, many of inner organs missing. Nymph undergoes several **ecdyses** (see **larva**), with some adult parts emerging each time.

Mature adult (**imago**)

- **Metamorphosis.** The growth and development of some animals involves intermediate forms which are very different from the adult form. Metamorphosis is a series of such changes, producing a complete or partial transformation from the young form to the adult. All insects, most marine **invertebrates***, e.g. lobsters, and most **amphibians***, e.g. frogs, undergo some degree of metamorphosis (intermediate larval forms are common, e.g. legless **tadpoles** in frogs and toads). Above are examples of insect metamorphosis (two different kinds – **complete** and **incomplete metamorphosis**).

* Amphibians, 113; Arthropods, 112; Fallopian tubes, 89; Invertebrates, 113 (Note 8); Uterus, Vagina, 89; Vertebrates, 113 (Craniata).

The skeleton

The human **skeleton** is a frame of over 200 bones which supports and protects the body organs (the **viscera**) and provides a solid base for the muscles to work against.

- **Cranium** or **skull**. A case protecting the brain and facial organs. It is made of **cranial** and **facial bones**, fused at lines called **sutures**. The upper jaw, for instance, consists of two fused bones called **maxillae** (sing. **maxilla**).

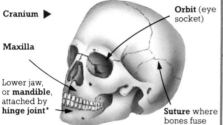

Cranium ▶

Maxilla

Lower jaw, or **mandible**, attached by **hinge joint***

Orbit (eye socket)

Suture where bones fuse

- **Rib cage**. A cage of bones forming the walls of the **thorax** or chest area. It is made up of 12 pairs of **ribs**, the **thoracic vertebrae** and the **sternum**. The ribs are joined to the sternum by bands of **cartilage*** called **costal cartilage**, but only the first seven pairs join it directly. The last five pairs are **false ribs**. The top three of these join the sternum indirectly – their costal cartilage joins that of the seventh pair. The bottom two pairs are **floating ribs**, only attached to the thoracic vertebrae at the back.

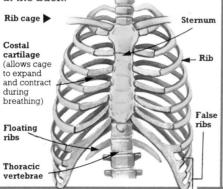

Rib cage ▶

Costal cartilage (allows cage to expand and contract during breathing)

Floating ribs

Thoracic vertebrae

Sternum

Rib

False ribs

- **Vertebral column**. Also called the **spinal column**, **spine** or **backbone**. A flexible chain of 33 **vertebrae** which protects the **spinal cord***, supports the head and provides points of attachment for the **pelvis** and **rib cage**.

- **Vertebrae** (sing. **vertebra**). The 33 bones of the **vertebral column**. A typical vertebra has a thick "chunk" (the **centrum** or **body**), various projections, or **processes** (named below) and a central hole – the **vertebral foramen** (pl. **foramina**). The foramina together form the **neural**, **spinal** or **vertebral canal**, through which the **spinal cord*** runs.

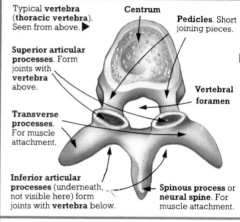

Typical **vertebra** (**thoracic vertebra**). Seen from above. ▶

Centrum

Pedicles. Short joining pieces.

Superior articular processes. Form joints with **vertebra** above.

Transverse processes. For muscle attachment.

Vertebral foramen

Inferior articular processes (underneath, not visible here) form joints with **vertebra** below.

Spinous process or **neural spine**. For muscle attachment.

The different vertebrae are named ▶ around the skeleton on the next page. The top 24 are movable and linked by **invertebral discs** of **cartilage***. The bottom nine are fused together. They all have the typical structure described above, except for the top two, the **atlas** and **axis**. The atlas (top vertebra) has a special joint with the **skull** which allows the head to nod. The axis has a "peg" (the **dens** or **odontoid process**) which fits into the atlas. This forms a **pivot joint**, a type of joint which allows head rotation.

* Cartilage, 53; **Hinge joint**, 52; **Spinal cord**, 74.

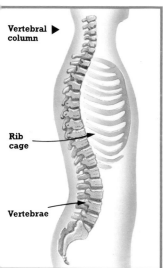

Vertebral column ▶

Rib cage

Vertebrae

The bones of the skeleton

7 **cervical vertebrae** support the neck. The top two are the **atlas** and **axis**.

Scapula or **shoulderblade**

Sternum or **breastbone**

12 **thoracic vertebrae** support the **ribs**.

The 5 **lumbar vertebrae** are in the lower back (**lumbar**) region.

The 5 **sacral vertebrae** at the base of the column are fused together to form the **sacrum**.

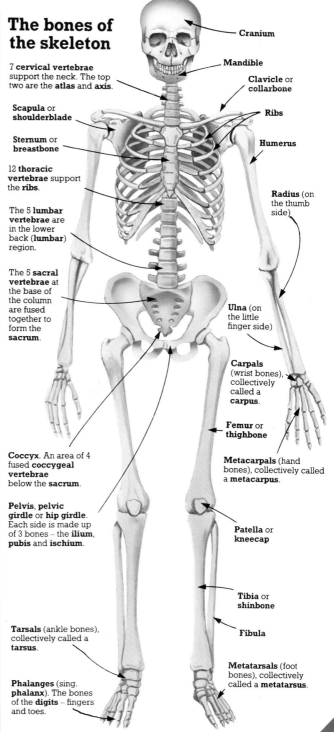

Cranium

Mandible

Clavicle or **collarbone**

Ribs

Humerus

Radius (on the thumb side)

Ulna (on the little finger side)

Carpals (wrist bones), collectively called a **carpus**.

Femur or **thighbone**

Metacarpals (hand bones), collectively called a **metacarpus**.

Patella or **kneecap**

Tibia or **shinbone**

Fibula

Metatarsals (foot bones), collectively called a **metatarsus**.

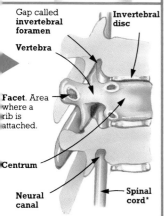

Gap called **invertebral foramen**

Vertebra

Invertebral disc

Facet. Area where a rib is attached.

Centrum

Neural canal

Spinal cord*

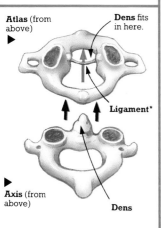

Atlas (from above) ▶

Dens fits in here.

Ligament*

Axis (from above) ▶

Dens

Coccyx. An area of 4 fused **coccygeal vertebrae** below the **sacrum**.

Pelvis, pelvic girdle or **hip girdle.** Each side is made up of 3 bones – the **ilium**, **pubis** and **ischium**.

Tarsals (ankle bones), collectively called a **tarsus**.

Phalanges (sing. **phalanx**). The bones of the **digits** – fingers and toes.

Joints and bone

The bones of the skeleton meet at many **joints**, or **articulations**. Some are **fixed joints**, allowing no movement, e.g. the **sutures*** of the skull. Most, however, are movable, and they give the body great flexibility. The most common are listed below.

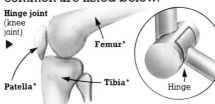

Hinge joint (knee joint)

Femur*

Patella*   Tibia*

Hinge

- **Hinge joints**. Joints (e.g. the knee joint) which work like any hinge. That is, the movable part (bone) can only move in one plane, i.e. in either of two opposing directions.

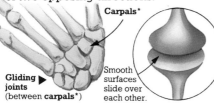

Carpals*

Gliding joints (between **carpals***)

Smooth surfaces slide over each other.

- **Gliding joints**. Also called **sliding** or **plane joints**. Joints in which one or more flat surfaces glide over each other, e.g. those between the **carpals***. They are more flexible than **hinge joints**.

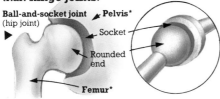

Ball-and-socket joint (hip joint)

Pelvis*

Socket

Rounded end

Femur*

- **Ball-and-socket joints**. The most flexible joints (e.g. the hip joint). The movable bone has a rounded end which fits into a socket in the fixed bone. The movable bone can swivel, or move in many directions.

Connective tissue

There are many different types of **connective tissue** in the body. They all protect and connect cells or organs and have a basis of non-living material (the **matrix**) in which living cells are scattered. The difference between them lies in the nature of this material. The various types of tissue found at a joint, including **bone** itself, are all types of connective tissue. They all contain protein fibres and are either tough (containing **collagen** fibres) or elastic (containing **elastin** fibres).

- **Periosteum**. A thin layer of elastic connective tissue. It surrounds all bones, except at the joints (where **cartilage** takes over), and contains **osteoblasts** – cells which make new bone cells, needed for growth and repair.

- **Ligaments**. Bands of connective tissue which connect the bones of joints (and also hold many organs in place). Most are tough, though some are elastic, e.g. between **vertebrae***.

- **Bone** or **osseous tissue**. A special type of tough connective tissue, made hard and resilient by large deposits of phosphorus and calcium compounds. The living bone cells, or **osteocytes**, are held in tiny spaces (**lacunae**, sing. **lacuna**) within this non-living material. ▶

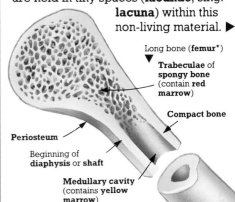

Long bone (**femur***)

▼ **Trabeculae** of spongy bone (contain **red marrow**)

Compact bone

Periosteum

Beginning of **diaphysis** or shaft

Medullary cavity (contains **yellow marrow**)

* **Carpals**, **Femur**, **Patella**, **Pelvis**, 51; **Sutures**, 50 (**Cranium**); **Tibia**, 51; **Vertebrae**, 50.

- **Synovial sac** or **synovial capsule**. A cushioning "bag" of lubricating fluid (**synovial fluid**), with an outer skin (**synovial membrane**) of elastic connective tissue. Most movable joints, e.g. the knee, have such a sac lying between the bones. They are known as **synovial joints**.

- **Tendons** or **sinews**. Bands of tough connective tissue joining muscles to bones. Each is a continuation of the membrane around the muscle, together with the outer membranes of its bundles of fibres.

- **Cartilage** or **gristle**. A tough connective tissue. In some joints (**cartilaginous joints**) it is the main cushion between the bones (e.g. **vertebrae***). In joints with **synovial sacs**, it covers the ends of the bones and is called **articular cartilage**.

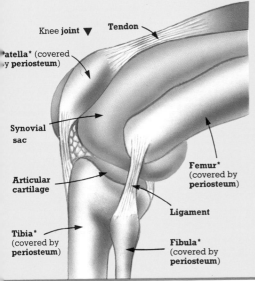

Knee joint ▼ Tendon

Patella* (covered by periosteum)

Synovial sac

Articular cartilage

Tibia* (covered by periosteum)

Femur* (covered by periosteum)

Ligament

Fibula* (covered by periosteum)

The end of the nose and the outer parts of the ears are made of cartilage, as are young skeletons, though these slowly turn to **bone** as minerals build up (a process called **ossification** or **osteogenesis**).

▶ There are two types of bone. **Spongy bone** is found in short and/or flat bones, e.g. the **sternum***, and fills the ends of long bones, e.g. the **femur***. It consists of a criss-cross network of flat plates called **trabeculae** (sing. **trabecula**), with many large spaces between them, filled by **red marrow** (see **bone marrow**). **Compact bone** forms the outer layer of all bones. It has far fewer spaces, and is laid in concentric layers (**lamellae**, sing. **lamella**) around channels called **Haversian canals**. These link with an complex system of tiny canals carrying blood vessels and nerves to the osteocytes.

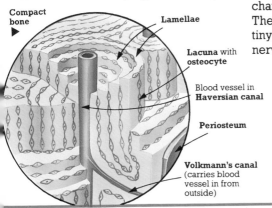

Compact bone ▶

Lamellae

Lacuna with osteocyte

Blood vessel in Haversian canal

Periosteum

Volkmann's canal (carries blood vessel in from outside)

- **Bone marrow**. Two types of soft tissue. **Red marrow**, found in spongy bone (see **bone**), is where all new red (and some white) blood cells are made. **Yellow marrow** is a fat store, found in hollow areas (**medullary** or **marrow cavities**) in long bone **shafts**.

* Femur, Fibula, Patella, Sternum, Tibia, 51; Vertebrae, 50.

Muscles

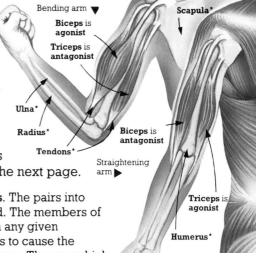

Muscles are areas of special elastic tissue (**muscle**) found all over the body. They may be either **voluntary muscles** (able to be controlled by conscious action) or **involuntary muscles** (not under conscious control). The main types of muscles are listed at the top of the next page.

Antagonistic pair ▶

Bending arm ▼
Biceps is agonist
Triceps is antagonist
Scapula*
Ulna*
Radius*
Tendons*
Biceps is antagonist
Straightening arm ▶
Triceps is agonist
Humerus*

- **Antagonistic pairs** or **opposing pairs**. The pairs into which almost all muscles are arranged. The members of each pair produce opposite effects. In any given movement, the muscle which contracts to cause the movement is the **agonist** or **prime mover**. The one which relaxes at the same time is the **antagonist**.

The structure of muscle tissue

The different types of muscles in the body are made up of different kinds of muscle tissue (groups of cells of different types). The tissue has many blood vessels, bringing food matter to be broken down for energy, and nerves, which stimulate the muscles to act.

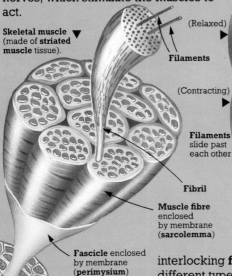

Skeletal muscle ▼
(made of **striated muscle** tissue).

Filaments

Fibril

Muscle fibre enclosed by membrane (**sarcolemma**)

Fascicle enclosed by membrane (**perimysium**)

Tough outer layer of **muscle** (**epimysium**)

- **Striated** or **striped muscle**. The type of muscle tissue which makes up **skeletal muscles**. It consists of long cells called **muscle fibres**, grouped together in bundles called **fascicles**.

Actin filaments   Myosin filaments

(Relaxed) ▶

(Contracting) ▶

Filaments slide past each other

Each fibre has a striped (**striated**) appearance and is made of many smaller cylinders, called **fibrils** or **myofibrils**, which are the parts that contract when a fibre is stimulated by a nerve. The fibrils themselves consist of interlocking **filaments**, or **myofilaments**, of two different types of protein – **actin** (thin filaments) and **myosin** (thicker filaments). These filaments slide past each other as a muscle contracts.

* Humerus, Radius, Scapula, 51; Tendons, 53; Ulna, 51.

Types of muscles

- **Skeletal muscles**. All the muscles attached to the bones of the skeleton, which contract together or in sequence to move all the body parts. They are all **voluntary muscles** (see introduction) and are made of **striated muscle** tissue. Some are named according to their position, shape or size, others are named after the movement they cause, e.g. **flexors** cause **flexion** (the bending of a limb at a joint), **extensors** straighten a limb.

These are all skeletal muscles

- **Cardiac muscle**. The muscle which makes up almost all of the wall of the heart. It is an **involuntary muscle** (see introduction) and is made of **cardiac muscle** tissue.

- **Visceral muscles**. The muscles in the walls of many internal organs, e.g. the intestines and blood vessels. They are all **involuntary muscles** (see introduction) and consist of **smooth muscle** tissue.

- **Cardiac muscle**. A special kind of **striated muscle** tissue, making up the **cardiac muscle** of the heart. Its constant rhythmical contractions are caused by stimulations from special areas of the tissue itself, which produce their own electrical impulses. Any nervous impulses just increase or decrease this heart rate.

- **Smooth muscle** or **visceral muscle**. The type of muscle tissue which makes up the **visceral muscles**. It consists of spindle-shaped cells, much shorter than the complex fibres of **striated muscle**. The way it contracts is not yet fully understood, but it contains **actin** and **myosin**, like striated muscle, and is also stimulated by nerves.

Nervous stimulation

Most muscles are stimulated to move by impulses from nerves running through the body. For more about this, see pages 80-81.

- **Motor end-plate**. The point where the end fibres of an "instruction-carrying" nerve cell (**motor neuron***) meet a **muscle fibre** (see **striated muscle**). The end fibres are branches from one main fibre (**axon***). This carries nervous impulses which make the muscle contract. Each impulse is duplicated and sent down each end branch, hence the whole muscle receives a multiplication of each impulse.

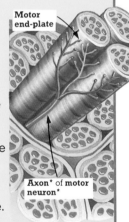

Motor end-plate

Axon* of motor neuron*

- **Muscle spindle**. A group of **muscle fibres** (see **striated muscle**) which has the end fibres of a sensory nerve cell (**sensory neuron***) wrapped round it. The end fibres are part of one main fibre (**dendron***). When the muscle stretches they are stimulated to send impulses to the brain, "telling" it about the new state of tension. The brain can then work out the changes needed for any further action.

Teeth

The **teeth** or **dentes** (sing. **dens**) help to prepare food for digestion by cutting and grinding it up. Each tooth is set into the jaw, which has a soft tissue covering called **gum (gingiva)**. During their lives, humans have two sets of teeth (**dentitions**) – a temporary set, or **deciduous dentition**, made up of 20 **deciduous teeth** (also called **milk** or **baby teeth**), and a later **permanent dentition** (32 **permanent teeth**).

Parts of a tooth

Molar (only one shown)
Crown
Enamel
Gum
Pulp cavity
Neck
Cement
Dentine
Root canals
Root
Nerve
Tiny blood vessels
Incisor (only one shown)
Chisel-shaped crown
Enamel
Gum
Cement
Neck
Dentine
Single root
Pulp cavity

- **Crown**. The exposed part of a tooth. It is covered by **enamel**. It is the part most subject to damage or tooth decay.

- **Root**. The part of a tooth that is fixed in a socket in the jaw. **Incisors** and **canines** have one root, **premolars** have one or two and **molars** have two or three. Each root is held in place by the tough fibres of a **ligament*** called the **periodontal ligament**. The fibres are fixed to the jawbone at one end, and to the **cement** at the other. They act as shock absorbers.

- **Neck** or **cervix**. The part of a tooth just below the surface, lying between the **crown** and the **root**.

- **Enamel**. A substance similar to bone, though it is harder (the hardest substance in the body) and has no living cells. It consists of tightly- packed crystals of **apatite**, a mineral made up of calcium, phosphorus and fluorine.

- **Cement** or **cementum**. A bone-like substance, similar to **enamel** but softer. It forms the thin surface layer of the **root** and is attached to the jaw by the **periodontal ligament** (see **root**).

- **Dentine** or **ivory**. A yellow substance which forms the second layer inside a tooth. Like **enamel**, it has many of the same constituents as bone, but it is softer and it also contains **collagen*** fibres and strands of **cytoplasm***. These run out from the **pulp** cells in the **pulp cavity**.

- **Pulp cavity**. The central area of a tooth, surrounded by **dentine**. It is filled with a soft tissue called **pulp**, which contains blood vessels and nerve fibre endings. These enter at the base of a **root** and run up to the cavity inside **root canals**. The blood vessels supply food and oxygen to the living tissue and the nerve fibre endings are **pain receptors***.

* Collagen, 52 (Connective tissue); Cytoplasm, 10; Ligaments, 52; Pain receptors, 83.

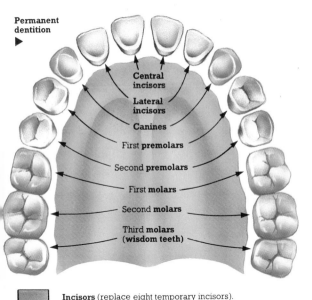

Permanent dentition ▶

Central incisors
Lateral incisors
Canines
First **premolars**
Second **premolars**
First **molars**
Second **molars**
Third **molars** (**wisdom teeth**)

Incisors (replace eight temporary incisors).

Canines (replace four temporary canines).

Premolars (replace eight temporary molars).

Molars (appear behind **premolars** and do not replace any **deciduous teeth**).

Types of teeth

- **Incisors**. Sharp, chisel-shaped teeth, used for biting and cutting. Each has one root, and there are four in each jaw, set at the front of the mouth.

- **Canines** or **cuspids**. Cone-shaped teeth (often called **eye** or **dog teeth**), used to tear food. Each has a sharp point (**cusp**) and one **root**. There are two in each jaw, one each side of the **incisors**. In animals which hunt and kill, they are long and curved.

- **Premolars** or **bicuspids**. Blunt, broad teeth, used for crushing and grinding (found in the permanent set of teeth only). There are four in each jaw, two behind each **canine**. Each has two sharp ridges (**cusps**) and one **root**, except the upper first premolars, which have two.

- **Molars**. Blunt, broad teeth, similar to **premolars** but with a larger surface area. They are also used for crushing and grinding, and each has four surface points (**cusps**). Lower molars have two **roots** each, and upper ones have three. In the permanent set of teeth there are six in each jaw, three behind each pair of **premolars**, and the third ones (at the back) are known as **wisdom teeth**.

- **Wisdom teeth**. Four **molars** (the third ones in line), lying at the end points of the jaws. They appear last of all, when a person is fully mature (hence their name). Often there is no room for them to come through and they get stuck in the jawbone, or **impacted**. A few people never develop wisdom teeth.

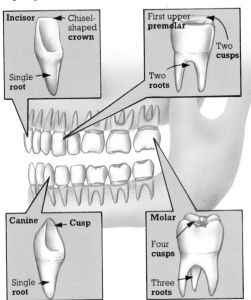

Incisor — Chisel-shaped **crown**
Single **root**

First upper **premolar** — Two **cusps**
Two **roots**

Canine — Cusp
Single **root**

Molar
Four **cusps**
Three **roots**

Blood

Blood is a vital body fluid, consisting of **plasma**, **platelets** and **red** and **white blood cells**. An adult human has about 5.5 litres (9.5 pints), which travel around in the **circulatory system*** – a system of tubes called **blood vessels**. The blood distributes heat and carries many important substances in its plasma. Its old, dying blood cells are constantly being replaced by new ones in a process called **haemopoiesis**.

Blood constituents

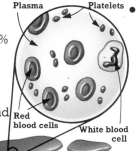

Plasma   Platelets

Red blood cells   White blood cell

- **Plasma.** The pale liquid (about 90% water) which contains the blood cells. It carries dissolved food for the body cells, waste matter and carbon dioxide secreted by them, **antibodies** to combat infection, and **enzymes*** and **hormones*** which control body processes.

- **Platelets** or **thrombocytes.** Very small, disc-shaped bodies with no **nuclei***, made in the **bone marrow***. They gather particularly at an injured area, where they are important in the **clotting** of blood.

- **White blood cells.** Also called **white corpuscles** or **leucocytes**. Large, opaque blood cells, important in body defence. There are several types. **Lymphocytes**, for example, are made in **lymphoid tissue*** and are found in the **lymphatic system*** as well as blood. They make **antibodies**. Other

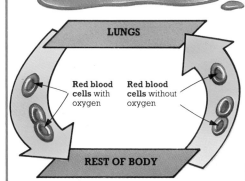

LUNGS

Red blood cells with oxygen   Red blood cells without oxygen

REST OF BODY

Lymphocyte

Different types of antibody

- **Red blood cells.** Also called **red corpuscles** or **erythrocytes**. Red, disc-shaped cells with no **nuclei***. They are made in the **bone marrow*** and contain **haemoglobin** (an iron compound which gives blood a dark red colour). This combines with oxygen in the lungs to form **oxyhaemoglobin**, and the blood becomes bright red. The red cells pass the oxygen to the body cells (by **diffusion***) and then return to the lungs with haemoglobin.

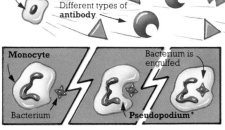

Monocyte   Bacterium is engulfed

Bacterium   Pseudopodium*

white cells – **monocytes** – are made in **bone marrow***. They "swallow up" foreign bodies, e.g. bacteria, in a process called **phagocytosis***. Many of them (**macrophages**) leave the blood vessels. They either travel around (**wandering macrophages**) or become fixed in an organ, e.g. a **lymph node*** (**fixed macrophages**).

58   * Bone marrow, 53; Circulatory system, 60; Diffusion, 99; Enzymes, 103; Hormones, 106; Lymphatic system, Lymph nodes, 65; Lymphoid tissue, 65 (Lymphoid organs); Nucleus, 10; Phagocytosis, 40 (Pseudopodium).

• **Blood groups**. The main way of classifying blood. The group depends on whether the **antigens** A or B are present in the **red blood cells**. Group A blood has A antigen, group B has B, group AB has both and group O has neither.

• **Rhesus factor** or **Rh factor**. A second way of classifying blood (as well as by **blood group**). If it contains the **Rhesus antigen**, it is **Rhesus positive** blood. If not, it is **Rhesus negative**.

Body defence

• **Antibodies**. "Defence" proteins in body fluids, e.g. **plasma**. They are made by **lymphocytes** (see **white blood cells**) when **antigens** appear in the body. A different antibody is made for each antigen, and they act in one of a number of different ways. **Anti-toxins** neutralize toxins (see **antigens**). Each one joins with a toxin molecule, making an **antigen-antibody complex**. **Agglutinins** stick together the bacteria or viruses with their antigens. **Lysins** kill them by dissolving their outer membranes.

Bacteria with antigens

Antibodies

Toxin

Antigen-antibody complex

Anti-toxin (antibody)

Toxin

Bacteria (and antigens) sticking together.

Agglutinin (antibody)

Antigen

Bacterium breaks down

Lysin (antibody)

• **Antigens**. Substances, mostly proteins, which cause the production of **antibodies** to combat them and any infection they may cause. They may form part of bacteria or viruses, or they may be toxins (poisons) released by them. Some are present in the body from birth, e.g. those determining **blood group**.

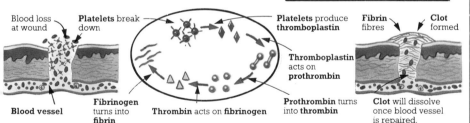

Blood loss at wound

Platelets break down

Blood vessel

Fibrinogen turns into fibrin

Thrombin acts on fibrinogen

Platelets produce thromboplastin

Thromboplastin acts on prothrombin

Prothrombin turns into thrombin

Fibrin fibres

Clot formed

Clot will dissolve once blood vessel is repaired.

• **Clotting** or **coagulation**. The thickening of blood into a mass (**clot**) at the site of a wound. First, disintegrating **platelets** and damaged cells release a chemical called **thromboplastin**. This causes **prothrombin** (a **plasma** protein) to turn into **thrombin** (an **enzyme***). This then causes **fibrinogen** (another plasma protein) to

harden into **fibrin**, a fibrous substance. A network of its fibres makes up the jelly-like clot.

• **Serum**. A yellow liquid consisting of the parts of the blood left after **clotting**. It contains many **antibodies** (produced to combat infections). When injected into other people, it can give temporary immunity to the infections.

* **Enzymes**, 103.

The circulatory system

The **circulatory** or **vascular system** is a network of blood-filled tubes, or **blood vessels**, of which there are three main types – **arteries**, **veins** and **capillaries**. A thin tissue layer called the **endothelium** lines arteries and veins, and is the only layer of capillary walls. Blood is kept flowing one way by the pumping of the heart, by muscles in artery and vein walls and by a decrease in pressure through the system (liquids flow from high to low pressure areas).

Passage of main substances in circulatory system.

➡ Arteries, arterioles, capillaries

➡ Capillaries, venules, veins

LUNGS

HEART

△ Dissolved food matter

△● Food and oxygen used by organ's cells

△ǁ Newly-digested food

● Oxygen

△ǀ Some food stored

○ Carbon dioxide

□ Waste

★ Some food used by organ's cells

◓ Oxygen breathed in, carbon dioxide out

■ Waste disposed

●**Arteries.** Wide, thick-walled blood vessels, making up the **arterial system** and carrying blood away from the heart. Smaller arteries (**arterioles**) branch off the main ones, and **capillaries** branch off the arterioles. Except in the **pulmonary arteries***, the blood contains oxygen (which makes it bright red). In all arteries it also carries dissolved food and waste, brought into the heart by **veins**, and there transferred to the arteries. These carry the food to the cells (via arterioles and capillaries) and the waste to the kidneys.

●**Veins.** Wide, thick-walled blood vessels, making up the **venous system** and carrying blood back to the heart. They contain valves to stop blood flowing backwards due to gravity, and are formed from merging **venules** (small veins). These are formed in turn from merging **capillaries**. The blood contains carbon dioxide (except in the **pulmonary veins***) and waste matter, both picked up from body cells by the capillaries. The blood in the veins leading from the digestive system and liver also carries dissolved food. This is transferred to the arteries in the heart.

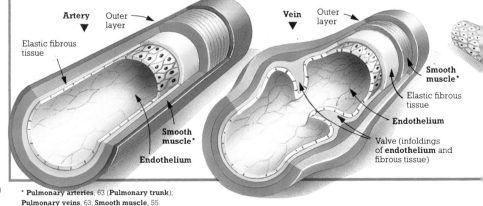

Artery ▼ Outer layer

Elastic fibrous tissue

Smooth muscle*

Endothelium

Vein ▼ Outer layer

Smooth muscle*

Elastic fibrous tissue

Endothelium

Valve (infoldings of **endothelium** and fibrous tissue)

* Pulmonary arteries, 63 (Pulmonary trunk);
Pulmonary veins, 63; Smooth muscle, 55.

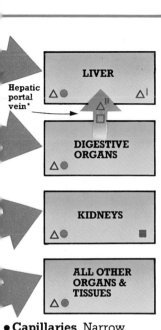

LIVER

Hepatic portal vein*

DIGESTIVE ORGANS

KIDNEYS

ALL OTHER ORGANS & TISSUES

• **Capillaries.** Narrow, thin-walled blood vessels, branching off **arterioles** (see **arteries**) to form a complex network. Oxygen and dissolved food pass out through their walls to the body cells, and carbon dioxide and waste pass in (see **tissue fluid**, page 64). The capillaries of the digestive organs and liver also pick up food. Capillaries finally join up again to form small veins (**venules**).

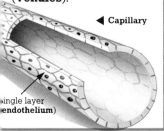

◀ **Capillary**

single layer (**endothelium**)

The main arteries and veins

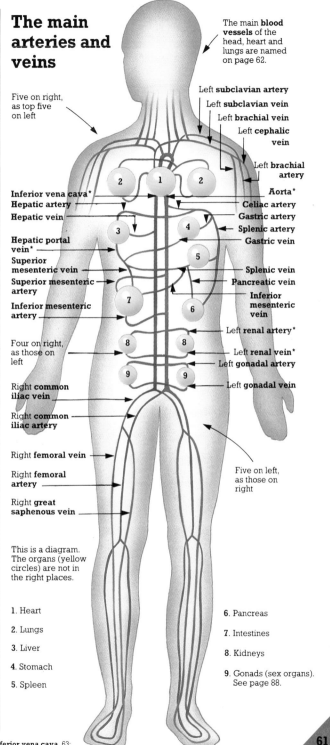

The main **blood vessels** of the head, heart and lungs are named on page 62.

Five on right, as top five on left

Left **subclavian artery**
Left **subclavian vein**
Left **brachial vein**
Left **cephalic vein**
Left **brachial artery**

Inferior vena cava*
Hepatic artery
Hepatic vein

Aorta*
Celiac artery
Gastric artery
Splenic artery
Gastric vein

Hepatic portal vein*
Superior mesenteric vein
Superior mesenteric artery
Inferior mesenteric artery

Splenic vein
Pancreatic vein
Inferior mesenteric vein

Left **renal artery***
Left **renal vein***
Left **gonadal artery**
Left **gonadal vein**

Four on right, as those on left

Right **common iliac vein**
Right **common iliac artery**

Right **femoral vein**
Right **femoral artery**
Right **great saphenous vein**

Five on left, as those on right

This is a diagram. The organs (yellow circles) are not in the right places.

1. Heart
2. Lungs
3. Liver
4. Stomach
5. Spleen

6. Pancreas
7. Intestines
8. Kidneys
9. Gonads (sex organs). See page 88.

* **Aorta**, 63; **Hepatic portal vein**, 68 (**Liver**); **Inferior vena cava**, 63; **Renal arteries, Renal veins**, 72 (**Kidneys**).

61

The heart

The **heart** is a muscular organ which pumps blood around the blood vessels (the heart and blood vessels together are the **cardiovascular system**). It is surrounded by the **pericardial sac**. This consists of an outer membrane (the **pericardium**) and the cavity (**pericardial cavity**) between it and the heart. This cavity is filled with a cushioning fluid (**pericardial fluid**). The heart has four chambers – two **atria** and two **ventricles**, all lined by a thin tissue layer called the **endocardium**.

Position of heart

The cardiac cycle

The **cardiac cycle** is the series of events which make up one complete pumping action of the heart, and which can be heard as the heartbeat (about 70 times a minute). First, both **atria** contract and pump blood into their respective **ventricles**, which relax to receive it. Then the atria relax and take in blood, and the ventricles ▶

The chambers of the heart

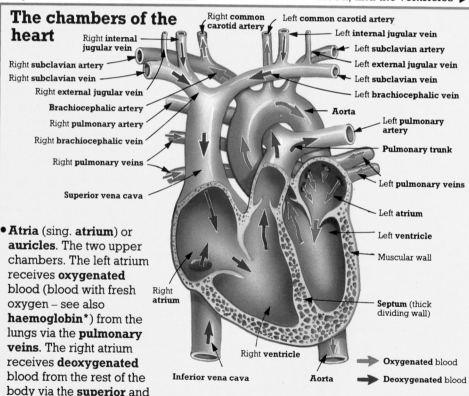

Right **common carotid artery**
Left **common carotid artery**
Right **internal jugular vein**
Left **internal jugular vein**
Right **subclavian artery**
Left **subclavian artery**
Right **subclavian vein**
Left **external jugular vein**
Right **external jugular vein**
Left **subclavian vein**
Brachiocephalic artery
Left **brachiocephalic vein**
Right **pulmonary artery**
Aorta
Right **brachiocephalic vein**
Left **pulmonary artery**
Right **pulmonary veins**
Pulmonary trunk
Superior vena cava
Left **pulmonary veins**
Left **atrium**
Left **ventricle**
Muscular wall
Right **atrium**
Septum (thick dividing wall)
Right **ventricle**
Inferior vena cava
Aorta

➡ **Oxygenated** blood
➡ **Deoxygenated** blood

- **Atria** (sing. **atrium**) or **auricles**. The two upper chambers. The left atrium receives **oxygenated** blood (blood with fresh oxygen – see also **haemoglobin***) from the lungs via the **pulmonary veins**. The right atrium receives **deoxygenated** blood from the rest of the body via the **superior** and **inferior vena cavae**. This is blood whose oxygen has been used by the cells and replaced by carbon dioxide.

- **Ventricles**. The two lower chambers. The left ventricle receives blood from the left **atrium** and pumps it into the **aorta**. The right ventricle receives blood from the right atrium and pumps it via the **pulmonary trunk** to the lungs.

* Haemoglobin, 58 (Red blood cells).

contract to pump it out. The relaxing phase of a chamber is its **diastole phase**; the contracting phase is its **systole phase**. There is a short pause after the systole phase of the ventricles, during which all chambers are in diastole phase (relaxing). The different **valves** which open and close during the cycle are defined below right.

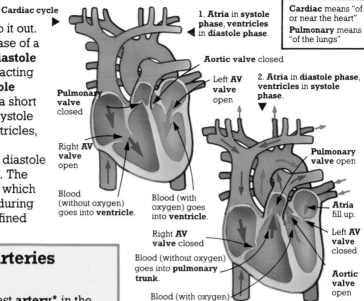

Cardiac cycle ▶

1. **Atria** in **systole phase**, **ventricles** in **diastole phase**.

Cardiac means "of or near the heart"
Pulmonary means "of the lungs"

Aortic valve closed

Left **AV valve** open

2. **Atria** in **diastole phase**, ventricles in **systole phase**. ▼

Pulmonary valve closed

Right **AV valve** open

Blood (without oxygen) goes into **ventricle**.

Blood (with oxygen) goes into **ventricle**.

Right **AV valve** closed

Blood (without oxygen) goes into **pulmonary trunk**.

Blood (with oxygen) goes into **aorta**.

Pulmonary valve open

Atria fill up.

Left **AV valve** closed

Aortic valve open

The main arteries and veins

Aorta. The largest **artery*** in the body. It carries blood with fresh oxygen out of the left **ventricle** to begin its journey round the body.

Pulmonary trunk. The **artery*** which carries blood needing fresh oxygen out of the right **ventricle**. After leaving the heart, it splits into the right and left **pulmonary arteries**, one going to each lung.

Superior vena cava. One of the two main **veins***. It carries blood needing fresh oxygen from the upper body to the right **atrium**. All the upper body veins merge into it.

Inferior vena cava. One of the two main **veins***, carrying blood needing fresh oxygen from the lower body to the right **atrium**. All the lower body veins merge into it.

Pulmonary veins. Four **veins*** which carry blood with fresh oxygen to the left **atrium**. Two right pulmonary veins come from the right lung, and two left pulmonary veins come from the left lung.

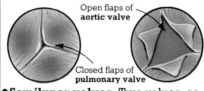

Open flaps of **aortic valve**

Closed flaps of **pulmonary valve**

- **Semilunar valves**. Two valves, so called because they have crescent-shaped flaps. One is the **aortic valve** between the left **ventricle** and the **aorta**. The other is the **pulmonary valve** between the right ventricle and the **pulmonary trunk**.

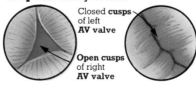

Closed **cusps** of left **AV valve**

Open cusps of right **AV valve**

- **Atrioventricular valves** or **AV valves**. Two valves, each between an **atrium** and its corresponding **ventricle**. The left AV valve, or **mitral valve**, is a **bicuspid valve**, i.e. it has two movable flaps, or **cusps**. The right AV valve is a **tricuspid valve**, i.e. it has three cusps.

Tissue fluid and the lymphatic system

The smallest blood vessels, called **capillaries***, are those in the most direct contact with the individual cells of the body, but even they do not touch the cells. The food and oxygen they carry finally reaches the cells in **tissue fluid**, a substance which forms the link between the **circulatory system*** and the body's drainage system, known as the **lymphatic system**.

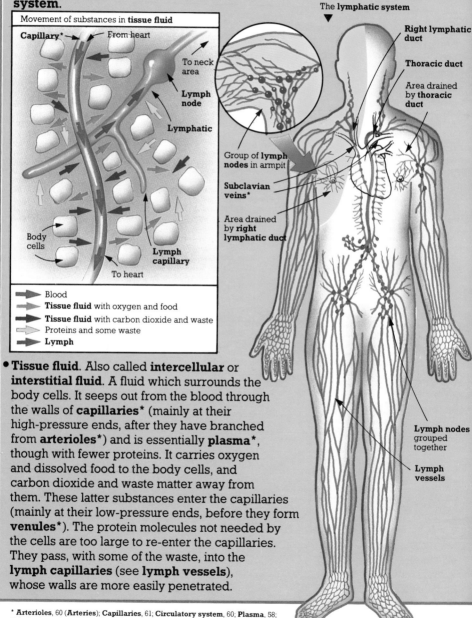

The **lymphatic system** ▼

Movement of substances in **tissue fluid**

Capillary* — From heart

To neck area

Lymph node

Lymphatic

Body cells

Lymph capillary

To heart

➡ Blood
➡ **Tissue fluid** with oxygen and food
➡ **Tissue fluid** with carbon dioxide and waste
➡ Proteins and some waste
➡ Lymph

Right lymphatic duct

Thoracic duct

Area drained by **thoracic duct**

Group of **lymph nodes** in armpit

Subclavian veins*

Area drained by **right lymphatic duct**

Lymph nodes grouped together

Lymph vessels

- **Tissue fluid**. Also called **intercellular** or **interstitial fluid**. A fluid which surrounds the body cells. It seeps out from the blood through the walls of **capillaries*** (mainly at their high-pressure ends, after they have branched from **arterioles***) and is essentially **plasma***, though with fewer proteins. It carries oxygen and dissolved food to the body cells, and carbon dioxide and waste matter away from them. These latter substances enter the capillaries (mainly at their low-pressure ends, before they form **venules***). The protein molecules not needed by the cells are too large to re-enter the capillaries. They pass, with some of the waste, into the **lymph capillaries** (see **lymph vessels**), whose walls are more easily penetrated.

64

Lymphoid organs

The **lymphoid organs**, or **lymphatic organs**, are bodies connected to the **lymphatic system**. They are all made of the same type of tissue (**lymphoid** or **lymphatic tissue**) and they all produce **lymphocytes*** – disease-fighting white blood cells.

- **Lymphatic system.** A system of tubes (**lymph vessels**) and small organs (**lymphoid organs**), important in the recycling of body fluids and in the fight against disease. The lymph vessels carry the liquid **lymph** around the body and empty it back into the **veins***, and the lymphoid organs are the source of disease-fighting cells.

- **Lymph vessels** or **lymphatic vessels**. Blind-ended tubes carrying **lymph** from all body areas towards the neck, where it is emptied back into the blood. They are lined with **endothelium***, and have valves to stop the lymph being pulled back by gravity. The thinnest ones are **lymph capillaries**, and include the important **lacteals***, which pick up fat particles (too large to enter the bloodstream directly). The capillaries join to form larger vessels called **lymphatics**, which finally unite to form two tubes – the **right lymphatic duct** (emptying into the right **subclavian vein***) and the **thoracic duct** (emptying into the left **subclavian vein***).

- **Lymph.** The liquid in **lymph vessels**. It contains **lymphocytes** (see **lymphoid organs**), some substances picked up from **tissue fluid** (especially proteins such as **hormones*** and **enzymes***) and also fat particles (see **lymph vessels**).

- **Lymph nodes** or **lymph glands**. Small lymphoid organs found along the course of **lymph vessels**, often in groups, e.g. in the armpits. They are the main sites of **lymphocyte** production (see above) and also contain a filter system which traps bacteria and foreign bodies. These are then engulfed by white blood cells (**fixed macrophages***).

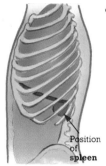

Position of spleen

- **Spleen.** The largest lymphoid organ, found just below the **diaphragm*** on the left side of the body. It holds an emergency store of red blood cells and also contains white blood cells (**fixed macrophages***) which destroy foreign bodies, e.g. bacteria, and old blood cells.

- **Tonsils.** Four lymphoid organs: one **pharyngeal tonsil** (the **adenoids**) at the back of the nose, one **lingual tonsil** at the base of the tongue and two **palatine tonsils** at the back of the mouth.

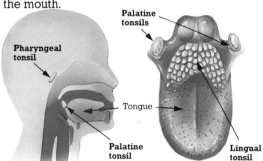

Palatine tonsils

Pharyngeal tonsil

Tongue

Palatine tonsil

Lingual tonsil

- **Thymus gland.** A lymphoid organ in the upper part of the chest. It is fairly large in children, reaches its maximum size at **puberty*** and then undergoes **atrophy**, i.e. wastes away.

The digestive system

After food is taken in, or **ingested**, it passes through the **digestive system**, gradually being broken down into simple soluble substances by a process called **digestion** (see also pages 108-109). The simple substances are absorbed into the blood vessels around the system and transported to the body cells. Here they are used to provide energy and build new tissue. For more about all these different processes, see pages 100-104. The main parts of the digestive system are listed on these two pages. The pancreas and liver (see page 68) also play a vital part in digestion, forming the two main **digestive glands*** (producing **digestive juices***).

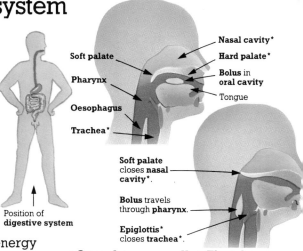

Position of
digestive system

Nasal cavity*
Soft palate
Hard palate*
Pharynx
Bolus in
oral cavity
Oesophagus
Tongue
Trachea*

Soft palate
closes **nasal
cavity***.

Bolus travels
through **pharynx**.

Epiglottis*
closes **trachea***.

●**Alimentary canal**. Also called the **alimentary tract**, **gastrointestinal (GI) tract**, **enteric canal** or the **gut**. A collective term for all the parts of the digestive system. It is a long tube running from the mouth to the **anus** (see **large intestine**). Most of its parts are in the lower body, or **abdomen**, inside the main body cavity, or **perivisceral cavity***. They are held in place by **mesenteries** – infoldings of the cavity lining (the **peritoneum**).

●**Pharynx**. A cavity at the back of the mouth, where the mouth cavity (**oral** or **buccal cavity**) and the **nasal cavities*** meet. When food is swallowed, the **soft palate** (a tissue flap at the back of the mouth) closes the nasal cavities and the **epiglottis*** closes the **trachea***.

●**Oesophagus** or **gullet**. The tube down which food travels to the **stomach**. A piece of swallowed food is a **bolus**.

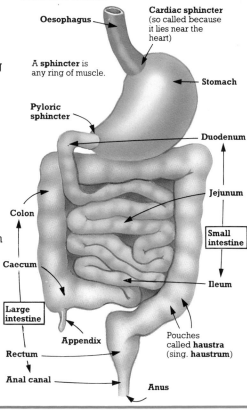

Oesophagus

Cardiac sphincter
(so called because
it lies near the
heart)

A **sphincter** is
any ring of muscle.

Stomach

Pyloric
sphincter

Duodenum

Jejunum

Small
intestine

Colon

Ileum

Caecum

Large
intestine

Appendix

Rectum

Anal canal

Pouches
called **haustra**
(sing. **haustrum**).

Anus

* Digestive juices, 68 (Digestive glands); Epiglottis, 70; Hard palate, 79; Nasal cavities, 79 (Nose); Perivisceral cavity, 37; Trachea, 70.

- **Cardiac sphincter**. Also called the **gastroesophageal sphincter**. A muscular ring between the **oesophagus** and **stomach**. It relaxes to open and let food through.

- **Stomach**. A large sac in which the first stages of digestion occur. Its lining has many folds (**rugae**, sing. **ruga**) which flatten out to let it expand. Some substances, e.g. water, pass through its wall into nearby blood vessels, but almost all the semi-digested food (**chyme**) goes into the **small intestine** (**duodenum**).

- **Small intestine**. The main site of digestion – a coiled tube with three parts, the **duodenum**, **jejunum** and **ileum**. Many tiny "fingers" called **villi** (sing. **villus**) project inwards from its lining. Each contains **capillaries*** (tiny blood vessels), into which most of the food is absorbed, and a **lymph vessel*** called a **lacteal**, which absorbs recombined fat particles (see **fats**, page 100). The remaining semi-liquid waste mixture passes into the **large intestine**.

- **Large intestine**. A thick tube receiving waste from the **small intestine**. It consists of the **caecum*** (a redundant sac), **colon**, **rectum** and **anal canal**. The colon contains bacteria, which break down any remaining food and make some important vitamins. Most of the water in the waste passes through the colon walls into nearby blood vessels. This leaves a semi-solid mass (**faeces**), which is pushed out of the body (**defaecation**) via the rectum, anal canal and **anus** – a hole surrounded by a muscular ring (the **anal sphincter**).

- **Appendix**. A small blind-ended tube off the **caecum** (see **large intestine**). It is a **vestigial** organ, i.e. one which our ancestors needed, but is now defunct.

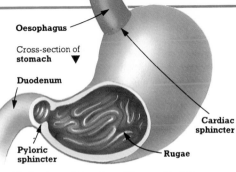

Oesophagus

Cross-section of stomach ▼

Duodenum

Cardiac sphincter

Pyloric sphincter

Rugae

- **Pyloric sphincter**. Also called the **pyloric valve** or **pylorus**. A muscular ring between the **stomach** and the **small intestine**. It relaxes to let food through only after certain digestive changes have occurred.

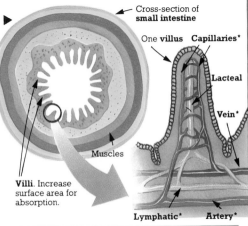

Cross-section of small intestine

One **villus**   Capillaries*

Lacteal

Vein*

Muscles

Villi. Increase surface area for absorption.

Lymphatic*   Artery*

- **Mucous membrane** or **mucosa**. A thin layer of tissue lining all digestive passages (also other passages, e.g. the air passages). It is a special type of **epithelium*** (a surface sheet of cells), containing many single-celled **exocrine glands***, called **mucous glands**. These secrete **mucus** – a lubricating fluid which, in the case of the digestive passages, also protects against the action of **digestive juices***.

- **Peristalsis**. The waves of contraction, produced by muscles in the walls of organs (especially digestive organs), which move substances along.

* Arteries, 60; Caecum, 43; Capillaries, 61; Digestive juices, 68 (Digestive glands); Epithelium, 82 (Epidermis); Exocrine glands, 68; Lymphatic, 65 (Lymph vessels); Veins, 60.

67

Glands

Glands are special organs (or sometimes groups of cells or single cells) which produce and secrete a variety of substances vital to life. There are two types of human gland – **exocrine** and **endocrine**.

Exocrine glands

Exocrine glands are glands which secrete substances through tubes, or **ducts**, onto a surface or into a cavity. Most body glands are exocrine, e.g. **sweat glands*** and **digestive glands**.

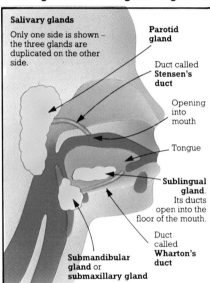

Salivary glands
Only one side is shown – the three glands are duplicated on the other side.

Parotid gland

Duct called **Stensen's duct**

Opening into mouth

Tongue

Sublingual gland. Its ducts open into the floor of the mouth.

Duct called **Wharton's duct**

Submandibular gland or **submaxillary gland**

• **Digestive glands**. Exocrine glands which secrete fluids called **digestive juices** into the digestive organs. The juices contain **enzymes*** which cause the breakdown of food (see chart, pages 108-109). Many of the glands are tiny, and set into the walls of the digestive organs, e.g. **gastric glands** in the stomach and **intestinal glands** (or **crypts of Lieberkühn**) in the small intestine. Others are larger and lie more freely, e.g. **salivary glands**. The largest are the **pancreas** and **liver**.

• **Pancreas**. A large gland which is both a **digestive gland** and an **endocrine gland**. It produces **pancreatic juice** (see chart, pages 108-109), which it secretes along the **pancreatic duct**, or **duct of Wirsung**. It also contains groups of cells called the **islets of Langerhans**. These make up the endocrine parts of the organ, and produce the **hormones* insulin*** and **glucagon***.

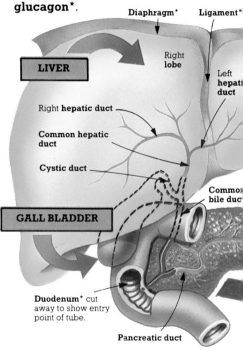

Diaphragm*   Ligament*

LIVER

Right lobe

Left hepatic duct

Right **hepatic duct**

Common hepatic duct

Cystic duct

Common bile duct

GALL BLADDER

Duodenum* cut away to show entry point of tube.

Pancreatic duct

• **Liver**. The largest organ. One of its many roles is that of a **digestive gland**, secreting **bile** (see chart, pages 108-109) along the **common hepatic duct**. Another of its vital jobs is the conversion and storage of newly-digested food matter (see diagram, page 101), which it receives along the **hepatic portal vein** (see picture, page 61). In particular, it regulates the amount of glucose in the blood. It also destroys worn-out red blood cells, stores vitamins and iron and makes important blood proteins.

* Diaphragm, 70; Duodenum, 67 (Small intestine); Enzymes, 103; Glucagon, Hormones, Insulin, 106; Ligaments, 52; Sweat glands, 83.

- **Gall bladder**. A sac which stores **bile** (made in the **liver**) in a concentrated form until it is needed (i.e. until there is food in the **duodenum***). Its lining has many folds (**rugae**, sing. **ruga**) which flatten out as it expands. When needed, the bile is squeezed along the **cystic duct** and **common bile duct**.

Left lobe

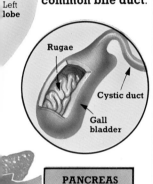

Rugae

Cystic duct

Gall bladder

PANCREAS

he two ducts join orm a duct called **ampulla of Vater**.

Common bile duct

Pancreatic duct

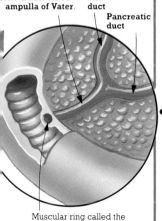

Muscular ring called the **sphincter of Oddi**. If it is closed, **bile** coming from the **liver** is forced back up into the **gall bladder**.

Endocrine glands

Endocrine or **ductless glands** are glands which secrete substances called **hormones** directly into the blood (i.e. into blood vessels in the glands). For more about hormones, and a chart including all those mentioned below, see pages 106-107. The glands may be separate bodies (e.g. those below) or cells inside organs, e.g. in the sex organs.

- **Pituitary gland**. Also called the **pituitary body** or **hypophysis**. A gland at the base of the brain, directly influenced by the **hypothalamus*** (see also **hormones**, page 106) and made up of an **anterior** (front) **lobe** (**adenohypophysis**) and a **posterior** (back) **lobe** (**neurohypophysis**). Many of its hormones are **tropic hormones**, i.e. they stimulate other glands to secrete hormones. It produces **ACTH, TSH, STH, FSH, LH, lactogenic hormone, oxytocin** and **ADH**.

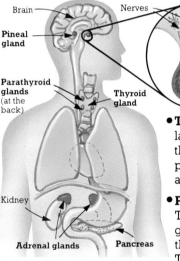

Brain

Pineal gland

Parathyroid glands (at the back)

Nerves

Thyroid gland

Hypothalamus*

Pituitary gland

Anterior lobe

Posterior lobe

Kidney

Adrenal glands

Pancreas

- **Adrenal glands** or **suprarenal glands**. A pair of glands, one gland lying above each kidney. Each has an outer layer (**cortex**), producing **aldosterone**, **cortisone** and **hydrocortisone**, and an inner layer (**medulla**), producing **adrenalin** and **noradrenalin**.

- **Thyroid gland**. A large gland around the **larynx***. It produces **thyroxin** and **thyrocalcitonin**.

- **Parathyroid glands**. Two pairs of small glands embedded in the **thyroid gland**. They produce **PTH**.

- **Pineal gland**. Also called the **pineal body**. A small gland at the front of the brain. Its role is not clear, but it is known to secrete **melatonin**, a hormone thought to influence **sex hormone*** production.

* Duodenum, 67 (Small intestine); Hypothalamus, 75; Larynx, 70; Sex hormones, 106.

The respiratory system

The term **respiration** covers three processes: **ventilation**, or breathing (taking in oxygen and expelling carbon dioxide), **external respiration** (the exchange of the gases between the **lungs** and the blood – see also red blood cells, page 58) and **internal respiration** (food breakdown, using oxygen and producing carbon dioxide – see pages 104-105). Listed here are the component parts of the human **respiratory system**.

Pharynx*

The **epiglottis** is a flap which closes the **trachea** while food goes down the **oesophagus***.

Oesophagus*

Larynx

Trachea

•**Lungs**. The two main breathing organs, inside which gases are exchanged. They contain many tubes (**bronchi** and **bronchioles**) and air sacs (**alveoli**).

Larynx

Trachea

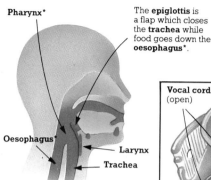

Vocal cords (open)

Rear view of **larynx** (cut away) ▼

Lung (blood vessels not shown) ▼

Cartilage* plates

Glottis

•**Trachea** or **windpipe**. The main tube through which air passes on its way to and from the **lungs**.

•**Larynx**. The "voice box" at the top of the **trachea**. It contains the **vocal cords** – two pieces of tissue folding inwards from the trachea lining and attached to plates of **cartilage***. The opening between the cords is called the **glottis**. During speech, muscles pull the cartilage plates (and hence the cords) together, and air passing out through the cords makes them vibrate, producing sounds.

•**Pleura** or **pleural membrane**. A layer of tissue surrounding each **lung** and lining the chest cavity (**thorax**). Between the pleura around a lung and the pleura lining the thorax there is a space (**pleural cavity**). This contains **pleural fluid**. The pleura and fluid-filled cavity make up a cushioning **pleural sac**.

Right **primary bronchus**

Secondary bronchus

Tertiary bronchus

Cut end of rib

Bronchiole

Pleura

Pleural cavity with **pleural fluid**

Diaphragm

The **lungs** and all the tubes are lined by **mucous membrane*** and **cilia***.

•**Diaphragm** or **midriff**. A sheet of muscular tissue which separates the chest from the lower body, or **abdomen**. At rest, it lies in an arched position, forced up by the abdomen wall below it.

* Cartilage, 53; Cilia, 40; Mucous membrane, 67; Oesophagus, Pharynx, 66.

- **Bronchi** (sing. **bronchus**). The main tubes into which the **trachea** divides. The first two branches are the right and left **primary bronchi**. Each carries air into a **lung** (via a hole called a **hilum**), alongside a **pulmonary artery*** bringing blood in. They then branch into **secondary bronchi**, **tertiary bronchi** and **bronchioles**, all accompanied by blood vessels, both branching from the pulmonary artery and merging to form **pulmonary veins*** (blood going out).

- **Bronchioles**. The millions of tiny tubes in the **lungs**, all accompanied by blood vessels. They branch off **tertiary bronchi** (see **bronchi**) and have smaller branches called **terminal bronchioles**, each one ending in a cluster of **alveoli**.

- **Alveoli** (sing. **alveolus**). The millions of tiny sacs attached to **terminal bronchioles** (see **bronchioles**). They are surrounded by **capillaries*** (tiny blood vessels) whose blood is rich in carbon dioxide. This passes out through the capillary walls and in through those of the alveoli (to be breathed out). The oxygen which has been breathed into the alveoli passes into the capillaries, which then begin to merge together (eventually forming **pulmonary veins***).

Breathing

- **Breathing** is made up of **inspiration** (breathing in) and **expiration** (breathing out). Both actions are normally automatic, controlled by nerves from the **respiratory centre** in the **medulla*** of the brain. This acts when it detects too high a level of carbon dioxide in the blood.

Inspiration ▶

Intercostal muscles contract, pulling ribs up and outwards.

Expiration ▶

Oxygen in

Carbon dioxide out

Diaphragm flattens

Intercostal muscles relax, ribs move down and inwards

Diaphragm relaxes

- **Inspiration** or **inhalation**. The act of breathing in. The **diaphragm** contracts and flattens, lengthening the chest cavity. The muscles between the ribs (**intercostal muscles**) also contract, pulling the ribs up and outwards and widening the cavity. The overall expansion lowers the air pressure in the **lungs**, and air rushes in to fill them (i.e. to equalize internal and external pressure).

- **Expiration** or **exhalation**. The act of breathing out. The **diaphragm** and **intercostal muscles** (see **inspiration**) relax, and air is forced out of the **lungs** as the chest cavity becomes smaller.

Tertiary bronchus

Terminal bronchioles

Bronchial means "of the bronchi or bronchioles"

To pulmonary vein*

Capillaries*

Cluster alveoli

From pulmonary artery*

Alveolus

The urinary system

The **urinary system** is the main system of body parts involved in **excretion**, which is the expulsion of unwanted substances. The parts are defined below and right. The lungs and skin are also involved in excretion (expelling carbon dioxide and sweat respectively).

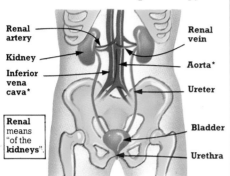

Renal artery

Kidney

Inferior vena cava*

Renal vein

Aorta*

Ureter

Renal means "of the **kidneys**".

Bladder

Urethra

- **Kidneys**. Two organs at the back of the body, just below the ribs. They are the main organs of excretion, filtering out unwanted substances from the blood and regulating the level and contents of body fluids (see also **homeostasis**, page 105). Blood enters a kidney in a **renal artery** and leaves it in a **renal vein**.

- **Ureters**. The two tubes which carry **urine** from the **kidneys** to the **bladder**.

Kidney (cut away)

Area shown in picture, top right

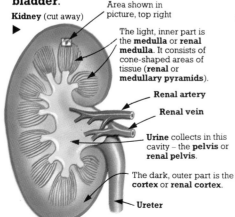

The light, inner part is the **medulla** or **renal medulla**. It consists of cone-shaped areas of tissue (**renal** or **medullary pyramids**).

Renal artery

Renal vein

Urine collects in this cavity – the **pelvis** or **renal pelvis**.

The dark, outer part is the **cortex** or **renal cortex**.

Ureter

Inside a kidney

> 1. **Glomerular filtration.** As blood squeezes through the **glomerulus**, most of its water, minerals, vitamins, glucose, **amino acids*** and **urea** are forced into the **Bowman's capsule**, forming **glomerular filtrate**.

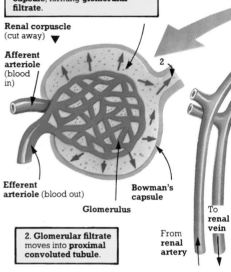

Renal corpuscle (cut away) ▼

Afferent arteriole (blood in)

2

Efferent arteriole (blood out)

Bowman's capsule

Glomerulus

To renal vein

From renal artery

> 2. **Glomerular filtrate** moves into **proximal convoluted tubule**.

- **Nephrons**. The tiny filtering units of the **kidneys** (there are about a million per kidney). Each consists of a **renal corpuscle** and a **uriniferous tubule**.

- **Renal corpuscles** or **Malpighian corpuscles**. The bodies which filter fluids out of the blood. Each consists of a **glomerulus** and a **Bowman's capsule**.

- **Bladder** or **urinary bladder**. A sac ▶ which holds stored **urine**. Its lining has many folds (**rugae**, sing. **ruga**) which flatten out as it fills up, letting it expand. Two muscular rings – the **internal** and **external urinary sphincters** – control the opening from the bladder into the **urethra**. When the volume of urine gets to a certain level, nerves stimulate the internal sphincter to open, but the external sphincter is under conscious control (except in young children), and can be held closed for longer.

* Amino acids, 100 (**Proteins**); Aorta, Inferior vena cava, 63.

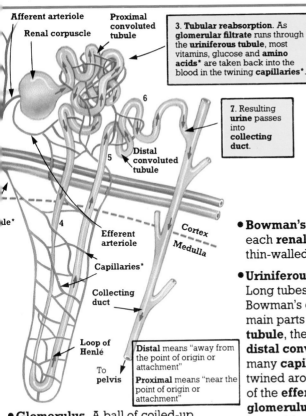

Afferent arteriole

Renal corpuscle

Proximal convoluted tubule

3. **Tubular reabsorption**. As **glomerular filtrate** runs through the **uriniferous tubule**, most vitamins, glucose and **amino acids*** are taken back into the blood in the twining **capillaries***.

4. Some minerals are also taken back. The **hormone* aldosterone*** controls reabsorption of more if needed.

6

7. Resulting **urine** passes into **collecting duct**.

5. Some water is also taken back. The **hormone* ADH*** controls reabsorption of more if needed.

Distal convoluted tubule

5

6. **Tubular secretion**. Some substances, e.g. ammonia and some drugs, pass from the blood into the **uriniferous tubule**.

le*   4

Efferent arteriole

Capillaries*

Collecting duct

Loop of Henlé

To **pelvis**

Cortex
Medulla

Distal means "away from the point of origin or attachment"

Proximal means "near the point of origin or attachment"

● **Bowman's capsule**. The outer part of each **renal corpuscle**. It is a thin-walled sac around the **glomerulus**.

● **Uriniferous tubules** or **renal tubules**. Long tubes, each one leading from a Bowman's capsule. Each has three main parts – the **proximal convoluted tubule**, the **loop of Henlé** and the **distal convoluted tubule** – and has many **capillaries*** (tiny blood vessels) twined around it. These are branches of the **efferent arteriole** (see **glomerulus**) and they re-unite to form larger blood vessels carrying blood from the **kidney**.

● **Glomerulus**. A ball of coiled-up **capillaries*** (tiny blood vessels) at the centre of each **renal corpuscle**. The capillaries branch from an **arteriole*** entering the corpuscle (an **afferent arteriole**) and re-unite to leave the corpuscle as an **efferent arteriole**.

● **Collecting duct** or **collecting tubule**. A tube which carries **urine** from several **uriniferous tubules** into the **pelvis** of a **kidney**.

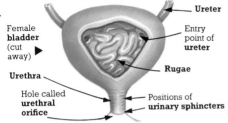

Ureter

Female bladder (cut away)

Entry point of ureter

Urethra

Rugae

Hole called **urethral orifice**

Positions of **urinary sphincters**

● **Urethra**. The tube carrying **urine** from the **bladder** out of the body (in men, it also carries **sperm*** – see **penis**, page 88). The expulsion of urine is called **urination** or **micturition**.

● **Urea**. A nitrogen-containing (**nitrogenous**) waste substance which is a product of the breakdown of excess **amino acids*** in the liver. It travels in the blood to the **kidneys**, together with smaller amounts of similar substances, e.g. creatinine.

● **Urine**. The liquid which leaves the **kidneys**. Its main constituents are **urea**, excess water and minerals.

* **ADH**, **Aldosterone**, 106; **Amino acids**, 100 (**Proteins**); **Arteriole**, 60 (**Arteries**); **Capillaries**, 61; **Hormones**, 106; **Sperm**, 93 (**Gametes**); **Venule**, 60 (**Veins**).

73

The central nervous system

The **central nervous system** (**CNS**) is the body's control centre. It co-ordinates all its actions, both mechanical and chemical (working with **hormones***) and is made up of the **brain** and **spinal cord**. The millions of nerves in the body carry "messages" (nervous impulses) to and from these central areas (see pages 78-81).

- **Brain.** The organ which controls most of the body's activities. It is the only organ able to produce "intelligent" action – action based on past experience (stored information), present events and future plans. It is made up of millions of **neurons*** (nerve cells), arranged into **sensory**, **association** and **motor areas**. The sensory areas receive information (nervous impulses) from all body parts and the association areas analyse the impulses and make decisions. The motor areas send impulses (orders) to muscles or glands. The impulses are carried by the fibres of 43 pairs of nerves – 12 pairs of **cranial nerves** serving the head and 31 pairs of **spinal nerves** (see **spinal cord**).

Brain

Spinal cord (inside vertebral column*)

- **Spinal cord.** A long string of nervous tissue running down from the **brain** inside the **vertebral column***. Nervous impulses from all parts of the body pass through it. Some are carried into or away from the **brain**, some are dealt with in the cord (see **involuntary actions**, page 81). 31 pairs of **spinal nerves** branch out from the cord through the gaps between the **vertebrae***. Each spinal nerve is made up of two groups of fibres: a **dorsal** or **sensory root**, made up of the fibres of **sensory neurons*** (bringing impulses in), and a **ventral** or **motor root**, made up of the fibres of **motor neurons*** (taking impulses out).

Parts of the brain

- **Cerebrum.** The largest, most highly developed area, with many deep folds. It is composed of two **cerebral hemispheres**, joined by the **corpus callosum** (a band of **nerve fibres***), and its outer layer is called the **cerebral cortex**. This contains all the most important **sensory**, **association** and **motor areas** (see **brain**). It controls most physical activities and is the centre for mental activities such as decision-making, speech, learning, memory and imagination.

- **Cerebellum.** The area which co-ordinates muscle movement and balance, two things under the overall control of the **cerebrum**.

- **Midbrain** or **mesencephalon.** An area joining the **diencephalon** to the **pons**. It carries impulses in towards the **thalamus**, and out from the **cerebrum** towards the **spinal cord**.

- **Pons** or **pons Varolii.** A junction of **nerve fibres*** which forms a link between the parts of the **brain** and the **spinal cord** (via the **medulla**).

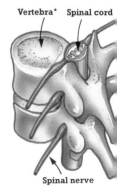

Vertebra*   Spinal cord

Spinal nerve

* Hormones, 106; Motor neurons, 77; Nerve fibres, Neurons, 76; Sensory neurons, 77; Vertebrae, Vertebral column, 50.

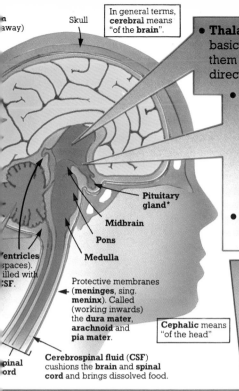

Skull

In general terms, **cerebral** means "of the **brain**".

Pituitary gland*

Midbrain

Pons

Medulla

Ventricles (spaces). filled with CSF.

Protective membranes (**meninges**, sing. **meninx**). Called (working inwards) the **dura mater**, **arachnoid** and **pia mater**.

Cephalic means "of the head"

Cerebrospinal fluid (CSF) cushions the **brain** and **spinal cord** and brings dissolved food.

spinal cord

- **Thalamus**. The area which carries out the first, basic sorting of incoming impulses and directs them to different parts of the **cerebrum**. It also directs some outgoing impulses.

  - **Hypothalamus**. The master controller of most inner body functions. It controls the **autonomic nervous system*** (the nerve cells causing unconscious action, e.g. food movement through the intestines) and the action of **pituitary gland***. Its activities are vital to **homeostasis*** – the maintenance of stable internal conditions.

  - **Diencephalon**. A collective term for the **thalamus** and **hypothalamus**.

Areas of **cerebrum**

☐ **Sensory areas**. Receive incoming impulses.
  1. General sensory area. Receives impulses from muscles, skin and inner organs.
  2. **Primary gustatory area**. Impulses from tongue.
  3. **Primary auditory area**. Impulses from ears.
  4. **Primary visual area**. Impulses from eyes.
  5. **Primary olfactory area**. Impulses from nose.

☐ **Motor areas**. Each tiny part sends out impulses to a specific muscle.

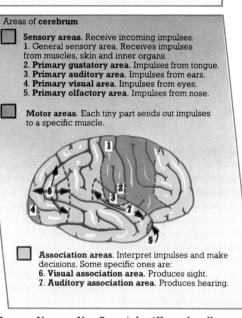

☐ **Association areas**. Interpret impulses and make decisions. Some specific ones are:
  6. **Visual association area**. Produces sight.
  7. **Auditory association area**. Produces hearing.

- **Medulla** or **medulla oblongata**. The area which controls the "fine tuning" of many unconscious actions (under the overall control of the **hypothalamus**). Different parts of it control different actions, e.g. the **respiratory centre** controls breathing.

- **Brain stem**. A collective term for the **midbrain**, **pons** and **medulla**.

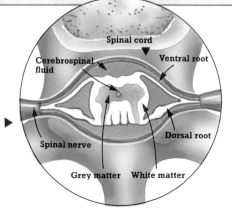

Spinal cord

Cerebrospinal fluid

Ventral root

Dorsal root

Spinal nerve

Grey matter   White matter

- **Neuroglia** or **glia**. Special stiffened cells which support and protect the nerve cells (**neurons***) of the CNS. Some produce a white fatty substance called **myelin** (see also **Schwann cells**, page 76). This coats the long fibres found in the connective areas of the **brain** and the outer layer of the **spinal cord**, and leads to these areas being known as **white matter**. **Grey matter**, by contrast, consists mainly of **cell bodies*** and their short fibres, and its neuroglia does not produce myelin.

* Autonomic nervous system, 80; Cell body, 76; Homeostasis, 105; Neurons, 76; Periosteum, 52; Pituitary gland, 69.

The units of the nervous system

The individual units of both the brain and spinal cord (**central nervous system***) and the nerves of the rest of the body (**peripheral nervous system**) are the nerve cells, or **neurons**. They are unique in being able to transmit electrical "messages" (the vital nervous impulses) around the body. Each neuron consists of a **cell body**, an **axon** and one or more **dendrites**, and there are three types of neuron – **sensory**, **association** and **motor neurons**.

The parts of a neuron

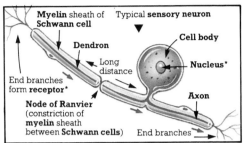

Myelin sheath of Schwann cell   Typical **sensory neuron**

Dendron

Long distance

End branches form **receptor***

Node of Ranvier (constriction of myelin sheath between **Schwann cells**)

Cell body

Nucleus*

Axon

End branches

- **Cell body** or **perikaryon**. The part of a neuron containing its **nucleus*** and most of its **cytoplasm***. The cell bodies of all **association**, some **sensory** and some **motor neurons** lie in the brain and spinal cord. Those of the other sensory neurons are found in special masses called **ganglia*** or as part of highly specialized **receptors*** in the nose and eyes. Those of the other motor neurons lie in **autonomic ganglia***.

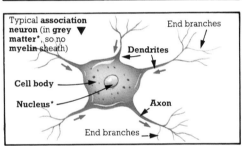

Typical **association neuron** (in **grey matter***, so no myelin sheath)

Cell body

Nucleus*

End branches

Dendrites

Axon

End branches

- **Nerve fibres**. The fibres (**axon** and **dendrites**) of a neuron. They are extensions of the **cytoplasm*** of the **cell body** and carry the vital nervous impulses. Most of the long nerve fibres which run out round the body (belonging to **sensory** or **motor neurons**) are accompanied by **neuroglial*** cells. These are called **Schwann cells** and they produce a sheath of **myelin*** around each fibre.

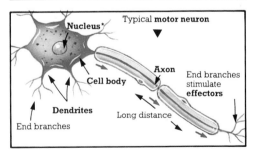

Nucleus*   Typical **motor neuron**

Axon

Cell body

Dendrites

End branches

Long distance

End branches stimulate effectors

- **Dendrites**. The **nerve fibres** carrying impulses towards a **cell body**. Most neurons have several short dendrites, but one type of **sensory neuron** has just one, elongated dendrite, often called a **dendron**. The endings of these dendrons form **receptors*** all over the body, and the dendrons themselves run inwards to the cell bodies (which are found in **ganglia*** just outside the spinal cord).

- **Axon**. The single long **nerve fibre** which carries impulses away from a **cell body**. The axons of all **association** and **sensory neurons** and some **motor neurons** lie in the brain and spinal cord. Those of the other motor neurons run out of the spinal cord to **autonomic ganglia***, or further to **effectors** (see **motor neurons**).

* Autonomic ganglia, 81; Central nervous system, 74; Cytoplasm, 10; Ganglia, 78; Grey matter, Myelin, 75 (Neuroglia); Nucleus, 10; Receptors, 79.

Types of neuron

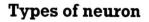

From receptor*

- **Sensory neurons** or **afferent neurons**. The neurons which carry "information" (nervous impulses) about sensations. The single **dendrites** (**dendrons**) of some sensory neurons run throughout the body, and their endings fire off impulses when stimulated. For more about these endings (**receptors**) and the different sensory neurons, see pages 78-79.

Long distance

Dendron

Axon

Cell body ↑

Sensory neurons (only one shown) bring impulses from eyes and fingers.

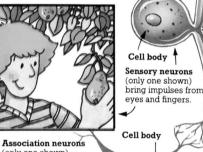

Association neurons (only one shown) analyse information and operate in decision-making.

Cell body

Cell body

Dendrites

Axon →

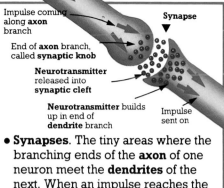

Impulse coming along **axon** branch

Synapse ▼

End of **axon** branch, called **synaptic knob**

Neurotransmitter released into **synaptic cleft**

Neurotransmitter builds up in end of **dendrite** branch

Impulse sent on

- **Synapses**. The tiny areas where the branching ends of the **axon** of one neuron meet the **dendrites** of the next. When an impulse reaches the end of the axon, a special chemical called a **neurotransmitter** is released into the minute gap (**synaptic cleft**) found at the junction. When enough of this has reached the other side, an impulse is sent on in the dendrites.

- **Motor neurons** or **efferent neurons**. The neurons which carry "instructions" (nervous impulses) away from the brain and spinal cord. The ends of the **axons** of some motor neurons make connections with muscles or glands (called **effectors**), and the impulses they carry (passed to them from **association neurons**) stimulate these organs into action. For more about the different motor neurons, see pages 80-81.

Cell body

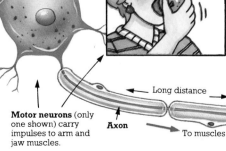

Long distance →

Motor neurons (only one shown) carry impulses to arm and jaw muscles.

Axon

To muscles

- **Association neurons**. Also called **relay**, **internuncial** or **connecting neurons**, or **interneurons**. Special linking neurons, present in vast numbers in the brain and spinal cord. They are involved in picking up impulses (from **sensory neurons**), interpreting the sensory information, and passing impulses to **motor neurons** to initiate actions.

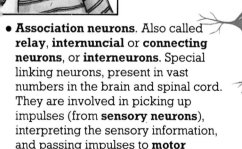

* Receptors, 79.

Nerves and nervous pathways

The **sensitivity** (**irritability**) of the body (its ability to respond to stimuli) relies on the transportation of "messages" (nervous impulses) by the fibres of nerve cells (**neurons***). The fibres which bring impulses into the brain and spinal cord are part of the **afferent system**. Those which carry impulses from the brain and cord are part of the **efferent system** (see pages 80-81). All the fibres outside the brain and cord make up the **nerves** of the body, known collectively as the **peripheral nervous system** (**PNS**).

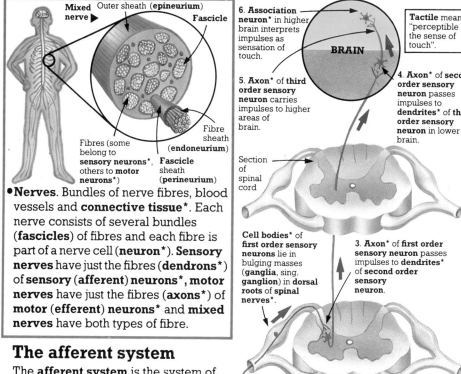

Mixed nerve ▶ Outer sheath (**epineurium**)

Fascicle

Fibres (some belong to **sensory neurons***, others to **motor neurons***)

Fibre sheath (**endoneurium**)

Fascicle sheath (**perineurium**)

6. Association neuron* in higher brain interprets impulses as sensation of touch.

BRAIN

Tactile means "perceptible by the sense of touch".

5. Axon* of third order sensory neuron carries impulses to higher areas of brain.

4. Axon* of second order sensory neuron passes impulses to dendrites* of third order sensory neuron in lower brain.

Section of spinal cord

3. Axon* of first order sensory neuron passes impulses to dendrites* of second order sensory neuron.

Cell bodies* of first order sensory neurons lie in bulging masses (**ganglia**, sing. **ganglion**) in dorsal roots of spinal nerves*.

•**Nerves**. Bundles of nerve fibres, blood vessels and **connective tissue***. Each nerve consists of several bundles (**fascicles**) of fibres and each fibre is part of a nerve cell (**neuron***). **Sensory nerves** have just the fibres (**dendrons***) of **sensory** (**afferent**) **neurons***, **motor nerves** have just the fibres (**axons***) of **motor** (**efferent**) **neurons*** and **mixed nerves** have both types of fibre.

The afferent system

The **afferent system** is the system of nerve cells (**neurons***) whose fibres carry sensory information (nervous impulses) towards the spinal cord, up inside it and into the brain. The nerve cells involved are all the **sensory** (**afferent**) **neurons*** of the body. The impulses originate in **receptors** and are interpreted by the brain as sensations.

Long distance (inside **nerve**)

Afferent means "leading towards".

2. Dendron* of first order sensory neuron carries impulses towards spinal cord.

1. Receptor in skin (**Meissner's corpuscle***) stimulated by contact.

The routes taken by nervous impulses are **neural pathways**. This is a simplified neural pathway of the **afferent system**. Only one of each type of **neuron*** is shown (in reality, there would be more involved).

* Association neurons, 77; Axon, Cell body, 76; Connective tissue, 52; Dendron, 76 (Dendrites); Meissner's corpuscles, 82; Motor neurons, 77; Neurons, 76; Sensory neurons, 77; Spinal nerves, 74 (Spinal cord).

- **Receptors**. The parts of the **afferent system** which fire off nervous impulses when they are stimulated. Most are either the single branched ending of the long **dendron*** of a **first order sensory neuron** (see picture) or a group of such endings. They are all embedded in body tissue, and many have some kind of structure formed around them (e.g. a **taste bud** – see **tongue**). They are found all over the body, both near the surface (in the skin, **sense organs**, **skeletal muscles***, etc.) and deeper inside (connected to inner organs, blood vessel walls, etc.).

- **Sense organs**. The highly specialized sensory organs of the body, each with many receptors. They are the **nose**, **tongue**, eyes and ears. For more about eyes and ears, see pages 84-87.

Divisions of the afferent system

Central and peripheral nervous systems. All nerve cells in body.

Afferent system. Nerve cells bringing impulses in and up.	Efferent system. Nerve cells taking impulses down and out (see pages 80-81).

Somatic afferent system. Nerve cells bringing impulses from **receptors** near body surface.	Visceral afferent system. Nerve cells bringing impulses from **receptors** deep inside body.

- **Nose**. The organ of smell. Each of its two nostrils opens into a **nasal cavity** which is lined with **mucous membrane*** and has many **olfactory hairs** extending from its roof. The hairs are the **dendrites*** of special **sensory neurons*** called **olfactory cells**. These are the **receptors** whose impulses are interpreted by the brain as sensations of smell (**olfactory sensations**).

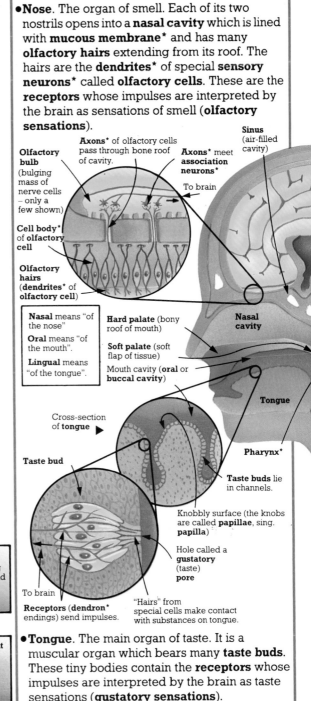

Axons* of olfactory cells pass through bone roof of cavity.

Olfactory bulb (bulging mass of nerve cells – only a few shown)

Axons* meet **association neurons***

To brain

Sinus (air-filled cavity)

Cell body* of **olfactory cell**

Olfactory hairs (**dendrites*** of **olfactory cell**)

Nasal means "of the nose"

Oral means "of the mouth".

Lingual means "of the tongue".

Hard palate (bony roof of mouth)

Soft palate (soft flap of tissue)

Mouth cavity (**oral or buccal cavity**)

Nasal cavity

Tongue

Pharynx*

Cross-section of **tongue** ▶

Taste bud

Taste buds lie in channels.

Knobbly surface (the knobs are called **papillae**, sing. **papilla**)

Hole called a **gustatory** (taste) **pore**

To brain

Receptors (**dendron*** endings) send impulses.

"Hairs" from special cells make contact with substances on tongue.

- **Tongue**. The main organ of taste. It is a muscular organ which bears many **taste buds**. These tiny bodies contain the **receptors** whose impulses are interpreted by the brain as taste sensations (**gustatory sensations**).

* **Association neurons**, 77; **Axon, Cell body**, 76; **Dendron**, 76 (**Dendrites**); **Mucous membrane**, 67; **Pharynx**, 66; **Sensory neurons**, 77; **Skeletal muscles**, 55.

The efferent system

The **efferent system** is the second system of nerve cells (**neurons***) in the body (see also **afferent system**, pages 78-79). The fibres of its nerve cells carry nervous impulses away from the brain, down through the spinal cord and out around the body. The nerve cells involved are all the **motor (efferent) neurons*** of the body. The impulses they carry stimulate action in the surface muscles (**skeletal muscles***) or in the glands and internal muscles (in the walls of inner organs and blood vessels). All these organs are known collectively as **effectors**.

Divisions of the efferent system

Central and peripheral nervous systems. All nerve cells in body.

Afferent system. Nerve cells bringing impulses in and up (see pages 78-79).

Efferent system. Nerve cells taking impulses down and out. **Efferent** means "leading away from".

Somatic efferent system. Nerve cells taking impulses to body surface (**skeletal muscles***). Cause **voluntary actions**.

Autonomic nervous system (visceral efferent system). Nerve cells taking impulses to inner organs. Cause **autonomic actions**.

Sympathetic division. Nerve cells whose impulses prepare body for action, e.g. increase heart rate.

Parasympathetic division. Nerve cells whose impulses restore and maintain normal body conditions, e.g. decrease heart rate.

The different actions

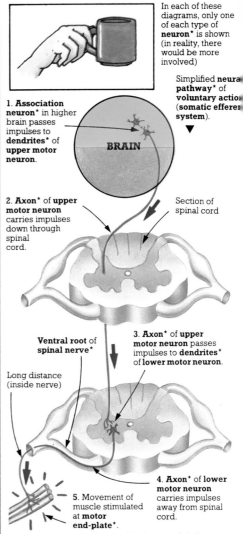

In each of these diagrams, only one of each type of **neuron*** is shown (in reality, there would be more involved)

Simplified **neural pathway*** of **voluntary action (somatic efferent system)**.

1. **Association neuron*** in higher brain passes impulses to **dendrites*** of **upper motor neuron**.

BRAIN

2. **Axon*** of **upper motor neuron** carries impulses down through spinal cord.

Section of spinal cord

Ventral root of spinal nerve*

3. **Axon*** of **upper motor neuron** passes impulses to **dendrites*** of **lower motor neuron**.

Long distance (inside nerve)

4. **Axon*** of **lower motor neuron** carries impulses away from spinal cord.

5. Movement of muscle stimulated at **motor end-plate***.

- **Voluntary actions.** Actions which result from conscious activity by the brain, i.e. ones it consciously decides upon, e.g. lifting a cup. We are always aware of these actions, which involve **skeletal muscles*** only. The impulses which cause them originate in higher areas of the brain (especially the **cerebrum***) and are carried by nerve cells of the **somatic efferent system**.

* Association neurons, 77; **Axon**, 76; **Cerebrum**, 74; Dendrites, 76; **Motor end-plate**, 55; **Motor neurons**, 77; **Neural pathways**, 78; Neurons, 76; Skeletal muscles, 55; Spinal nerves, 74 (**Spinal cord**).

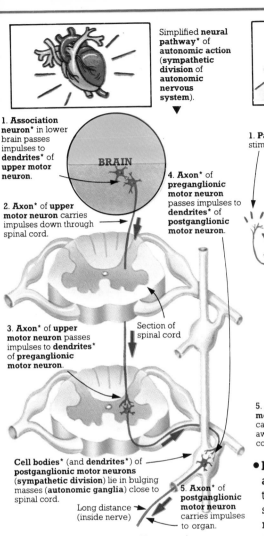

Simplified **neural pathway*** of autonomic action (**sympathetic division** of autonomic nervous system).

▼

1. **Association neuron*** in lower brain passes impulses to **dendrites*** of **upper motor neuron**.

BRAIN

2. **Axon*** of **upper motor neuron** carries impulses down through spinal cord.

4. **Axon*** of **preganglionic motor neuron** passes impulses to **dendrites*** of **postganglionic motor neuron**.

3. **Axon*** of **upper motor neuron** passes impulses to **dendrites*** of **preganglionic motor neuron**.

Section of spinal cord

Cell bodies* (and **dendrites***) of **postganglionic motor neurons** (**sympathetic division**) lie in bulging masses (**autonomic ganglia**) close to spinal cord.

Long distance (inside nerve)

5. **Axon*** of **postganglionic motor neuron** carries impulses to organ.

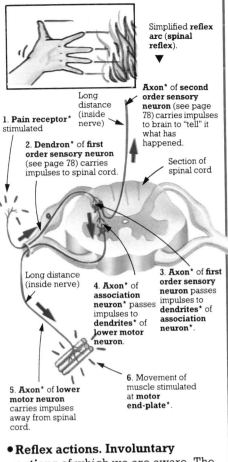

Simplified **reflex arc** (**spinal reflex**).

▼

Long distance (inside nerve)

1. **Pain receptor*** stimulated

Axon* of **second order sensory neuron** (see page 78) carries impulses to brain to "tell" it what has happened.

2. **Dendron*** of **first order sensory neuron** (see page 78) carries impulses to spinal cord.

Section of spinal cord

Long distance (inside nerve)

4. **Axon*** of **association neuron*** passes impulses to **dendrites*** of **lower motor neuron**.

3. **Axon*** of **first order sensory neuron** passes impulses to **dendrites*** of **association neuron***.

5. **Axon*** of **lower motor neuron** carries impulses away from spinal cord.

6. Movement of muscle stimulated at **motor end-plate***.

● **Involuntary actions**. Automatic actions (ones the brain does not consciously decide upon). There are two types. Firstly, there are the constant actions of inner organs, e.g. the beating of the heart, of which we are not normally aware. The impulses which cause them originate in the lower brain (especially the **hypothalamus***) and are carried by nerve cells of the **autonomic nervous system**. They are called **autonomic actions**. The other involuntary actions are **reflex actions**.

● **Reflex actions. Involuntary actions** of which we are aware. The term is most often used to refer to sudden actions of **skeletal muscles***, e.g. snatching the hand away from something hot. The impulses which cause such an action are carried by nerve cells of the **somatic efferent system** and the entire **neural pathway*** is a "short-circuited" one, called a **reflex arc**. In the case of **cranial reflexes** (those of the head, e.g. sneezing), this pathway involves a small part of the brain; with **spinal reflexes** (those of the rest of the body), the brain is not actively involved, only the spinal cord.

* Association neurons, 77; Axon, Cell body, 76; Dendron, 76 (Dendrites); Hypothalamus, 75; Motor end-plate, 55; Nerve, Neural pathways, 78; Pain receptors, 83; Skeletal muscles, 55; Spinal nerves, 74 (Spinal cord).

81

The skin

The **skin** or **cutis** is the outer body covering, made up of several tissue layers. It registers external stimulation, protects against damage or infection, prevents drying out, helps regulate body temperature, excretes waste (**sweat**), stores fat and makes **vitamin D***. It contains many tiny structures, each type with a different function. The entire skin (tissue layers and structures), is called the **integumentary system**.

The different layers

Epidermal layers

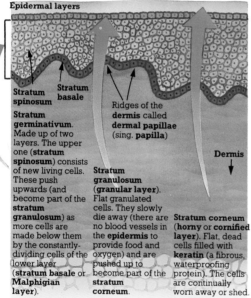

Stratum spinosum **Stratum basale**

Stratum germinativum. Made up of two layers. The upper one (**stratum spinosum**) consists of new living cells. These push upwards (and become part of the **stratum granulosum**) as more cells are made below them by the constantly-dividing cells of the lower layer (**stratum basale** or **Malphigian layer**).

Ridges of the **dermis** called **dermal papillae** (sing. **papilla**)

Stratum granulosum (**granular layer**). Flat granulated cells. They slowly die away (there are no blood vessels in the **epidermis** to provide food and oxygen) and are pushed up to become part of the **stratum corneum**.

Dermis

Stratum corneum (**horny** or **cornified layer**). Flat, dead cells filled with **keratin** (a fibrous, waterproofing protein). The cells are continually worn away or shed.

• **Epidermis**. The thin outer layer of the skin which forms its **epithelium** (a term for any sheet of cells which forms a surface covering or a cavity lining). It is made up of several layers (**strata**, sing. **stratum**), shown above.

• **Dermis**. The thick layer of **connective tissue*** under the **epidermis**, containing most of the embedded structures (see introduction). It also contains many **capillaries*** (tiny blood vessels) which supply food and oxygen.

• **Subcutaneous layer** or **superficial fascia**. The layer of fatty tissue (**adipose tissue**) below the **dermis** (it is a fat store). Elastic fibres run through it to connect the dermis to the organs below, e.g. muscles. It forms an insulating layer.

Structures in the skin

• **Meissner's corpuscles**. Special bodies formed around nerve fibre endings. There are especially large numbers on the fingertips and palms. They are touch **receptors***, i.e. they send impulses to the brain when the skin makes contact with an object.

• **Sebaceous glands. Exocrine glands*** which open into **hair follicles**. They produce an oil called **sebum** which waterproofs the hairs and **epidermis** and keeps them supple.

• **Hair erector muscles**. Special muscles, each attached to a **hair follicle**. When they contract (in the cold), the hairs straighten. This traps more air and improves insulation (especially in animals with lots of hair, feathers or fur). It also causes "goose-pimples".

• **Hair follicles**. Long narrow tubes, each containing a hair. The hair grows as new cells are added to its base from the cells lining the follicle. Its older cells die as **keratin** forms inside them (see **stratum corneum**).

* Capillaries, 61; Connective tissue, 52; Exocrine glands, 69; Receptors, 79; Vitamin D, 109.

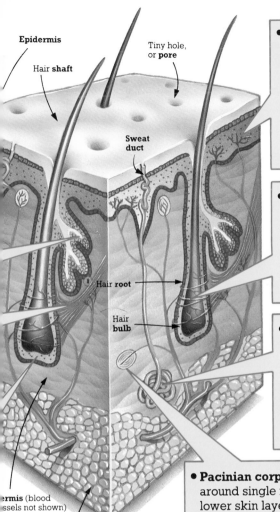

Epidermis

Hair shaft

Tiny hole, or **pore**

Sweat duct

Hair **root**

Hair **bulb**

ermis (blood ssels not shown)

ubcutaneous layer (**subcutaneous** means beneath the skin", i.e. this layer is ot regarded as part of the skin).

- **Pain receptors**. Nerve fibre endings in the tissue of most inner organs and in the skin (in the **epidermis** and the top of the **dermis**). They are the **receptors*** which send impulses when any stimulation (e.g. pressure, heat, touch) becomes excessive. This is what causes a sensation of pain.

- **Hair plexuses** or **root hair plexuses**. Special groups of nerve fibre endings. Each forms a network around a **hair follicle** and is a **receptor***, i.e. it sends nervous impulses to the brain, in this case when the hair moves.

- **Sweat glands** or **sudoriferous glands**. Coiled **exocrine glands*** which excrete **sweat**. Each has a narrow tube (**sweat duct**) going to the surface. Sweat consists of water, salts and **urea***, which enter the gland from the cells and **capillaries*** (blood vessels).

- **Pacinian corpuscles**. Special bodies formed around single nerve fibre endings, lying in the lower skin layers and the walls of inner organs. They are pressure **receptors***, i.e. they send impulses to the brain when the tissue is receiving deep pressure rather than light touch.

Fair skin (**melanin** in lower layers of **epidermis**)

The **pigment*** **carotene**, together with **melanin**, causes yellow skin

Dark skin (**melanin** in all epidermal layers)

- **Melanin**. A brown **pigment*** which shields against ultra-violet light by absorbing the light energy. It is found in all the layers of the **epidermis** of people from tropical areas, giving them dark skin. Fair-skinned people only have melanin in their lower epidermal layers, but produce more when in direct sunlight, causing a suntan.

The eyes

The **eyes** are the organs of **sight**, sending nervous impulses to the brain when stimulated by light rays from external objects. The brain interprets the impulses to produce images. Each eye consists of a hollow, spherical capsule (**eyeball**), made up of several layers and structures. It is set into a socket in the skull (an **orbit**), and is protected by eyelids and eyelashes.

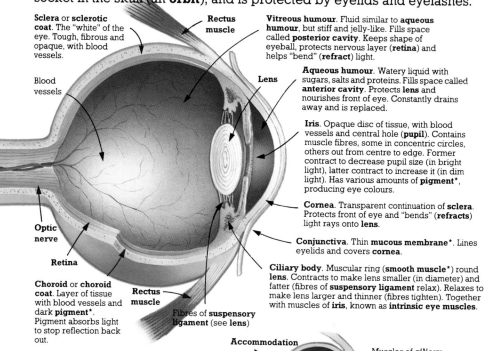

Sclera or **sclerotic coat**. The "white" of the eye. Tough, fibrous and opaque, with blood vessels.

Blood vessels

Optic nerve

Retina

Choroid or **choroid coat**. Layer of tissue with blood vessels and dark **pigment***. Pigment absorbs light to stop reflection back out.

Rectus muscle

Rectus muscle

Fibres of suspensory ligament (see **lens**)

Vitreous humour. Fluid similar to **aqueous humour**, but stiff and jelly-like. Fills space called **posterior cavity**. Keeps shape of eyeball, protects nervous layer (**retina**) and helps "bend" (**refract**) light.

Lens

Aqueous humour. Watery liquid with sugars, salts and proteins. Fills space called **anterior cavity**. Protects **lens** and nourishes front of eye. Constantly drains away and is replaced.

Iris. Opaque disc of tissue, with blood vessels and central hole (**pupil**). Contains muscle fibres, some in concentric circles, others out from centre to edge. Former contract to decrease pupil size (in bright light), latter contract to increase it (in dim light). Has various amounts of **pigment***, producing eye colours.

Cornea. Transparent continuation of **sclera**. Protects front of eye and "bends" (**refracts**) light rays onto **lens**.

Conjunctiva. Thin **mucous membrane***. Lines eyelids and covers **cornea**.

Ciliary body. Muscular ring (**smooth muscle***) round **lens**. Contracts to make lens smaller (in diameter) and fatter (fibres of **suspensory ligament** relax). Relaxes to make lens larger and thinner (fibres tighten). Together with muscles of **iris**, known as **intrinsic eye muscles**.

•**Lens**. The transparent body whose role, like that of any lens, is to focus the light rays passing through it, i.e. "bend" (**refract**) them so that they come to a point, in this case on the **retina**. It consists of many thin tissue layers and is held in place by the fibres of a **ligament*** called the **suspensory ligament**. These fibres join it to the **ciliary body**, which can alter the shape of the lens so that light rays are always focused on the retina, whatever the distance of the object being looked at. This is known as **accommodation**. The rays form an upside-down image on the retina, but this is corrected by the brain.

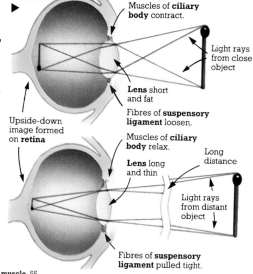

Accommodation

Muscles of **ciliary body** contract.

Light rays from close object

Lens short and fat

Fibres of **suspensory ligament** loosen.

Upside-down image formed on **retina**

Muscles of **ciliary body** relax.

Lens long and thin

Long distance

Light rays from distant object

Fibres of **suspensory ligament** pulled tight.

* Ligaments, 52; **Mucous membrane**, 67; **Pigments**, 27; **Smooth muscle**, 55.

The inner nervous layer

- **Retina**. The innermost layer of tissue at the back of the eyeball, made up of a layer of **pigment*** and a nervous layer consisting of millions of sensory nerve cells (**sensory neurons***) and their fibres. These lie in chains and carry nervous impulses to the brain. The first cells in the chains are **receptors***, i.e. their end fibres (**dendrons***) fire off the impulses when they are stimulated (by light rays). These fibres are called **rods** and **cones** because of their shapes. The receptors are **photoreceptors** (i.e. stimulated by light).

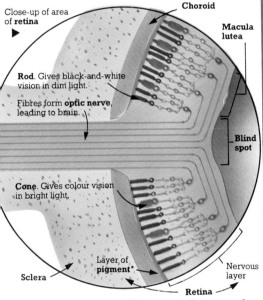

Close-up of area of **retina**

Choroid

Macula lutea

Rod. Gives black-and-white vision in dim light.

Fibres form **optic nerve**, leading to brain.

Blind spot

Cone. Gives colour vision in bright light.

Sclera

Layer of **pigment***

Nervous layer

Retina

- **Macula lutea** or **yellowspot**. An area of yellowish tissue in the centre of the **retina**. It has a small central dip, called the **fovea** or **fovea centralis**. This has the highest concentration of **cones** (see **retina**) and is the area of acutest vision. If you look directly at a specific object, its light rays are focused on the fovea.

- **Blind spot** or **optic disc**. The point in the **retina** where the **optic nerve** leaves the eye. It has no **receptors** (see **retina**) and so cannot send any impulses.

Structures around the eyeballs

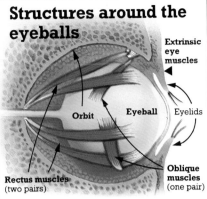

Extrinsic eye muscles

Orbit Eyeball Eyelids

Rectus muscles (two pairs)

Oblique muscles (one pair)

- **Extrinsic eye muscles**. The three pairs of muscles joining the eyeball to the eye socket (**orbit**). They contract to make the eyeball swivel around.

- **Lachrymal glands** or **tear glands**. Two **exocrine glands***, one at the top of each eye socket (**orbit**). They secrete a watery fluid onto the lining of the upper eyelids via tubes called **lachrymal ducts**. The fluid contains salts and an anti-bacterial **enzyme***, and it washes over the surface of the eyes, keeping them moist and clean. It

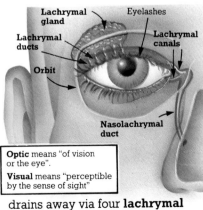

Lachrymal gland Eyelashes

Lachrymal ducts

Lachrymal canals

Orbit

Nasolachrymal duct

Optic means "of vision or the eye".
Visual means "perceptible by the sense of sight"

drains away via four **lachrymal canals**, two at the inside corner of each eye, which join to form a **nasolachrymal duct**. This empties into a **nasal cavity***.

---

* Dendron, 76 (Dendrites); Enzymes, 103; Exocrine glands, 69; Nasal cavity, 79 (Nose); Pigments, 27; Receptors, 79; Sensory neurons, 77.

The ears

The two **ears** are the organs of hearing and balance. Each one is divided into three areas – the **outer ear**, the **middle ear** and the **inner ear**.

● **Outer ear** or **external ear**. An outer "shell" of skin and **cartilage*** (**pinna** or **auricle**), together with a short tube (**ear canal** or **external auditory canal**). The tube lining contains special **sebaceous glands*** (**ceruminous glands**) which secrete **cerumen** (ear wax).

● **Middle ear** or **tympanic cavity**. An air-filled cavity which contains a chain of three tiny bones (**ear ossicles** or **auditory ossicles**) called the **malleus** (or **hammer**), **incus** (or **anvil**) and **stapes** (or **stirrup**).

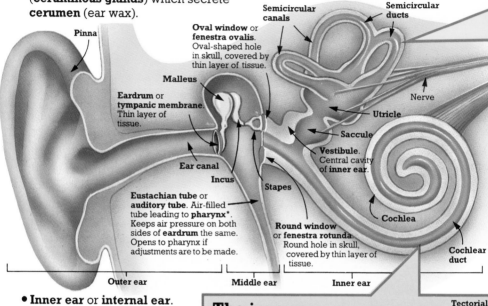

Pinna

Oval window or fenestra ovalis. Oval-shaped hole in skull, covered by thin layer of tissue.

Semicircular canals

Semicircular ducts

Malleus

Eardrum or tympanic membrane. Thin layer of tissue.

Nerve

Utricle

Saccule

Vestibule. Central cavity of inner ear.

Ear canal

Incus

Stapes

Eustachian tube or auditory tube. Air-filled tube leading to pharynx*. Keeps air pressure on both sides of eardrum the same. Opens to pharynx if adjustments are to be made.

Round window or fenestra rotunda. Round hole in skull, covered by thin layer of tissue.

Cochlea

Cochlear duct

Outer ear

Middle ear

Inner ear

● **Inner ear** or **internal ear**. A connected series of cavities in the skull, with tubes and sacs inside them. The cavities (**cochlea**, **vestibule** and **semicircular canals**) are called the **bony labyrinth** and are filled with one fluid (**perilymph**). The tubes and sacs are filled with another fluid (**endolymph**) and are called the **membranous labyrinth**. They are the **cochlear duct**, **saccule**, **utricle** and **semicircular ducts**.

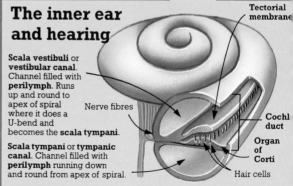

The inner ear and hearing

Scala vestibuli or **vestibular canal**. Channel filled with **perilymph**. Runs up and round to apex of spiral where it does a U-bend and becomes the **scala tympani**.

Scala tympani or **tympanic canal**. Channel filled with **perilymph** running down and round from apex of spiral.

Tectorial membrane

Nerve fibres

Cochlear duct

Organ of Corti

Hair cells

● **Cochlea**. A spiralling tubular cavity, part of the **inner ear**. It contains **perilymph** (see **inner ear**) in two channels (continuous with each other), and also a third channel – the **cochlear duct**.

 * Cartilage, 53; Pharynx, 66; Sebaceous glands, 82.

The inner ear and balance

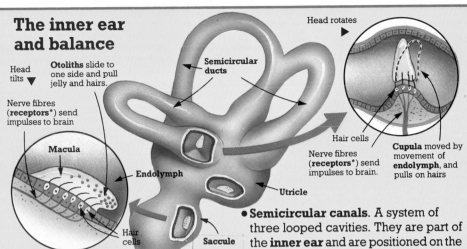

Head tilts ▼ **Otoliths** slide to one side and pull jelly and hairs.

Nerve fibres (**receptors***) send impulses to brain

Macula

Endolymph

Hair cells

Saccule

Semicircular ducts

Head rotates ▶

Hair cells

Nerve fibres (**receptors***) send impulses to brain.

Cupula moved by movement of **endolymph**, and pulls on hairs

Utricle

- **Saccule** (**sacculus**) and **utricle** (**utriculus**). Two sacs lying between the **semicircular ducts** and the **cochlear duct**. They contain **endolymph** (see **inner ear**) and have special hair cells in patches in their linings. These cells have nerve fibres (**dendron*** endings) attached to them and hairs embedded in a jelly-like mass called a **macula** (pl. **maculae**). This contains grains of calcium carbonate (**otoliths**). The maculae send the brain information about forward, backward, sideways or tilting motion of the head.

- **Semicircular canals**. A system of three looped cavities. They are part of the **inner ear** and are positioned on the three different planes of movement, at right angles to each other.

- **Semicircular ducts**. Three looped tubes inside the **semicircular canals**. Each contains **endolymph** (see **inner ear**) and a special sensory body, which lies across the basal swelling (**ampulla**, pl. **ampullae**) of the duct. The sensory bodies (**cupulae**, sing. **cupula**) work in a very similar way to **maculae** (see **saccule**) – each consists of a jelly-like mass (without **otoliths**) and hair cells. They send the brain information about rotation and tilting of the head.

- **Cochlear duct**. A spiralling tube within the **cochlea**, connected to the **saccule**. It contains **endolymph** (see **inner ear**) and a long body called the **organ of Corti**. This contains special hair cells whose hairs project into the endolymph and touch a shelf-like tissue layer (**tectorial membrane**). The bases of the cells are attached to nerve fibres (**dendron*** endings).

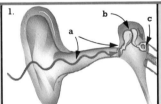

1.

a b c

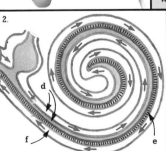

2.

d f e

a) Sound waves (air vibrations) come in along **ear canal** and make **eardrum** vibrate.

b) **Ear ossicles** pick up vibrations and pass them to **oval window** (lever action magnifies vibrations about 20 times).

c) Vibrations of **oval window** cause waves in **perilymph** of **vestibule**.

d) Waves in **perilymph** of **scala vestibuli** cause waves in **endolymph** of **cochlear duct**.

e) Hairs move and cause nerve fibres (**receptors***) to send impulses to brain (which interprets them as sensation of hearing).

f) Waves gradually fade out.

---

* Dendron, 76 (Dendrites); Receptors, 79.

The reproductive system

Reproduction is the process of producing new life. Humans reproduce by **sexual reproduction*** (described on pages 90-91) and the reproductive organs involved (making up the **reproductive system**) are called the **genital organs** or **genitalia**. They consist of the primary reproductive organs, or **gonads** (two **ovaries** in women, two **testes** in men) and a number of additional organs. In both women and men, cells in the gonads also act as **endocrine glands***, secreting many important **hormones***.

The male reproductive system

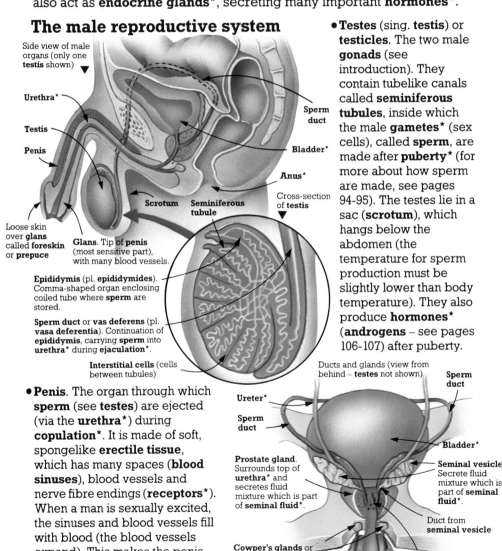

Side view of male organs (only one **testis** shown) ▼

Urethra*

Testis

Penis

Scrotum

Seminiferous tubule

Sperm duct

Bladder*

Anus*

Cross-section of **testis** ▼

Loose skin over **glans** called **foreskin** or **prepuce**

Glans. Tip of **penis** (most sensitive part), with many blood vessels.

Epididymis (pl. **epididymides**). Comma-shaped organ enclosing coiled tube where **sperm** are stored.

Sperm duct or **vas deferens** (pl. **vasa deferentia**). Continuation of **epididymis**, carrying **sperm** into **urethra*** during **ejaculation***.

Interstitial cells (cells between tubules)

• **Testes** (sing. **testis**) or **testicles**. The two male **gonads** (see introduction). They contain tubelike canals called **seminiferous tubules**, inside which the male **gametes*** (sex cells), called **sperm**, are made after **puberty*** (for more about how sperm are made, see pages 94-95). The testes lie in a sac (**scrotum**), which hangs below the abdomen (the temperature for sperm production must be slightly lower than body temperature). They also produce **hormones*** (**androgens** – see pages 106-107) after puberty.

• **Penis.** The organ through which **sperm** (see **testes**) are ejected (via the **urethra***) during **copulation***. It is made of soft, spongelike **erectile tissue**, which has many spaces (**blood sinuses**), blood vessels and nerve fibre endings (**receptors***). When a man is sexually excited, the sinuses and blood vessels fill with blood (the blood vessels expand). This makes the penis stiff and erect.

Ducts and glands (view from behind – **testes** not shown)

Ureter*

Sperm duct

Sperm duct

Bladder*

Prostate gland. Surrounds top of **urethra*** and secretes fluid mixture which is part of **seminal fluid***.

Seminal vesicle Secrete fluid mixture which is part of **seminal fluid***.

Duct from **seminal vesicle**

Cowper's glands or **bulbourethral glands.** Secrete **mucus***.

Opening of duct from **prostate gland**

Urethra*

* Anus, 67 (Large intestine); Bladder, 72; Ejaculation, 91 (Copulation); Endocrine glands, 69; Gametes, 93; Hormones, 106; Mucus, 67 (Mucous membrane); Puberty, 90; Receptors, 79; Seminal fluid, 91 (Copulation); Sexual reproduction, 92; Ureters, 72; Urethra, 73.

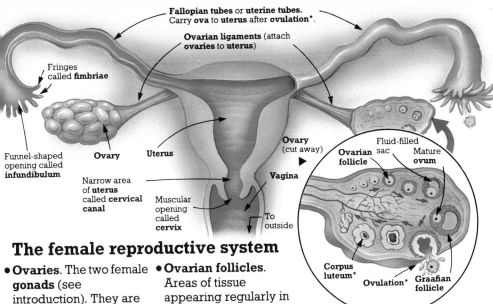

Fallopian tubes or uterine tubes. Carry ova to uterus after ovulation*.

Ovarian ligaments (attach ovaries to uterus)

Fringes called fimbriae

Funnel-shaped opening called infundibulum

Ovary

Uterus

Narrow area of uterus called cervical canal

Muscular opening called cervix

Vagina

To outside

Ovary (cut away)

Ovarian follicle

Fluid-filled sac

Mature ovum

Corpus luteum*

Ovulation*

Graafian follicle

The female reproductive system

- **Ovaries.** The two female **gonads** (see introduction). They are held in place in the lower abdomen (below the kidneys) by **ligaments***. These attach them to the walls of the pelvis. The female **gametes*** (sex cells), called **ova** (sing. **ovum**), are produced regularly in the ovaries (in **ovarian follicles**) after **puberty***. For more about how ova are made, see pages 94-95.

- **Ovarian follicles.** Areas of tissue appearing regularly in the **ovaries** after **puberty***. Each contains a maturing **ovum** (see **ovaries**). The follicles gradually get larger and begin to secrete **hormones*** (see **oestrogen**, page 106). Each round of follicle production results in only one fully mature follicle (**Graafian follicle**).

- **Uterus** or **womb**. The hollow organ, inside which a developing baby (**foetus***) is held, or from which the **ova** (see **ovaries**) are discharged (see **menstrual cycle**, page 90). It has a lining of **mucous membrane*** (the **endometrium**), covering a muscular wall with many blood vessels.

- **Vagina.** The muscular canal leading from the **uterus** out of the body. It carries away the **ova** (see **ovaries**) and inner uterus lining during the **menstrual** **cycle***, receives the **penis** during **copulation*** and forms the birth canal. Its lining produces a lubricating fluid.

- **Vulva** or **pudendum**. A collective term for the outer parts of the female reproductive system – the **labia** and the **clitoris**. The labia are two folds of skin (one inside the other) which surround the openings from the **vagina** and the **urethra***. The clitoris is the most sensitive part. Like the **penis**, it is made of **erectile tissue** and has many **receptors***.

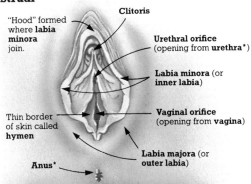

"Hood" formed where labia minora join.

Clitoris

Urethral orifice (opening from urethra*)

Labia minora (or inner labia)

Thin border of skin called hymen

Vaginal orifice (opening from vagina)

Labia majora (or outer labia)

Anus*

* Anus, 67 (Large intestine); Copulation, 91; Corpus luteum, 90 (Menstrual cycle); Foetus, 91 (Pregnancy); Gametes, 93; Hormones, 106; Ligaments, 52; Mucous membrane, 67; Ovulation, 90 (Menstrual cycle); Puberty, 90; Receptors, 79; Urethra, 73.

89

Development and reproduction

Humans reproduce by **sexual reproduction***. The main processes this involves are described on these two pages, as well as the initial developments which allow it to happen.

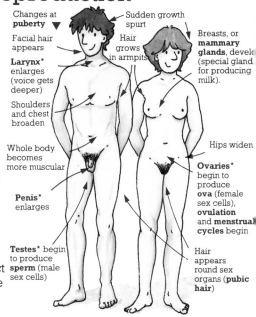

Changes at **puberty** ▼

Facial hair appears

Larynx* enlarges (voice gets deeper)

Shoulders and chest broaden

Whole body becomes more muscular

Penis* enlarges

Testes* begin to produce **sperm** (male sex cells)

Sudden growth spurt

Hair grows in armpits

Breasts, or **mammary glands**, develo (special gland for producing milk).

Hips widen

Ovaries* begin to produce **ova** (female sex cells), **ovulation** and **menstrual cycles** begin

Hair appears round sex organs (**pubic hair**)

• **Puberty.** The point when the reproductive organs mature, and a person becomes capable of reproducing – roughly between the ages of 11 and 15 in girls, and 13 and 15 in boys. It involves a number of significant changes, all stimulated by **hormones*** (see **oestrogen** and **androgens**, pages 106-107). All the new resulting features are called **secondary sex characters**, as distinct from the **primary sex characters** – the sex organs present from birth (see pages 88-89).

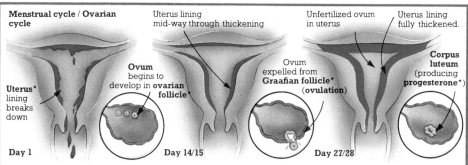

Menstrual cycle / Ovarian cycle

Uterus lining mid-way through thickening

Unfertilized ovum in uterus

Uterus lining fully thickened.

Ovum begins to develop in **ovarian follicle***

Ovum expelled from **Graafian follicle*** (**ovulation**)

Corpus luteum (producing **progesterone***)

Uterus* lining breaks down

Day 1

Day 14/15

Day 27/28

• **Menstrual cycle.** A series of preparatory changes in the **uterus*** lining (**endometrium**), in case of **fertilization**. The lining gradually develops a new inner layer rich in blood vessels. If a fertilized **ovum** (female sex cell) does not appear, this new layer breaks down and leaves the body via the **vagina***

(**menstruation**). Each menstrual cycle lasts about 28 days and they occur continuously from **puberty** to **menopause** (usually between the ages of 45 and 50), when ova production ceases.

The events of the menstrual cycle run in conjunction with the **ovarian cycle** – the regular maturation of an ovum in an **ovarian**

follicle*, followed by **ovulation** (the release of the ovum into a **Fallopian tube***), and the breakdown of the **corpus luteum**. This body is formed from the burst **Graafian follicle*** (it does not break down if an ovum is fertilized). Both cycles are controlled by a group of **hormones*** (see pages 106-107).

* Fallopian tubes, 89; Graafian follicle, 89 (Ovarian follicles); Hormones, 106; Larynx, 70; Ovaries, 89; Penis, 88; Progesterone, 106; Sexual reproduction, 92; Testes, 88; Uterus, Vagina, 89.

- **Copulation**. Also called **coitus** or **sexual intercourse**. The insertion of the **penis*** into the **vagina***, followed by rhythmical movements of the pelvis in one or both sexes. Its culmination in the male is **ejaculation** – the ejection of **semen** from the **urethra*** (in the penis) into the vagina. Semen consists of **sperm** (male sex cells) and a fluid mixture (**seminal fluid**).

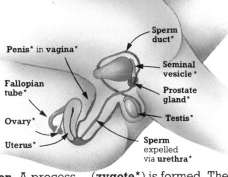

Penis* in vagina*

Sperm duct*

Seminal vesicle*

Fallopian tube*

Prostate gland*

Ovary*

Testis*

Uterus*

Sperm expelled via **urethra***

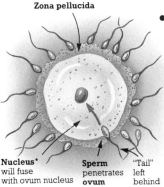

Zona pellucida

Nucleus* will fuse with ovum nucleus

Sperm penetrates **ovum**

"Tail" left behind

- **Fertilization**. A process which occurs after **ejaculation** if the **sperm** (male sex cells) meet an **ovum** (female sex cell) in a **Fallopian tube***. One sperm penetrates the ovum's outer skin (**zona pellucida**). Its **nucleus*** fuses with that of the ovum, and the first cell of a new baby (**zygote***) is formed. The new cell travels towards the **uterus***, undergoing many cell divisions (**cleavage***) as it does so. The ball of cells formed from these divisions then becomes embedded in the uterus wall (**implantation**), after which it is called an **embryo***.

Pregnancy

- **Pregnancy**, or **gestation**, is the state of carrying young. The time between **fertilization** and giving birth (**parturition**) is the **gestation period** (about 9 months in humans) and the new developing individual in the **uterus*** is called a **foetus**, a term usually used instead of **embryo*** after about 2 months of pregnancy. A series of powerful muscular contractions called **labour** occur just before parturition.

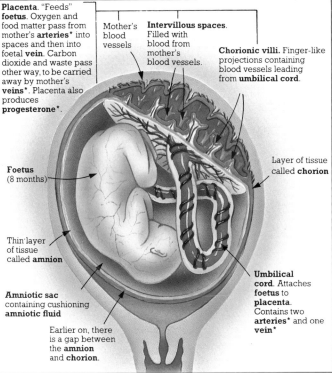

Placenta. "Feeds" foetus. Oxygen and food matter pass from mother's **arteries*** into spaces and then into foetal **vein**. Carbon dioxide and waste pass other way, to be carried away by mother's **veins***. Placenta also produces **progesterone***.

Mother's blood vessels

Intervillous spaces. Filled with blood from mother's blood vessels.

Chorionic villi. Finger-like projections containing blood vessels leading from **umbilical cord**.

Foetus (8 months)

Layer of tissue called **chorion**

Thin layer of tissue called **amnion**

Umbilical cord. Attaches foetus to placenta. Contains two arteries* and one vein*

Amniotic sac containing cushioning amniotic fluid

Earlier on, there is a gap between the **amnion** and **chorion**.

* **Arteries**, 60; **Cleavage**, 93 (**Embryo**); **Fallopian tubes**, 89; **Nucleus**, 10; **Ovaries**, 89; **Penis**, 88; **Progesterone**, 106; **Prostate gland**, **Seminal vesicles**, **Sperm ducts**, **Testes**, 88; **Urethra**, 73; **Uterus**, **Vagina**, 89; **Veins**, 60; **Zygote**, 93.

Types of reproduction

Reproduction is the creation of new life, a process which occurs in all living things. The two main types are **asexual** and **sexual reproduction**, but there is also a special case called **alternation of generations**.

Asexual reproduction

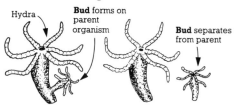

Hydra — **Bud** forms on parent organism — **Bud** separates from parent

- **Asexual reproduction** is the simplest form of reproduction, occurring in many simple plants and animals. There are a number of different types, e.g. **binary fission***, **vegetative reproduction***, **gemmation** and **sporulation**, but they all share two main features. Firstly, only one parent is needed and secondly, the new individual produced is always genetically identical to this parent.

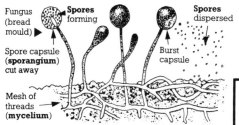

Fungus (bread mould) ▶ — **Spores** forming — **Spores** dispersed — Spore capsule (**sporangium**) cut away — **Burst** capsule — Mesh of threads (**mycelium**)

- **Sporulation.** The production of bodies called **spores** by simple plants, e.g. fungi and mosses. After dispersal by wind or water, these develop into new plants. There are two types of spore and, though only one parent is needed in both cases, true **asexual reproduction** really only occurs with one type. These spores are produced in plants such as simple fungi by ordinary cell division (see pages 12-13) and develop into plants which are identical to the parent (an important feature of asexual reproduction). The second kind of spore, however, is produced (e.g. in mosses and ferns) by a special kind of cell division (see pages 94-95) which is a feature of **sexual reproduction**. The new plants are not the same as the parent (see **alternation of generations**).

- **Gemmation.** Called **budding** in animals. A type of **asexual reproduction** occurring in many simple plants and animals, e.g. Hydra. It involves the formation of a group of cells which grows out of the organism and develops into a new individual. It either breaks away from the parent or (in **colonial*** animals, e.g. corals) it stays attached (though self-contained).

Sexual reproduction

- **Sexual reproduction** is the type of reproduction shown by all flowering plants and most animals. It involves the joining (**fusion**) of two **gametes** (sex cells), one male and one female. This process is called **fertilization**, and is further described on pages 30 (flowering plants), 91 (humans and similar animals) and 48 (other animals). The two gametes each have only half the number of **chromosomes*** (called the **haploid number***) as the plant or animal which produced them. This is achieved by a special kind of cell division (see pages 94-95) and ensures that when the gametes come together, the new individual produced has the correct, original number of chromosomes (called the **diploid number***).

92   * Binary fashion, 12 (Cell division); Chromosones, 96; Colonial, 114; Diploid number, 12 (Mitosis); Haploid number, 94 (Meiosis); Vegetative reproduction, 34.

- **Alternation of generations.** A reproductive process found in many simple animals and plants, e.g. jellyfish and mosses. In the animals, a form produced by **sexual reproduction** alternates with one produced **asexually**. In the plants, though, the alternation is really between two stages of sexual reproduction. One plant body (**gametophyte**) produces another (**sporophyte**) by sexual reproduction. This then produces **spores** (see **sporulation**) which grow into new gametophytes. However, the spores are made in the same way as **gametes** (see pages 94-95) and they (and the gametophytes) have only half the original number of **chromosomes***. The gametophytes produce gametes by ordinary cell division (see pages 12-13), as there is no need to halve the chromosomes again.

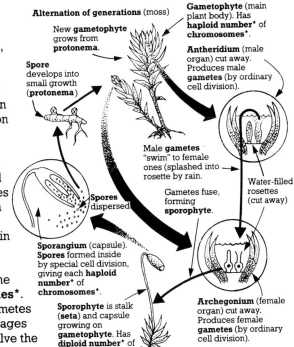

Alternation of generations (moss)

Gametophyte (main plant body). Has **haploid number*** of **chromosomes***.

New **gametophyte** grows from **protonema**.

Spore develops into small growth (**protonema**)

Antheridium (male organ) cut away. Produces male **gametes** (by ordinary cell division).

Male **gametes** "swim" to female ones (splashed into rosette by rain.

Water-filled rosettes (cut away)

Gametes fuse, forming **sporophyte**.

Spores dispersed

Sporangium (capsule). **Spores** formed inside by special cell division, giving each **haploid number*** of **chromosomes***.

Sporophyte is stalk (**seta**) and capsule growing on **gametophyte**. Has **diploid number*** of **chromosomes***.

Archegonium (female organ) cut away. Produces female **gametes** (by ordinary cell division).

- **Gametes** or **germ cells.** The sex cells which join in **sexual reproduction** to form a new living thing. They are made by a special kind of cell division (see pages 94-95). In animals and simple plants, male gametes are known as **sperm**, short for **spermatozoa** (sing. **spermatozoon**) in animals and **spermatozooids** in simple plants. In flowering plants, they are just **nuclei*** (rather than cells) and are called **male nuclei** (see also pages 30 and 95). Female gametes are called **ova** (sing. **ovum**) or **egg cells** (egg cell is usually used in the case of plants). A sperm is smaller than an ovum and has a "tail" (**flagellum***).

Ovum   Sperm

"Head"

"Tail"

Human **embryo** (eight weeks)

- **Zygote.** The first cell of a new living thing. It is formed when a male and female **gamete** join (see **sexual reproduction**).

- **Embryo.** A new developing individual. It grows from one cell (the **zygote**) by a series of cell divisions (see pages 12-13) called **cleavage**. In humans, this first produces a ball of cells (**morula**) from the one original), and then a larger, hollow ball (**blastocyst**). After **implantation***, this is called the embryo. As it grows, the cells become **differentiated**, i.e. each develops into one kind of cell, e.g. a nerve cell.

* **Chromosomes**, 96; **Diploid number**, 12 (**Mitosis**); **Flagella**, 40; **Haploid number**, 94 (**Meiosis**); **Implantation**, 91 (**Fertilization**); **Nucleus**, 10.

Cell division for reproduction

Many cells within a living thing can divide to produce new cells for growth and repair (see pages 12-13). There is, however, a second type of cell division, which happens specifically to produce the **gametes*** (sex cells) needed for **sexual reproduction*** (and also one of the two types of **spore***). The division of the **nucleus*** in this type of cell division is called **meiosis**. The production of gametes, including both the cell division and the subsequent maturing of the gametes, is called **gametogenesis**.

● **Meiosis**. The division of the **nucleus*** when a cell divides to produce sex cells (see introduction). It can be split into two separate divisions – the **first meiotic division** (or **reduction division**) and the **second meiotic division** (each is followed by division of the **cytoplasm***). These can be divided into different phases (as in **mitosis***). Meiosis in general, and the first meiotic division in particular, ensures that each new **daughter nucleus** receives exactly half the number of **chromosomes*** as the original nucleus. The original number is the **diploid number** (see **mitosis**, page 12); the halved amount is the **haploid number**.

Crossing over (occurs in early **prophase**)

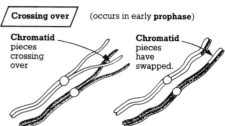

Chromatid pieces crossing over

Chromatid pieces have swapped.

Chromatids of each **tetrad** cross over each other at places called **chiasmata** (sing. **chiasma**). Two chromatid pieces (one from each pair) break off and swap over. Causes mixing of **genes*** (helping to ensure new living things are never identical to parents, i.e. always a new variety of types).

Prophase (later stage)

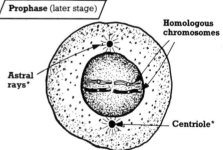

Homologous chromosomes

Astral rays*

Centriole*

First meiotic division

These pictures show an animal cell, but only four **chromosomes*** are shown.

Prophase (early stage)

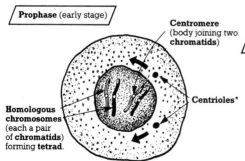

Centromere (body joining two chromatids)

Centrioles*

Homologous chromosomes (each a pair of chromatids) forming **tetrad**.

Threads of **chromatin*** in **nucleus*** coil up to form **chromosomes***. Paired chromosomes (**homologous chromosomes**) line up side by side, forming pairs called **bivalents**. Each chromosome duplicates, becoming a pair of **chromatids** (each group of four chromatids now called a **tetrad**). **Centrioles*** move to opposite poles of cell.

Homologous chromosomes (each a pair of **chromatids**) move together to equator of cell.

Metaphase

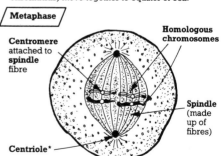

Homologous chromosomes

Centromere attached to **spindle** fibre

Spindle (made up of fibres)

Centriole*

Nuclear membrane* disappears, two **centrioles*** form a **spindle** (see **metaphase** of **mitosis**, page 13). **Chromosomes*** (pairs of **chromatids**) become attached to spindle by **centromeres**.

* **Astral rays**, 13; **Centrioles**, 12; **Chromatin**, 10 (**Nucleus**); **Chromosomes**, 96; **Cytoplasm**, 10; **Gametes**, 93; **Genes**, 97; **Mitosis**, 12; **Nuclear membrane**, 10 (**Nucleus**); **Sexual reproduction**, 92; **Spores**, 92 (**Sporulation**).

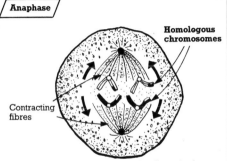

Anaphase

Homologous
chromosomes

Contracting
fibres

Homologous chromosomes (each still a pair of
chromatids) separate (see **Law of segregation**, page
98), dragged apart by fibres of **spindle**.

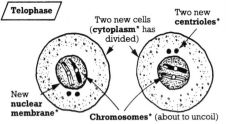

Telophase

Two new cells
(**cytoplasm*** has
divided)

Two new
centrioles*

New
**nuclear
membrane***

Chromosomes* (about to uncoil)

Spindle disappears, **centrioles*** duplicate. Happens in
conjunction with **cytokinesis** (division of **cytoplasm***).
Two new cells formed, each with half the original
number of **chromosomes*** (each two **chromatids**).
Interphase* (intervening period) usually follows, in
which case **nuclear membranes*** form and
chromosomes uncoil again to form threadlike mass
(**chromatin***).

Second meiotic division

The **second meiotic division** happens
in the cells produced by the **first
meiotic division**. It occurs in exactly
the same way, and with the same
phases, as **mitosis*** (when the
nucleus* divides as part of cell
division for growth and repair) and is
followed in the same way by the
division of the **cytoplasm***. The only
difference is that each dividing nucleus
now has only the **haploid number** of
chromosomes* (see **meiosis**) so the
resulting new sex cells (**gametes***) will
also be haploid. The second division
differs according to whether male or
female gametes are to be produced,
and the final maturing of the gametes
after the second division is different in
animals and plants (see text right).

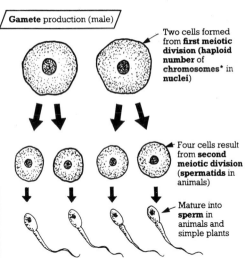

Gamete production (male)

Two cells formed
from **first meiotic
division (haploid
number** of
chromosomes* in
nuclei)

Four cells result
from **second
meiotic division
(spermatids** in
animals)

Mature into
sperm in
animals and
simple plants

Two cells formed from **first meiotic division** divide
again (see **second meiotic division**). In animals,
resulting four cells called **spermatids** and mature into
male **gametes*** (sex cells), or **sperm**. In simple plants,
four cells either develop into spore or into type of
spore* involved in **alternation of generations***. In
flowering plants, **nuclei*** of four cells each divide again
(**mitosis***). Resulting cells (**pollen*** grains) each have
two nuclei (one later divides again to form two **male
nuclei***).

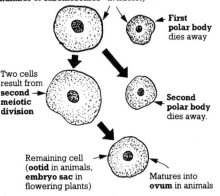

Gamete production (female)

Two cells formed from **first meiotic division (haploid
number** of **chromosomes*** in **nuclei**)

First
polar body
dies away

Two cells
result from
**second
meiotic
division**

Second
polar body
dies away.

Remaining cell
(**ootid** in animals,
embryo sac in
flowering plants)

Matures into
ovum in animals

One of two cells formed by **first meiotic division** dies
away (called **first polar body**). Other divides again (see
second meiotic division). Of two resulting cells, one
(**second polar body**) dies away. In animals, other one
called **ootid** and matures into female **gamete*** (sex cell),
or **ovum**. In flowering plants, other one called **embryo
sac** and its **nucleus*** divides three more times (by
mitosis*). Of eight new nuclei, six have cells form
around them, two stay naked. One of six cells is female
gamete, or **egg cell** (see **ovule**, page 30). Formation of
egg cell in simple plants is very similar.

* **Alternation of generations**, 93; **Centrioles**, 12; **Chromatin**, 10 (Nucleus); **Chromosomes**, 96; **Cytoplasm**, 10; **Gametes**, 93; **Interphase**,
13; **Male nuclei**, 93 (Gametes); **Mitosis**, 12; **Nuclear membrane**, 10 (Nucleus); **Pollen**, 30; **Spores**, 92 (Sporulation).

Genetics and heredity

Genetics is a branch of biology. It is the study of **inheritance** – the passing of characteristics from one generation to the next. The bodies which are instrumental in this process are called **chromosomes**. Each chromosome is made up of **genes** – the "coded" instructions for the appearance and constituents of an organism. For more about inheriting genes, see page 98.

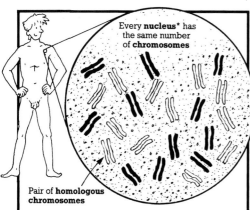

Every **nucleus*** has the same number of **chromosomes**

Pair of **homologous chromosomes**

• **Chromosomes.** Structures present at all times in the **nuclei*** of all cells, though they only become independently visible (as thread-like bodies of differing shapes and sizes) when a cell is dividing (and has been stained with a dye). Each one is made of a single molecule of **DNA** (see **nucleic acids**), plus proteins called **histones**. The DNA molecule is a chain of many connected **genes**.

Every **species*** has its own number of chromosomes per cell, called the **diploid number** (humans have 46). These are arranged in pairs called **homologous chromosomes**.

• **Nucleic acids.** Two different acids, called **DNA (deoxyribonucleic acid)** and **RNA (ribonucleic acid)**. Both are found in the **nuclei*** of all cells, hence their name (RNA is also found in the **cytoplasm*** – see **ribosomes**, page 11). Each molecule of a nucleic acid is very large, and is composed of many individual units called **nucleotides**. A DNA molecule consists of two chains of nucleotides twisted around each other, forming a shape called a **double helix** (rather like a twisted ladder). An RNA molecule consist of one chain of nucleotides (and looks like a ladder cut in half lengthwise).

Nucleic acid structure

DNA ▶

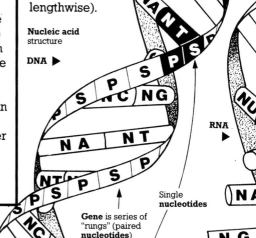

RNA ▶

Single **nucleotides**

Gene is series of "rungs" (paired **nucleotides**)

N = **nitrogen base** (linked nitrogen, carbon, hydrogen and oxygen atoms). 5 types:
A = **adenine T** =**thymine** (always paired in **DNA**)
G = **guanine C** =**cytosine** (always paired in **DNA**)
U = **uracil** (only found in **RNA**, replaces thymine of **DNA**)

S = sugar (linked carbon, hydrogen and oxygen atoms). **Deoxyribose** in **DNA**, **ribose** in **RNA**.
P = **phosphate group***.

  * Cytoplasm, Nucleus, 10; Phosphate group, 105 (**ADP**); Species, 110.

- **Genes.** Sets of "coded" instructions which make up the **DNA** molecule of a **chromosome** (in humans, each DNA molecule is thought to contain about 1000 genes). Each gene is a connected series of about 250 "rungs" on the DNA "ladder". Since the order of the "rungs" varies, each gene has a different "code", relating to one specific characteristic (**trait**) of the organism, e.g. its **blood group*** or the composition of a **hormone***. With the exception of the **sex chromosomes**, the genes carried on paired **homologous chromosomes** (see **chromosomes**) are also paired, and run down the chromosomes in the same order (one member of each pair on each chromosome). These paired genes control the same characteristic and may give identical instructions. However, their instructions may also be different, in which case the instructions from one gene (the **dominant** gene) will "mask out" those from the other (the **recessive** gene), unless **incomplete dominance** or **codominance** is shown. Two such non-identical genes are called **alleles** or **allelomorphs**.

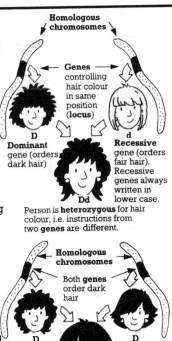

Homologous chromosomes

Genes controlling hair colour in same position (**locus**)

Dominant gene (orders dark hair) **D**

Recessive gene (orders fair hair). Recessive genes always written in lower case. **d**

Dd
Person is **heterozygous** for hair colour, i.e. instructions from two **genes** are different.

Homologous chromosomes

Both **genes** order dark hair

D   **D**

DD
Person is **homozygous** for hair colour, i.e. instructions from two genes are identical.

The two examples have different **genotypes** for hair colour, i.e. different sets of instructions (**DD** and **Dd**), but are the same **phenotype**, i.e. the resulting characteristic is the same (dark hair).

- **Codominance.** A special situation where a pair of **genes** controlling the same characteristic give different instructions, neither is **dominant** (see **genes**), but both are represented in the result. The human **blood group*** AB, for example, results from equal dominance between a gene for group A and one for group B.

- **Incomplete dominance** or **blending**. A situation where a pair of **genes** which control the same characteristic give different instructions, but neither is **dominant** (see **genes**) or obvious in the result. For example, a lack of dominance between a gene for red colour and one for white results in the intermediate roan colour of some cows.

- **Sex chromosomes.** One pair of **homologous chromosomes** (see **chromosomes**) in all cells (all the others are called **autosomes**). There are two different kinds of sex chromosomes, called the **X** and **Y** chromosomes. A male has one X and one Y. The Y chromosome carries the genetic factor (not a **gene** as such) determining maleness, thus all individuals with two X chromosomes are female.

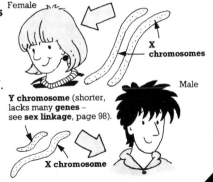

Female

X chromosomes

Male

Y chromosome (shorter, lacks many **genes** – see **sex linkage**, page 98).

X chromosome

* **Blood group**, 59; **Hormones**, 106.

Inheriting genes

Every new organism inherits its **chromosomes*** (and **genes***) from its parents. In **sexual reproduction***, the **sperm*** and **ovum*** (sex cells) which come together to form this new individual each have only half the normal number of chromosomes (the **haploid number** – see pages 94-95). This ensures that the **zygote*** (first new cell) formed from the two sex cells will have the normal number (see **chromosomes**, page 96). Two laws (**Mendel's laws**) point out genetic factors which are always true when cells divide to produce sex cells.

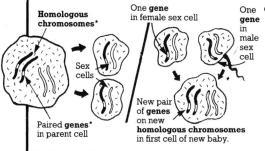

Homologous chromosomes*

Sex cells

Paired **genes*** in parent cell

One **gene** in female sex cell

New pair of **genes** on new **homologous chromosomes** in first cell of new baby.

One **gene** in male sex cell

• **Law of segregation (Mendel's first law). Homologous chromosomes*** always separate when the **nucleus*** of a cell divides to produce **gametes*** (sex cells – see pages 94-95), hence so too do the paired **genes*** controlling the same characteristic. The offspring thus always have paired genes (one member of each pair coming from each parent).

• **Law of independent assortment (Mendel's second law).** Each member of a pair of **genes*** can join with either of the two members of another pair when a cell divides to form **gametes*** (sex cells). Hence all the different mixes are possible in a new individual.

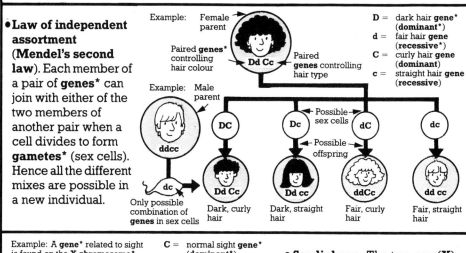

Example: Female parent

Paired **genes*** controlling hair colour

Dd Cc

Paired **genes** controlling hair type

Example: Male parent

ddcc

DC   Dc   dC   dc   ← Possible sex cells

← Possible offspring

dc

Dd Cc
Dark, curly hair

Dd cc
Dark, straight hair

ddCc
Fair, curly hair

dd cc
Fair, straight hair

Only possible combination of **genes** in sex cells

D = dark hair **gene*** (**dominant***)
d = fair hair **gene** (**recessive***)
C = curly hair **gene** (**dominant**)
c = straight hair **gene** (**recessive**)

Example: A **gene*** related to sight is found on the **X chromosome***

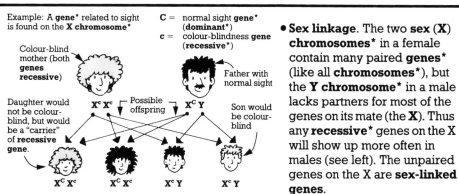

Colour-blind mother (both **genes** recessive)

Daughter would not be colour-blind, but would be a "carrier" of **recessive** gene.

Father with normal sight

Son would be colour-blind

$X^c X^c$ ← Possible offspring → $X^C Y$

$X^C X^c$ $X^C X^c$ $X^c Y$ $X^c Y$

C = normal sight **gene*** (**dominant***)
c = colour-blindness **gene** (**recessive***)

• **Sex linkage.** The two **sex (X) chromosomes*** in a female contain many paired **genes*** (like all **chromosomes***), but the **Y chromosome*** in a male lacks partners for most of the genes on its mate (the **X**). Thus any **recessive*** genes on the X will show up more often in males (see left). The unpaired genes on the X are **sex-linked genes**.

* **Homologous chromosomes**, 96 (**Chromosomes**); **Nucleus**, 10; **Ovum**, 93 (**Gametes**); **Recessive**, 97 (**Genes**); **Sexual reproduction**, 92; **Sperm**, 93 (**Gametes**); **X** and **Y chromosomes**, 97 (**Sex chromosomes**); **Zygote**, 93.

Fluid movement

The movement of substances around the body, especially their movement into and out of cells, is essential to the life of an organism. Food matter must be able to pass into the cells, and waste matter and harmful material must be able to move out. Most solids and gases travel around in **solutions**, i.e. they (the **solutes**) are dissolved in a fluid (the **solvent** – normally water).

● **Diffusion.** The movement of molecules of a substance from an area where they are in higher concentration to one where their concentration is lower. This is a two-way process (where the concentration of a **solute** is low, that of the **solvent** will be high, so its molecules will move the other way) and it ceases when the molecules are evenly distributed. Many substances, e.g. oxygen and carbon dioxide, diffuse into and out of cells.

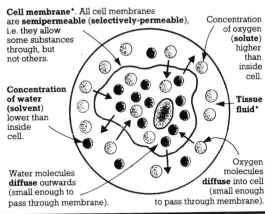

Cell membrane*. All cell membranes are **semipermeable (selectively-permeable)**, i.e. they allow some substances through, but not others.

Concentration of oxygen (**solute**) higher than inside cell.

Concentration of water (solvent) lower than inside cell.

Tissue fluid*

Water molecules **diffuse** outwards (small enough to pass through membrane).

Oxygen molecules **diffuse** into cell (small enough to pass through membrane).

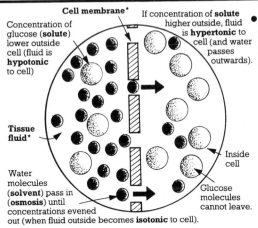

Cell membrane*

Concentration of glucose (**solute**) lower outside cell (fluid is **hypotonic** to cell)

If concentration of **solute** higher outside, fluid is **hypertonic** to cell (and water passes outwards).

Tissue fluid*

Water molecules (**solvent**) pass in (**osmosis**) until concentrations evened out (when fluid outside becomes **isotonic** to cell).

Inside cell

Glucose molecules cannot leave.

● **Osmosis.** The movement of molecules of a **solvent** through a **semipermeable** membrane (see above) in order to lower the concentration of a **solute** on the other side of the membrane, and even out the concentrations either side. This is a one-way type of **diffusion**, occurring when the molecules of the solute cannot pass the other way. **Osmotic pressure** is the pressure which builds up in an enclosed space, e.g. a cell, when a **solvent** enters by osmosis.

● **Active transport.** A process which occurs when substances need to travel in the opposite direction to that in which they would travel by **diffusion** (i.e. from low to high concentration, e.g. when cells take in large amounts of glucose for breakdown). It is not yet fully understood, but it is thought that special "carrier" molecules outside a cell "pick up" particles, "carry" them through the **cell membrane***, release them and return to the outside for more. Energy is needed for this action (since it opposes the natural tendency). This is supplied in the form of **ATP***.

● **Pinocytosis.** The taking in of a fluid droplet by inward-folding and separation of a section of **cell membrane*** (forming a **vacuole***). Most cells can do this.

* **ATP**, 105; **Cell membrane**, 10; **Tissue fluid**, 64; **Vacuoles**, 10.

Food and how it is used

Food is vital to all organisms, providing all the materials needed to be broken down for energy, to regulate cellular activities and to build and repair tissues (see pages 102-105). Of the various food substances, **carbohydrates**, **proteins** and **fats** are called **nutrients**, and **minerals**, **vitamins** (not needed by plants) and water are **accessory foods**. Plants build their own nutrients, and take in minerals and water; animals take in all the substances they need and break them down by digestion (see pages 108-109).

- **Carbohydrates**. A group of substances made up of carbon, hydrogen and oxygen, which exist in varying degrees of complexity (see "terms used", page 109). In animals, complex carbohydrates are taken in and broken down by digestion (see chart, pages 108-109) into the simple carbohydrate **glucose**. The breakdown of glucose (**internal respiration***) provides almost all the energy for life's activities. Plants build up glucose from other substances (see **photosynthesis**, page 26).

- **Proteins**. A group of substances made up of simpler units called **amino acids**. These contain carbon, hydrogen, oxygen, nitrogen and, in some cases, sulphur. Most protein molecules consist of hundreds, maybe thousands, of amino acids, joined together by links called **peptide links** into one or more chains called **polypeptides***. The many different types of protein each have a different arrangement of amino acids. They include the **structural proteins** (the basic components of new cells) and **catalytic proteins** (**enzymes***), which play a vital role in controlling cell processes.

  Plants build up amino acids from the substances they take in (see **photosynthesis**, page 26), and then build proteins from these amino acids. Animals take in proteins and break them down into single amino acid molecules by digestion (see chart, pages 108-109). These are then transported in the blood to all the body cells and reassembled into the different proteins needed (see **ribosomes**, page 11).

- **Fats**. A group of substances made up of carbon, hydrogen and a small amount of oxygen. Plants build up fats from the substances they take in and their seeds hold most of them as a store of food. This can be converted to extra **glucose** (see **carbohydrates**) to provide energy for the growing plant. Digestion of fats in animals produces **fatty acids** and **glycerol** (see chart, pages 108-109). If these need to be broken down for energy (as well as glucose), they are further broken down in the liver. This results in some products which the liver can convert to glucose, but others it cannot. These are instead converted elsewhere to a substance which forms a later stage of glucose breakdown. Fatty acids and glycerol not needed for energy are immediately recombined to form fat particles and stored in various body areas, e.g. under the skin (see **subcutaneous layer**, page 82).

100 * Enzymes, 103; Internal respiration, 104; Polypeptides, 109.

- **Vitamins**. A group of substances vital to animals, though only needed in tiny amounts. The most important function of many vitamins is to act as co-enzymes*, i.e. to help **enzymes*** catalyse chemical reactions. See page 109 for a list of vitamins and their functions.

- **Minerals**. Simple chemicals, e.g. phosphorus and calcium. They are vital constituents of plant and animal tissue, e.g. in the bones and teeth of animals, and some also act as **co-enzymes*** (see **vitamins**). They include **trace elements**, e.g. copper and iodine, present in tiny amounts.

- **Roughage**. Bulky fibrous food, e.g. bran, which cannot be digested by an animal. Much of it is made up of **cellulose**, a **carbohydrate** found in plant **cell walls***. Unlike most carbohydrates, this cannot be digested by most animals, including humans, because they do not have the necessary **digestive enzyme***, called **cellulase**. (Some animals, e.g. snails, do have this enzyme, and others, who must digest cellulose, do so in another way – see **rumen**, page 43.) The fact that roughage is bulky means that food can be gripped by intestinal muscles, and so moved on through the system.

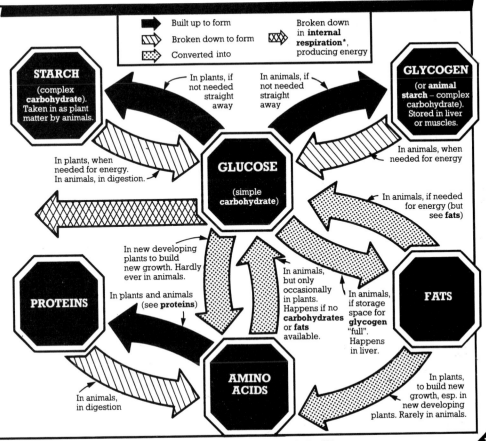

* Cell wall, 10; Co-enzymes, 103 (**Enzymes**); **Digestive enzymes**, 108; **Internal respiration**, 104.

Metabolism

Metabolism is a collective term for all the complex, closely-coordinated chemical reactions occurring inside an organism. These can be split into two opposing sets of reactions, called **catabolism** and **anabolism**. The rates of the reactions vary in response to variations in the organism's internal and external environments, and they play a major role in keeping internal conditions stable (see **homeostasis**, page 105).

● **Catabolism**. A collective term for all the reactions which break down substances in the body (**decomposition reactions**). One example is digestion in animals, which breaks down complex substances into simpler ones (see chart, pages 108-109). Another is the further breakdown of these simple substances in the cells (**internal respiration***). Catabolism always liberates energy (in digestion, most is lost as heat, but in internal respiration, it is used for the body's activities). This is despite the fact that, as with all chemical reactions, catabolism itself requires energy. This energy (needed) is taken from the much greater amount of energy produced during the reactions. The rest of this is released, hence the overall result is always an energy "profit".

● **Anabolism**. A collective term for all the reactions which build up substances in the body (**synthesis reactions**). One example is the linking together of amino acids to form proteins (see page 100). Anabolism always needs energy to be taken in, since the small amount produced during the reactions is never enough (i.e. the overall result of anabolism is an energy "loss"). The extra energy is taken from the **catabolism** "profit".

● **Metabolic rate**. The overall rate at which metabolic reactions occur in an individual. In human beings, it varies widely from person to person, and in the same individual under different conditions. It increases under stress, when the body temperature rises and during exercise, hence the true and accurate measurement of a person's metabolic rate is a measurement taken when the subject is resting, has a normal body temperature, and has not recently exercised. This is called the **basal metabolic rate** (**BMR**) and is expressed in **Calories** or **kilojoules** (see **Calories**) per square metre of body surface per hour (see calculations opposite).

People with high BMR can eat large amounts without putting on weight, because their **catabolism** of food matter (in the cells) happens so fast that not much fat is stored. This fast rate of reactions also often results in "excess" energy (i.e. energy not needed for **anabolism**), so they may appear to have a lot of "nervous energy". People with low BMR put on weight easily and often appear to have little energy.

The metabolic rate is influenced by a number of **hormones***, especially **STH**, **thyroxin**, **adrenalin** and **noradrenalin**. or more about these, see pages 106-107.

* **Hormones**, 106; **Internal respiration**, 104.

- **Calorie**. A unit of heat energy. One **calorie** (small c) is the amount of heat energy needed to raise the temperature of 1 gram of water by 1°C. The unit Calorie (large c) is equal to 1000 calories (a **kilocalorie**), i.e. it is the amount of heat energy needed to raise the temperature of 1000 grams of water by 1°C. It is the preferred unit in biology since large amounts of heat energy are involved. In many cases nowadays, though, a different unit, called a **kilojoule**, is used instead (one Calorie equals 4.2 kilojoules).

To work out a person's **basal metabolic rate** (**BMR** = $Cal/m^2/hr.$)

Facts known (worked out using a piece of apparatus called a calorimeter):
1. If 1 litre of oxygen is used to break down carbohydrates, c.5.05 Cal are produced (i.e. enough heat energy to heat c.5050g water by 1°C).
2. With fats, the result from 1 litre oxygen is c.4.7 Cal.
3. With proteins – c.4.6 Cal.

First calculation:
Heat energy generated when food (in general) is broken down using 1 litre of oxygen = the average of the three figures above, i.e. 4.78 Cal (provided subject measured has taken in equal amounts of the three foodstuffs).

Measure the oxygen used by a subject's body in a fixed time. Done using a spirometer (respirometer): ▶

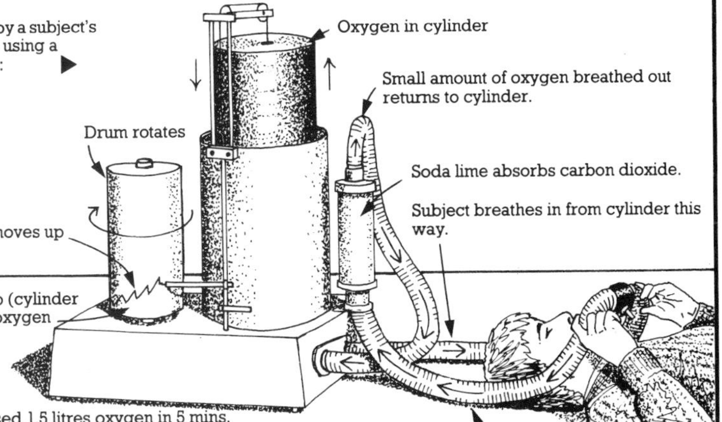

Oxygen in cylinder

Drum rotates

Small amount of oxygen breathed out returns to cylinder.

Soda lime absorbs carbon dioxide.

Subject breathes in from cylinder this way.

Trace drawn as cylinder moves up and down.

Overall trend of trace is up (cylinder moves down as its vol. of oxygen decreases).

Calculations (example):
1. (Measured) Subject used 1.5 litres oxygen in 5 mins.
2. Hence he would use 18 litres in 1 hr (1.5 x 12).
3. (Known) 4.78 Cal produced when food broken down by 1 litre oxygen.
4. Hence 86.04 Cal produced if food broken down by 18 litres (4.78 x 18).
5. Hence 86.04 Cal produced by breakdown of food in whole of subject's body in 1 hr. (he would use 18 litres per hour – see point 2).
6. But **BMR** is measured in Cal *per sq. metre of body surface* per hr.
7. Standard chart used to work out body surface in sq. metres.
8. 86.04 divided by body surface (e.g. $2m^2$) = 43.02 $Cal/m^2/hr$ (**BMR**)

Subject breathes out to cylinder this way.

- **Enzymes**. Special proteins (**catalytic proteins**) found in all living things and vital to the chemical reactions of life. They act as **catalysts**, i.e. they speed up reactions without themselves being changed. Many enzymes are aided by other substances, called **co-enzymes**, whose molecules are able to "carry" the products of one reaction (catalysed by an enzyme) on to the next reaction.

There are many different types of enzyme, e.g. **digestive enzymes**, which control the breakdown of complex food material into simple soluble substances (see text and chart, pages 108-109), and **respiratory enzymes**, which control the further breakdown of these simple substances in the cells to liberate energy (i.e. **internal respiration***).

Energy for life and homeostasis

A living thing needs energy for its activities. This energy comes from a series of chemical reactions inside its cells, known as **internal respiration**, **tissue respiration** or **cellular respiration**. The cells contain various simple food substances, which are the results of digestive breakdown in animals (see pages 108-109) and **photosynthesis*** in plants. These substances all contain stored energy, which is released when internal respiration breaks them down. In almost all cases, glucose is the substance broken down (see **carbohydrates** and diagram, pages 100-101). There are two kinds of internal respiration – **anaerobic** and **aerobic respiration**.

●**Anaerobic respiration**. A type of **internal respiration** which does not need free oxygen (oxygen taken into the body). It takes place in the cells of all organisms and releases a small amount of energy. In most organisms, it consists of a chain of chemical reactions called **glycolysis**, which break down glucose into **pyruvic acid**. In normal circumstances this is then immediately followed by **aerobic respiration**, which breaks down this poisonous acid in the presence of oxygen. This breakdown releases the bulk of the energy. In abnormal conditions, however, it may not be possible for the aerobic stage to follow immediately, in which case a further stage of anaerobic respiration occurs (see **oxygen debt**).

In some microscopic organisms, e.g. yeast and some bacteria, anaerobic respiration always runs through all its stages, providing enough energy for their needs without requiring oxygen.

●**Aerobic respiration**. A type of **internal respiration** which can only take place in the presence of free oxygen (oxygen taken into the body). It is the way in which most living things obtain the bulk of their energy and follows a stage of **anaerobic respiration**. Oxygen (brought by the blood) is taken into each cell and reacts in the **mitochondria*** with the **pyruvic acid** produced in anaerobic respiration. Carbon dioxide and water are the final products of the reactions, and chemical energy is released, which is then "stored" as **ATP**.

Aerobic respiration is an example of **oxidation** – the breakdown of a substance in the presence of oxygen.

●**Oxygen debt**. A situation which occurs when extreme physical exercise is undertaken by an organism which shows **aerobic respiration**. Under these circumstances, the oxygen in the organism's cells is used up faster than it can be taken in. This means that there is not enough to break down the poisonous **pyruvic acid** produced in the first, **anaerobic**, stage of respiration. Instead, the acid undergoes further anaerobic reactions to convert it to **lactic acid** (much less harmful). This begins to build up, and the organism is said to have acquired an oxygen debt. This is "paid off" later by taking in oxygen faster than usual to break down the lactic acid.

- **ADP** (**adenosine diphosphate**) and **ATP** (**adenosine triphosphate**). Two substances which consist of a chemical grouping called **adenosine**, combined with two and three **phosphate groups** respectively. A phosphate group consists of linked phosphorus, oxygen and hydrogen atoms. It can combine with other substances (either by itself or linked with other phosphate groups in a chain). When **aerobic respiration** occurs, the chemical energy released is involved in reactions which result in a conversion of ADP molecules into ATP molecules (by attachment of a third phosphate group in each case). The energy taken in to effect these reactions can be regarded as being "stored" in the form of ATP. This is a substance which can be easily stored in all cells (it is found in especially large quantities in cells which require a lot of energy, e.g. muscle cells). When the energy is needed, reactions occur which convert ATP back into ADP. These reactions result in an overall release of energy – the "stored" energy. In this way, power is supplied for the cell's activities.

Homeostasis

Homeostasis is the maintenance, by an organism, of a stable **internal environment**, i.e. a constant temperature, stable composition, level and pressure of body fluids, constant **metabolic rate***, etc. This is vital if the organism is to function properly. It requires the detection of any deviation from the norm (caused by new internal or external factors) and the means to correct such deviations, and is practised most efficiently in birds and **mammals***, e.g. humans. Their detection of deviations is achieved by the **feedback** of information to controlling organs. The blood glucose level, for example, is constantly being detected by the pancreas (i.e. information is "fed back"). The correction of deviations is achieved by **negative feedback**, i.e. feedback which "tells" of deviations and results in a change of action. If the glucose level gets too high, for example, the pancreas reacts by producing more insulin* to reduce it (see also **antagonistic hormones**, page 106). Most homeostatic actions are, like this example, controlled by hormones, many of which are in turn controlled by the **hypothalamus*** in the brain. An example of the importance of the hypothalamus in homeostasis is the control of body temperature. All birds and mammals, e.g. humans, are **homiothermic** (warm-blooded), i.e. they can keep a constant temperature (about 37°C in humans) regardless of external conditions (the opposite is **poikilothermic**, or cold-blooded). A "thermostat" area of the hypothalamus, called the **preoptic area**, detects any changes in body temperature and sends impulses either to the **heat-losing centre** or to the **heat-promoting centre** (both also found in the hypothalamus). These areas then send out nervous impulses to cause various heat-losing or heat-promoting actions in the body.

Hormones

Hormones are special chemical "messengers" which control various activities inside an organism. These pages deal with the hormones produced by humans and their related groups. Plants also produce hormones (**phytohormones**), though these are not yet fully understood (see **abscission layer**, page 21, and **photoperiodism** and **growth hormones**, page 23). Human hormones are secreted by **endocrine glands***. Some act only on specific body parts (**target cells** or **target organs**), others cause a more general response. The principal controller of hormone production is the **hypothalamus*** (part of the brain). It controls the secretions of many glands, mainly through its control of the **pituitary gland***, which itself controls many other glands. The hypothalamus "tells" the pituitary to produce its hormones by sending **regulating factors** to its **anterior lobe** and nervous impulses to its **posterior lobe**. Hormone secretion is vital to **homeostasis***.

●**Regulating factors**. Special chemicals which control the production of a number of hormones, and hence many vital body functions. They are sent to the **anterior lobe** of the **pituitary gland*** by the **hypothalamus*** (part of the brain). There are two types – **releasing factors**, which make the gland secrete specific hormones, and **inhibiting factors**, which make it stop its secretion. For example, **FSHRF** (**FSH releasing factor**) and **LHRF** (**LH releasing factor**) cause the release of the hormones **FSH** and **LH** (see chart), and hence the onset of **puberty***. Many regulating factors are vital to **homeostasis***.

●**Antagonistic hormones**. Hormones that produce opposite effects. **Glucagon** and **insulin** (see chart) are examples. When the blood glucose level drops too far, the pancreas produces glucagon to raise it again. A high glucose level causes the pancreas to produce insulin to lower the level (see also **homeostasis**, page 105).

HORMONES
ACTH (adrenocorticotropic hormone) or **adrenocorticotropin**
TSH (thyroid-stimulating hormone) or **thyrotropin**
STH (somatotropic hormone) or somatotropin or **HGH** (human growth hormone)
FSH (follicle-stimulating hormone)
LH (luteinizing hormone). Also called **luteotropin** in women and **ICSH** (interstitial cell stimulating hormone) in men.
Lactogenic hormone or **PR** (prolactin)
Oxytocin
ADH (anti-diuretic hormone) or vasopressin
Thyroxin
TCT (thyrocalcitonin) or calcitonin
PTH (parathyroid hormone) or parathyrin or parathormone
Adrenalin or **adrenin** or **epinephrin** **Noradrenalin** or norepinephrin
Aldosterone
Cortisone Hydrocortisone or cortisol
Oestrogen (female **sex hormone**) **Progesterone** (female **sex hormone**)
Androgens (male **sex hormones**), esp. **testosterone**
Gastrin
CCK (cholecystokinin)
Secretin PZ (pancreozymin)
Enterocrinin
Insulin
Glucagon

* Endocrine glands, 69; Homeostasis, 105; Hypothalamus, 75; Pituitary gland, 69; Puberty, 90.

WHERE PRODUCED	EFFECTS
Pituitary gland (p.69) **(anterior lobe)**	Stimulates production of hormones in **cortex** of **adrenal glands** (p.69).
Pituitary gland (p.69) **(anterior lobe)**	Stimulates production of **thyroxin** by **thyroid gland** (p.69).
Pituitary gland (p.69) **(anterior lobe)**	Stimulates growth by increasing rate at which amino acids are built up to make proteins in cells.
Pituitary gland (p.69) **(anterior lobe)**	In women, works with **LH** to stimulate development of **ova** in **ovarian follicles** (p.89) and secretion of **oestrogen** by follicles in early stages of **menstrual cycle** (p.90). In men, causes formation of **sperm** (p.93).
Pituitary gland (p.69) **(anterior lobe)**	Stimulates **ovulation** (p.90), formation of **corpus luteum** (p.90) and its secretion of oestrogen and **progesterone**. Works with oestrogen and progesterone to stimulate thickening of lining of **uterus** (p.89). In men, causes production of **androgens**.
Pituitary gland (p.69) **(anterior lobe)**	Works with **LH** to cause secretion of hormones by **corpus luteum** (p.90). Causes milk production after giving birth.
Hypothalamus (p.75). Builds up in pituitary gland (**posterior lobe**).	Stimulates contraction of muscles of **uterus** (p.89) during labour and ejection of milk after giving birth.
Hypothalamus (p.75). Builds up in pituitary gland (**posterior lobe**).	Increases amount of water re-absorbed into blood from **uriniferous tubules** (p.73) in kidneys.
Thyroid gland (p.69)	Increases rate of food breakdown, hence increasing energy and raising body temperature. Works with **STH** in the young to control rate of growth and development. Contains iodine.
Thyroid gland (p.69)	Decreases level of calcium and phosphorus in blood by reducing their release from bones (where they are stored).
Parathyroid glands (p.69)	Increases level of calcium in blood by increasing its release from bone (see above). Decreases phosphorus level.
Adrenal glands (p.69) **(medulla)**. Also at nerve endings. Secreted at times of excitement or danger.	Stimulate liver to release more glucose into blood, to be broken down for energy. Stimulate increase in heart rate, faster breathing and blood vessel constriction.
Adrenal glands (p.69) **(cortex)**	Increases amount of sodium and water in blood by causing re-absorption of more from **uriniferous tubules** (p.73) in kidneys.
Adrenal glands (p.69) **(cortex)**	Stimulate increase in rate of food breakdown for energy, and thus increase resistance to stress. Lessen inflammation.
Mostly in **ovarian follicles** (p.89) and **corpus luteum** (p.90) in **ovaries** (female sex organs, p.89). Also in **placenta** (p.91) during pregnancy.	Oestrogen activates development of **secondary sex characters** at **puberty** (p.90), e.g. breast growth. Both prepare **mammary** (milk) **glands** for milk production and work with **LH** to cause thickening of lining of **uterus** (p.89). Progesterone dominates towards end of **menstrual cycle** (p.90) and during pregnancy, when it maintains uterus lining and mammary gland readiness.
Mostly in **interstitial cells** in **testes** (male sex organs, p.88).	Activate development and maintenance of **secondary sex characters** at **puberty** (p.90), e.g. beard growth.
	Stimulates production of **gastric juice** (p.108).
Cells in small intestine	Stimulates opening of **sphincter of Oddi**, contraction of **gall bladder** and release of **bile** (all p.69) into **duodenum** (p.67).
Cells in small intestine	Stimulate pancreas to produce **pancreatic juice** (p.108) and secrete it into **duodenum** (p.67).
Cells in small intestine	Stimulates production of **intestinal juice** (p.108).
Pancreas, when blood glucose level too high.	Stimulates liver to convert more glucose to glycogen for storage (p.101). Also speeds up transport of glucose to cells.
Pancreas, when blood glucose level too low.	Stimulates faster conversion of glycogen to glucose in liver (p.101), and conversion of fats and proteins to glucose.

Digestive juices and enzymes

All the **digestive juices*** of the human body (secreted into the intestines by **digestive glands***) contain **enzymes*** which control the breakdown of food into simple soluble substances. These are called **digestive enzymes** and can be divided into three groups. **Amylases** (or **diastases**) promote the breakdown of **carbohydrates*** (the final result being **monosaccharides** – see terms used, right). **Proteinases** (or **peptidases**) promote the breakdown of **proteins** into **amino acids*** by attacking the **peptide links** (see **proteins**, page 100). **Lipases** promote the breakdown of **fats** into **glycerol** and **fatty acids** (see **fats**, page 100). The chart below lists the different digestive juices of the body, together with their enzymes and the action of these enzymes.

Digestive juice: Saliva

Produced by: Salivary glands* in mouth

Digestive enzyme: Salivary amylase (or ptyalin)

Actions: Starts breakdown of **carbohydrates*** starch and **glycogen** (**polysaccharides** – see p.101).

Products: Some **dextrin** (shorter **polysaccharide**). See note 1.

Digestive juice: Gastric juice

Produced by: Gastric glands* in stomach lining. Secreted into stomach (see **gastrin**, p. 106).

Digestive enzymes (and one other constituent):
1. **Pepsin** (**proteinase**). See note 2.
2. **Rennin** (**proteinase**). Found only in the young.
3. **Hydrochloric acid**
4. **Gastric lipase**. Found mainly in the young.

Actions:
1. Starts breakdown of **proteins*** (**polypeptides**).
2. Works (with calcium) to curdle milk, i.e. to act on its **protein** (**casein**). See note 3.
3. Activates **pepsin** (see note 2) and kills bacteria.
4. Starts breakdown of **fat*** molecules in milk.

Products:
1. Shorter **polypeptides**
2,3. **Curds**, i.e. milk solids
4. Intermediate compounds

Digestive juice: Bile

Produced by: Liver. Stored in **gall bladder***, secreted into small intestine (see **CCK**, p. 106).

Constituents: Bile salts and bile acids

Actions: Break up **fats*** (and intermediate compounds) into smaller particles, a process called **emulsification**.

Digestive juice: Pancreatic juice

Produced by: Pancreas. Secreted into small intestine (see **secretin/PZ**, p.106).

Digestive enzymes:
1. **Trypsin** (**proteinase**). See note 2.
2. **Chymotrypsin** (**proteinase**). See note 2.
3. **Carboxypeptidase** (**proteinase**). See note 2.
4. **Pancreatic amylase** (or **amylopsin**)
5. **Pancreatic lipase**

Actions:
1, 2, 3. Continue breakdown of **proteins*** (long and shorter **polypeptides**).
4. Continues breakdown of **carbohydrates***.
5. Breaks down **fat*** particles.

Products:
1,2,3. **Dipeptides** and some **amino acids***.
4. **Maltose** (**disaccharide**)
5. **Glycerol** and fatty acids (see **fats**, p. 100).

Digestive juice: Intestinal juice (or **succus entericus**)

Produced by: Intestinal glands* in small intestine lining. Final secretion into small intestine (see **enterocrinin**, p.106).

Digestive enzymes:
1. **Maltase** (**amylase**)
2. **Sucrase** (or **invertase** or **saccharase**) (**amylase**)
3. **Lactase** (**amylase**)
4. **Enterokinase**. See note 2.

Actions:
1. Breaks down **maltose** (**disaccharide**)
2. Breaks down **sucrose** (**disaccharide**)
3. Breaks down **lactose** (**disaccharide**)
4. Completes breakdown of **proteins*** (**dipeptides**)

Products:
1. **Glucose** (or **dextrose**) (**monosaccharide**)
2. **Glucose** and **fructose** (**monosaccharides**)
3. **Glucose** and **galactose** (**monosaccharides**)
4. **Amino acids***

Notes

1. Not much **dextrin** is produced at this stage, since food is not in the mouth long enough. Most carbohydrates pass through unchanged.

2. **Proteinases** are first secreted in inactive forms, to prevent them digesting the digestive tube (made of **protein***, like most of the body). Once in the tube (beyond a protective layer of **mucous membrane***),

these are converted into active forms. **Hydrochloric acid** changes **pepsinogen** (inactive) into **pepsin**, **enterokinase** changes **trypsinogen** into **trypsin**, and trypsin then changes **chymotrypsinogen** and **procarboxypeptidase** into **chymotrypsin** and **carboxypeptidase**.

3. The action of **rennin** and **hydrochloric acid** in curdling milk is vital, since liquid milk would pass through the system too fast to be digested.

* Amino acids, 100 (Proteins); Carbohydrates, 100; Digestive juices, 68 (Digestive glands); Enzymes, 103; Fats, 100; Gall bladder, 69; Gastric glands, Intestinal glands, 68 (Digestive glands); Mucous membrane, 67; Salivary glands, 68.

Terms used

Polysaccharides. The most complex **carbohydrates***. Each is a chain of **monosaccharide** molecules. Most carbohydrates taken into the body are polysaccharides, e.g. **starch** (the main polysaccharide in edible plants) and **glycogen** (the main one in animal matter). For more about starch and glycogen, see page 101.

Disaccharides. Compounds of 2 **monosaccharide** molecules, either forming intermediate stages in the breakdown of **polysaccharides** or (in the case of **sucrose** and **lactose**) taken into the body as such. (Sucrose is found in sugar beet and sugar cane, lactose occurs in milk.)

Monosaccharides. The simplest **carbohydrates***. Almost all result from **polysaccharide** breakdown, though **fructose** is taken into the body as such (e.g. in fruit juices), as well as resulting from **sucrose** breakdown. **Glucose** is the final result of all action on carbohydrates (fructose and **galactose** are converted to glucose in the liver).

Polypeptides. The complex form taken by all **proteins** entering the body. Each is a chain of hundreds (or thousands) of **amino acid*** molecules (see **proteins**, page 100).

Dipeptides. Chains of 2 **amino acid*** molecules, forming intermediate stages in the breakdown of **polypeptides**.

Vitamins and their uses

Vitamin A (retinol)

Sources: Liver, kidneys, fish-liver oils, eggs, dairy products, margarine, **pigment*** (**carotene**) in green and yellow fruit and vegetables, esp. tomatoes, carrots (carotene converted to vitamin A in intestines).

Uses: Maintains general health of **epithelial*** cells (lining cells), aids growth, esp. bones and teeth. Essential for vision in dim light – involved in formation of light-sensitive **pigment*** (**rhodopsin**), found in **rods** of **retina***. Aids in resistance against infection.

Vitamin B complex

Group of at least 10 vitamins, usually occurring together. Include: **Thiamine** (or **aneurin**) (**B1**), **Riboflavin** (**B2**), **Niacin** (or **nicotinic acid** or **nicotinamide**) (**B3**), **Pantothenic acid** (**B5**), **Pyridoxine** (**B6**), **Cyanocobalamin** (or **cobalamin**) (**B12**), **Folic acid** (**Bc** or **M**), **Biotin** (sometimes called **vitamin H**), **Lecithin**.

Sources: All found in yeast, liver. All except B12 found in wholewheat cereals and bread, wheatgerm, green vegetables, e.g. beans (B12 not found in any vegetable products). B2 and B12 found especially in dairy products. Most also found in eggs, nuts, fish, lean meat, kidneys, potatoes. B6, folic acid and biotin also made by bacteria in intestines.

Uses: Most needed for growth and maintenance of healthy tissues, e.g. muscles (B1, B6) nerves (B1, B3, B6, B12), skin (B2, B3, B5, B6, B12), hair (B2, B5) and a number aid continuous function of body organs (B5, B6, lecithin). Most (B1, B2, B3, B5, B6, B12) are essential **co-enzymes***, aiding in breakdown of foods for energy (**internal respiration***). Many (esp. B2, B6, B12) also co-enzymes aiding build up of substances (**proteins***) for growth, regulatory or defence purposes. B12 and folic acid vital to formation of blood cells, B5 and B6 to manufacture of nerve chemicals (**neurotransmitters***).

Vitamin C (ascorbic acid)

Sources: Green vegetables, potatoes, tomatoes, citrus fruit, e.g. oranges, grapefruit, lemons.

Uses: Needed for growth and maintenance of healthy tissues, esp. skin, blood vessels, bones, gums, teeth. Essential **co-enzyme*** in many metabolic reactions, esp. **protein*** breakdown and build-up of **amino acids*** into new proteins (esp. **collagen** – see **connective tissue**, page 52). Aids in resistance against infection and healing of wounds.

Vitamin D (calciferol)

Sources: Liver, fish-liver oils, oily fish, dairy products, egg yolk, margarine, special substance (provitamin D3) in skin cells (converted to vitamin D when exposed to sunlight).

Uses: Essential for absorption of calcium and phosphorus, and their deposition in bones and teeth. May work with **PTH*** (**hormone**).

Vitamin E (tocopherol)

Sources: Meat, egg yolk, leafy green vegetables, nuts, dairy products, margarine, cereals, wholemeal bread, wheatgerm, seeds, seed and vegetable oils.

Uses: Not yet fully understood. Believed to be involved in formation of **DNA***, **RNA*** and red blood cells, and promotion of fertility and food breakdown in muscle cells.

Vitamin K (phylloquinone or menaquinone)

Sources: Liver, fruit, nuts, cereals, tomatoes, green vegetables, esp. cabbage, cauliflower, spinach. Also made by bacteria in intestines.

Uses: Essential to formation of **prothrombin*** in liver (needed to cause clotting of blood).

* **Amino acids**, 100 (**Proteins**); **Carbohydrates**, 100; **Co-enzymes**, 103 (**Enzymes**); **DNA**, 96 (**Nucleic acids**); **Epithelium**, 82 (**Epidermis**); **Internal respiration**, 104; **Neurotransmitters**, 77 (**Synapse**); **Pigments**, 27; **Prothrombin**, 59 (**Clotting**); **PTH**, 106; **Retina**, 85; **RNA**, 96 (**Nucleic acids**).

The classification of living things

Classification, or **taxonomy**, is the grouping together of living things, according to characteristics which they share. The main, formal type of classification (**classical taxonomy**) bases its groups primarily on structural characteristics (but see also page 114). The resulting classification charts first list the largest groups (**Kingdoms**), and then go on to list the smaller and smaller divisions within these groups.

The first groups after the Kingdoms are called **Sub-kingdoms** and the next are **Phyla** (sing. **Phylum**) in the case of animals and **Divisions** in the case of plants (though some plant classification charts have no Sub-kingdoms). After these come **Classes, Orders, Families, Genera** (sing. **Genus**) and finally **Species** – the smallest groupings. Some Divisions or Phyla, especially those with only a few members, may not have all these groups (e.g. the next group after a Phylum may be an Order, Family, Genus or even a Species) and there are also further "mid-way" groups in some cases, e.g. **Sub-classes** or **Sub-phyla**. The charts on the next four pages only classify as far as Classes in most cases, with some Sub-classes and also special **Infraclasses** in the case of **mammals** (see page 113).

It should be noted that there are areas which are still under dispute in both plant and animal classification. The classification of plants in particular varies so much so that one, two or even three groups are regarded by many taxonomists as completely separate Kingdoms, and not plants at all. The notes accompanying both the plant charts here and the animal chart on pages 112-113 cover some of the major differences. In addition, two of the most commonly-used plant classification charts are shown on these two pages, instead of just one, as given for the animal Kingdom.

The Plant Kingdom (Kingdom Plantae)

Chart 1

SUB-KINGDOM: Thallophyta. No roots, stems or leaves, no **embryo*** as such.

DIVISION: Schizophyta or **Schizomycophyta. Bacteria** (sing. **bacterium**). Single-celled organisms found everywhere in large numbers. Some are **pathogenic**, that is, they cause disease, but others are useful, decomposing dead organisms for example.

DIVISION: Myxomycophyta or **Myxomycota.** Slime moulds. Very simple organisms with no **cell walls*** and no **chlorophyll***. Live on decaying plants or animals. Reproduce with **spores***.

DIVISION: Eumycophyta or **Eumycota.** True **fungi** (sing. **fungus**). May be single-celled or made of intertwined threads called **hyphae** (sing. **hypha**) which form a mesh (**mycelium**) over dead material on which fungus feeds. Have **cell walls*** but no **chlorophyll***. Useful in causing decay, also in some industrial processes (e.g. brewing). Some are important antibiotics, e.g. Penicillium. Reproduce with **spores***. E.g. mushrooms.

All the remaining Divisions in the Sub-kingdom are types of **algae** (sing. **alga**) – simple plants found in salt or freshwater or damp places. All possess **chlorophyll*** (but see note 2) and the larger ones (seaweeds) each have a ribbon-like plant body called a **thallus**.

DIVISION: Cyanophyta. Blue-green algae. Primitive single-celled or many-celled algae with **cell walls***. Have bluish-green **pigment*** called **phycocyanin**. Found even in hot springs and arctic water.

DIVISION: Euglenophyta. Single-celled algae with no **cell walls***. Have **flagella***. Commonly found in freshwater.

DIVISION: Chrysophyta. Golden algae. Single-celled, with **cell walls***. Have **flagella***. Highly diverse group – salt or freshwater, also damp places.

DIVISION: Pyrrophyta. Fire algae. Single-celled, no **cell walls***. Have **flagella***.

DIVISION: Bacillariophyta. Diatoms. Single-celled, with silica "shells". Water-living (salt or freshwater). May occur singly, though often **colonial*** (living together in a mass).

DIVISION: Xanthophyta. Yellow-green algae. Mostly single-celled, with **cell walls*** and **pigment*** called **xanthophyll**. Found in salt or freshwater, also damp places.

DIVISION: Rhodophyta. Red algae (seaweeds). Many-celled with **cell walls*** and red and blue **pigments***. Mainly found in salt water. E.g. Dulse.

DIVISION: Phaeophyta. Brown algae (seaweeds). Many-celled, all with **cell walls***. Includes all common seaweeds, brown to olive-green in colour. Each has special disc-like attachment called a **holdfast**, which fixes it to a surface. E.g. kelps.

DIVISION: Chlorophyta. Green algae (seaweeds). Largest group of algae – includes many single-celled and many-celled algae. All have **cell walls***. Mostly freshwater, though some found in salt water and some in damp places, e.g. tree trunks and soil. Exist in enormous quantities (single-celled ones often **colonial** – see **Bacilliarophyta**).

SUB-KINGDOM: Embryophyta. All have **cell walls***, **chlorophyll***, roots, stems and leaves. Also a distinct protective layer of cells around new developing plant (**embryo***).

DIVISION: Bryophyta. Have some kind of roots, stems and leaves but no **vascular tissue***. Most have short stem-like structure called a **seta**, which bears tightly-packed leaves (in mosses) or flat leaf-like expansions (in liverworts). Have thread-like roots called **rhizoids** which cling to a surface instead of going into ground. Mainly land plants with wide distribution in damp areas. 3 Classes:

*Cell wall, 10; Chlorophyll, 27; Embryo, 93; Flagella, 40; Pigment, 27; Spores, 92 (Sporulation); Vascular tissue, 14.

Classes:
  Hepaticae. Liverworts.

  Musci. Mosses.

  Anthocerotae. Hornworts.

DIVISION: Tracheophyta. Have roots, stems and leaves and **vascular tissue***.

Sub-Division: Pteridophyta. No flowers or seeds. 4 Classes:

Classes:
  Psilotales. Primitive, loosely related to ferns.

  Lycopodiales. Clubmosses. Creeping **evergreens***, related to ferns. Date back to prehistoric times.

  Equisetales. Horsetails. Related to ferns, but can live with less moisture and shade. Giant forms abundant in prehistoric times.

  Filicales. Ferns. Live in moist, shady areas. Have **fronds** – **bipinnate*** structures (stalks and leaves combined) which bear **spores***.

Sub-Division: Spermatophyta. Have seeds. 2 Classes:

Class:
  Gymnospermae. Seeds not enclosed in a fruit, no flowers.
Sub-classes:
  Cycadales. Cycads. Primitive, palm-like.

  Coniferales. Conifers, e.g. firs. **Evergreens***, most with sharp pointed leaves (**needles**) and all with reproductive bodies called **cones**. **Ovules*** develop on external **scales** of female cones (no flowers), **pollen*** on scales of male cones.

  Ginkgoales. Only one living member – Gingko (maidenhair tree).

  Gnetales. Only 3 genera, e.g. Welwitschia (desert plant with large leathery leaves).
Class:
  Angiospermae. Seeds enclosed in a fruit. Have flowers.
Sub-classes:
  Dicotyledonae. Have 2 **cotyledons***, e.g. buttercup, rose.

  Monocotyledonae. Have 1 **cotyledon***, e.g. grasses, lily.

Chart 2 (for descriptions, see chart 1)

Thallophytes is an informal term only.

DIVISION: Schizophyta or **Schizomycophyta**.

DIVISION: Myxomycophyta or **Myxomycota**.

DIVISION: Eumycophyta or **Eumycota**.

DIVISION: Cyanophyta.

DIVISION: Euglenophyta.

DIVISION: Chrysophyta.

DIVISION: Pyrrophyta.

DIVISION: Bacillariophyta.

DIVISION: Xanthophyta.

DIVISION: Rhodophyta.

DIVISION: Phaeophyta.

DIVISION: Chlorophyta.

Embryophytes is an informal term only.

DIVISION: Bryophyta.

Classes:
  Hepaticae
  Musci
  Anthocerotae

Tracheophytes is an informal term only.

Pteridophytes is an informal term only.

DIVISION: Psilophyta. Was Class **Psilotales**.

DIVISION: Lycophyta. Was Class **Lycopodiales**.

DIVISION: Sphenophyta. Was Class **Equisetales**.

DIVISION: Pterophyta. Was Class **Filicales**.

Spermatophytes is an informal term only.

Gymnosperms is an informal term only.

DIVISION: Cycadophyta. Was Sub-class **Cycadales**.

DIVISION: Coniferophyta. Was Sub-class **Coniferales**.

DIVISION: Ginkgophyta. Was Sub-class **Ginkgoales**.

DIVISION: Gnetophyta. Was Sub-class **Gnetales**.

Angiosperms is an informal term only.

DIVISION: Anthophyta. Was Class **Angiospermae**.

Class:
  Dicotyledonae. Was Sub-class **Dicotyledonae**.

Class:
  Monocotyledonae. Was Sub-class **Monocotyledonae**.

Notes

1. The bacteria and blue-green algae (Divisions **Schizophyta** and **Cyanophyta**) do not have **nuclei*** and are thus not true plants or animals. For this reason, some classifications put them in a separate Kingdom (before plants and animals) called the Kingdom **Monera** or **Prokaryota** (**prokaryotic** means "without a nucleus", the opposite is **eukaryotic).**

2. Some of the single-celled algae (especially those of the Divisions **Euglenophyta**, **Chrysophyta** and **Pyrrophyta**) have both animal and plant characteristics (e.g. they can "eat" food as well as

making it by **photosynthesis***, some have **flagella*** and some have no **cell walls***). For this reason, some classifications put them in a separate Kingdom called the Kingdom **Protista** (after note 1) and before plants and animals). The Kingdom may be further expanded to include the **Protozoa** (see page 112).

3. The slime moulds and fungi (Divisions **Myxomycophyta** and **Eumycophyta**) have doubtful affinity with the plants (they lack **chlorophyll***) but no closer links with animals. For this reason, some classifications put them in a separate Kingdom called the Kingdom **Fungi** (after **Monera** and **Protista** (see notes 1 and 2) and before plants and animals).

---

*Bipinnate, 22; Cell wall, 10; Chlorophyll, 27; Cotyledon, 33; Evergreen, 8; Flagella, 40; Nucleus, 10; Ovules, 30; Photosynthesis, 26; Pollen, 30; Spores, 92 (Sporulation); Vascular tissue, 14.

The Animal Kingdom (Kingdom Animalia)

See introduction, page 110. As with the plant classification chart, this chart lists its members in order of complexity, beginning with the most primitive. The main characteristics which appear as animals become more complex are mentioned in this chart in the first instance they occur, but are assumed from then on. These are a true gut, a circulatory system, a nervous system, a true body cavity, some type of **segmentation***, some type of skeleton and the existence of lungs (see also pages 36-37). All other characteristics mentioned refer specifically to the group being defined.

In the classification of animals, there are a number of relatively primitive animals (especially particular kinds of worms) which belong together in small groups. These are normally only included in the most comprehensive classification charts (as minor **Phyla**), and are not listed here.

SUB-KINGDOM: Protozoa

PHYLUM: Protozoa. The only Phylum, with the same name as the Sub-kingdom. Single-celled animals. Mostly aquatic, though many are **parasitic***. E.g. Amoeba, Paramecium.

Classes: Mastigophora (or Flagellata), Sarcodina, Ciliophora (or Ciliata), Sporozoa, Microspora.

SUB-KINGDOM: Parazoa

PHYLUM: Porifera. The only Phylum. Sponges. Porous, non-mobile living mass, consisting of millions of single-celled organisms (see **colonial**, page 114).

Classes: Calcarea, Demospongiae, Sclerospongiae, Hexactinellida (or Triaxonida or Hyalospongiae).

SUB-KINGDOM: Metazoa. All the rest of the Animal Kingdom, i.e. all the many-celled (**multicellular**) animals.

PHYLUM: Coelenterata (coelenterates) or **Cnidaria**. Aquatic animals with **tentacles***. Only one body opening (for substances in and out). Move by muscular action. E.g. sea anemones, jellyfish, Hydra.

Classes: Hydrozoa, Scyphozoa, Anthozoa (or Actinozoa).

PHYLUM: Ctenophora. Marine, jelly-like animals, very similar to **coelenterates** but moving by means of tiny "hairs" (**cilia***).

Classes: Tentaculata, Nuda.

PHYLUM: Platyhelminthes. Flatworms. Have a mouth and a primitive excretory system. E.g. **parasitic*** flukes and tapeworms.

Classes: Turbellaria, Cestoidea (or Cestoda or Eucestoda), Cestodaria, Monogenoidea (or Monogenea), Digenoidea (or Digenea), Aspidogastrea (or Aspidobothrea or Aspidocotylea).

PHYLUM: Nemertea or **Rhynchocoela**. Ribbon worms. Marine worms with a true gut (i.e. running from mouth to **anus***), a primitive circulatory system and a sucking organ (**proboscis**) with a hooked end.

Classes: Anopla, Enopla.

PHYLUM: Aschelminthes. Worm-like aquatic animals. Mostly **parasitic***. E.g. roundworms, hookworms, threadworms.

Classes: Nematoda, Rotifera (or Rotatoria), Gastrotricha, Kinorhyncha (or Echinodera), Priapulida, Nematomorpha (or Gordiacea).

PHYLUM: Annelida (annelids) or **Annulata**. Most advanced worms. Have tubular, segmented bodies with a body cavity, circulatory and nervous system. Have fine bristles (**chaetae***) to grip soil or sand.

Classes: Aclitellata (marine worms), Clitellata (freshwater worms, earthworms and leeches).

PHYLUM: Mollusca (molluscs). Soft-bodied animals with a limey shell, a head and a muscular "foot" for creeping or digging. Mostly aquatic.

Classes: 3 minor ones – **Scaphopoda, Monoplacophora, Amphineura.** 3 more important:

Gastropoda (gastropods). Univalves, i.e. with a shell made of one piece only. E.g. snails, limpets.

Lamellibranchiata (lamellibranchs) or **Bivalvia (bivalves)** or **Pelecypoda.** Have a shell in two parts hinged together. E.g. oysters, clams, mussels.

Cephalopoda (cephalopods) or **Siphonopoda.** Molluscs with **tentacles*** and well-developed eyes. E.g. octopuses, squid, cuttlefish.

PHYLUM: Arthropoda (arthropods). Animals with many jointed limbs and a hard outer skeleton.

Sub-Phylum: Chelicerata (chelicerates). Common characteristics include pincer-like mouthparts (**chelicerae**, sing. **chelicera**).

Classes: 2 minor ones – **Merostomata** (king crabs), **Pycnogonida** (sea spiders). 1 more important:

Arachnida (arachnids). Animals with 8 legs. E.g. spiders, mites, scorpions.

Sub-Phylum: Crustacea (crustaceans). 1 Class with same name:

Class: Crustacea (crustaceans). Mostly aquatic animals, with **gills*** on their legs and 2 pairs of **antennae***. E.g. crabs, woodlice, lobsters.

Sub-Phylum: Uniramia. 1 pair of **antennae***, mostly land-living.

Classes: 3 minor ones – **Onychophora** (velvet worms), **Symphyla** (tiny, centipede-like), **Pauropoda** (tiny, millipede-like). 3 more important:

Chilopoda. Centipedes. Each body segment has 1 pair of legs. **Carnivorous***.

Diplopoda. Millipedes. Each body segment has 2 pairs of legs. **Herbivorous***.

Insecta (insects) or **Hexapoda.** Animals with 6 legs and usually 2 pairs of wings. E.g. beetles, moths, ants.

---

* Antennae, 46; Anus, 67 (**Large intestine**); Carnivores, 6; Chaetae, 40 (**Parapodia**); Cilia, 40; Gills, 45; Herbivores, 6; Parasites, 114; Segmentation, 36; Tentacles, 47.

PHYLUM: Echinodermata (echinoderms). Marine animals, all with a limey skeleton just below the skin. Usually have a 5-rayed arrangement and a spiny skin.

Classes: Asteroidea (starfish), **Ophiuroidea** (brittle stars), **Echinoidea** (sea urchins), **Holothuroidea** (sea cucumbers), **Crinoidea** (sea lilies).

PHYLUM: Chordata (chordates). At some time in their life, all have a **notochord** – a stiff "rod" of cells running lengthwise between the spinal cord and the gut.

Sub-Phyla: 2 minor ones – **Urochordata** (or **Tunicata**) (sea squirts), **Cephalochordata** (or **Acrania**) (lancets). 1 more important:

Craniata (craniates) or **Vertebrata (vertebrates)**. Notochord (see **Chordata**) replaced by spine (see note 7). Have well-developed brain.

Classes: 2 minor ones, both Classes of jawless fish – **Myxini** (hagfish), **Cephalaspidomorphi** (lampreys). 6 more important:

Elasmobranchiomorphi (elasmobranchs) or **Chondrichthyes**. Fishes with a skeleton made of **cartilage***. Have fins and breathe with **gills***. E.g. sharks, rays.

Osteichthyes. Fishes with a skeleton made of bone. Have fins and scales, and breathe with **gills***. E.g. sturgeon, cod, herring.

Amphibia (amphibians) or **Batrachia (batrachians)**. Animals which can live on land but must be near water. Most have lungs and lay eggs in water. E.g. frogs, newts, toads.

Reptilia (reptiles). Animals with dry, scaly skin. Live on land, and lay shelled eggs on land. E.g. snakes, lizards, crocodiles, turtles.

Aves. Birds. All have feathers and lay shelled eggs. E.g. penguins, robins, ostriches, hawks.

Mammalia (mammals). All females produce milk. Nearly all have hair or fur. Has 2 Sub-classes:

Sub-classes: Prototheria. Lay shelled eggs. Has just 1 Order – **Monotremata (monotremes)** – spiny anteaters and duck-billed platypuses.

Theria. Do not lay eggs. Has 2 special **Infraclasses** before the Orders:

Infraclasses: Metatheria, Marsupalia (marsupials) or **Didelphia**. Young develop in the **uterus*** for only a short time, completing their development attached to the openings of the mother's milk glands and normally held within a pouch of skin called a **marsupium**. E.g. kangaroos, opossums.

Eutheria or **Placentalia (placental mammals)**. Young develop in the **uterus*** until birth, attached by a highly-developed **placenta***. E.g. cows, mice, whales, humans.

Notes

1. In some charts, the Class **Sarcodina** of the Phylum **Protozoa** has 2 Sub-classes – **Rhizopoda** and **Actinopoda**. In others, these two are omitted as Sub-classes, and their members grouped together under the Class Sarcodina. In this case, the Class has the alternative name of Rhizopoda.

2. Some charts show another Sub-kingdom, called **Mesozoa**, between the **Parazoa** and the **Metazoa**. It has only one Phylum, also called Mesozoa, and is made up of obscure **parasites***. Its rank as a Sub-kingdom, or even as a Phylum, is in much doubt. Many people regard its members as peculiar forms of flatworms (Phylum **Platyhelminthes**).

3. The Classes **Monogenoidea** and **Digenoidea** of the Phylum **Platyhelminthes** are grouped together in some charts as the Class **Trematoda (trematodes)**.

4. The Class **Onychophora** of the Phylum **Arthropoda** is made a separate Phylum in some charts, since its members (velvet worms) show characteristics of both the Arthropoda and the **Annelida**.

5. In some charts, the Phylum **Arthropoda** does not have any Sub-phyla, merely the same 10 Classes. In others still, there are no Sub-phyla and only 7 Classes. The Classes **Pauropoda, Symphyla, Chilopoda** and **Diplopoda** are grouped together in one Class called **Myriapoda** ("many feet"). In most cases, however, the term **myriapods** is only an informal one.

6. The Sub-phyla **Urochordata** and **Cephalochordata** of the Phylum **Chordata** are sometimes known collectively as the **Protochordata (protochordates)**, though this term is purely an informal one. It is also sometimes extended to include the minor Phylum **Hemichordata** (acorn worms), since

the members of this show certain features characteristic of the Chordata (the name implies a "half-way" stage).

7. The term **craniate** means "with a skull" – this is true of all members of the Sub-phylum **Craniata**. The alternative Sub-phylum name of **vertebrates** means "animals with backbones". This is not strictly true, since the most primitive Class – **Myxini** (hagfish) – do not have backbones.

8. The **invertebrates** are all the animals without backbones, i.e. everything on the chart up to the Sub-phylum **Craniata** – the **vertebrates**. (But see above, note 7.)

9. The two Classes **Myxini** (hagfish) and **Cephalaspidomorphi** (lampreys), the only jawless members of the Sub-phylum **Craniata**, are sometimes known collectively as the **Agnatha** and the remaining, jawed, Classes are called the **Gnathostomata**. However, these terms are only informal ones.

10. The Classes **Myxini** (hagfish), **Cephalaspidomorphi** (lampreys), **Elasmobranchiomorphi (cartilaginous fish)** and **Osteichthyes (bony fish)** of the Sub-phylum **Craniata** are sometimes known collectively as **Pisces** (fish), though this term is only an informal one.

11. The Classes of the Sub-phylum **Craniata** are sometimes put into two informal groups – the **Amniota** (amniotes – **Reptilia, Aves, Mammalia**) and **Anamniota** (all the other Classes). The amniotes are those whose **embryos*** (developing young) have an **amnion, chorion** and **allantois** (see pages 48 and 91).

* **Cartilage**, 53; **Embryo**, 93; **Gills**, 45; **Parasites**, 114; **Placenta**, 91; **Uterus**, 89.

Informal group terms

Listed here are the main terms used to group living things together according to their general life styles (i.e. their ecological similarities – see also page 9). These are informal terms, as opposed to the formal terms of the classification charts (pages 110-113), which are based on structural similarities.

Plants

• **Xerophytes**. Plants which can survive long periods of time without water, e.g. cacti.

• **Hydrophytes**. Plants which grow in water or very wet soil, e.g. reeds.

• **Mesophytes**. Plants which grow under average conditions of moisture.

• **Halophytes**. Plants which can withstand very salty conditions, e.g. sea pinks.

• **Lithophytes**. Plants which grow on rock, e.g some mosses.

• **Epiphytes**. Plants which grow on other plants, but only to use them for support, not to feed off them, e.g. some mosses.

• **Saprophytes**. Plants which live on decaying plants or animals, feed off them, but are not the agents of their decay, e.g. some fungi.

Animals

• **Predators**. Animals which kill and eat other animals (their **prey**), e.g. lions. Bird predators, e.g. hawks, are called **raptors**.

• **Detritus feeders**. Animals which feed on debris from decayed plant or animal matter, e.g. worms.

• **Scavengers**. Large **detritus feeders**, e.g. hyenas, which feed only on dead flesh (animal matter).

• **Territorial**. Holding and defending a **territory** (an area of land or water) either singly or in groups, e.g. many fish, birds and mammals. This is usually linked with attracting a mate and breeding.

• **Abyssal**. Living at great depths in a lake or the sea, e.g. oarfish and gulper eels.

• **Demersal**. Living at the bottom of a lake or the sea, e.g. angler fish and prawns.

• **Sedentary**. In the case of birds, this term describes those which do not **migrate***; with other animals, it is synonymous with **sessile**.

• **Nocturnal**. Active at night and sleeping during the day, e.g. owls and bats.

Plants and animals

• **Insectivores**. Specialized organisms which eat only insects, e.g. pitcher plants (which trap and digest insects) and hedgehogs.

• **Parasites**. Plants or animals which live in or on other living plants or animals (the **hosts**), and feed off them, e.g. mistletoe and fleas. Not all are harmful to the host.

• **Symbionts** or **symbiotes**. A pair of living things which associate closely with each other and derive mutual benefit from such close existence (**symbiosis**). **Lichens**, normally found on bare rock, are an example. Each is in fact two plants (a fungus and an alga). The alga produces food (by **photosynthesis***) for the fungus (which otherwise could not live on bare rock). The fungus uses its fine threads to hold the moisture the alga needs.

• **Commensals**. A pair of living things which associate closely with each other, may derive some benefit from such close existence (**commensalism**), e.g. shared food, but are not strictly **symbionts**. One type of worm, for instance, is very often found in the same shell as a hermit crab. One of the commonest examples of commensalism is the existence of house mice wherever there are humans.

• **Social** or **colonial**. Living together in groups. The two terms are synonymous in the case of plants, and refer to those which grow in clusters. In the case of animals, there is a difference of numbers between the terms. Lions, for example, are social, but their groups (**prides**) are not large enough to be called colonies. With true colonial animals, there is also a great difference in the level of interdependence between colony members. In a gannet colony, for example, this is relatively low (they only live close together because there is safety in numbers). In an ant colony, by contrast, different groups (**castes**) have very different jobs, e.g. gathering food or guarding the colony, so each member relies heavily on others. The highest level of colonial interdependence is shown by the tiny, physically inseparable, single-celled organisms which form one living mass, e.g. a sponge.

• **Sessile**. In the case of animals, this term refers to those which are not free to move around, i.e. they are permanently fixed to the ground or other solid object, e.g. sea anemones. With plants, it describes those without stalks, e.g. algae.

• **Pelagic**. Living in the main body of a lake or the sea, as opposed to at the bottom or at great depths. Pelagic creatures range from tiny **plankton** through medium-sized fishes and sharks to very large whales. The medium-sized and large ones are all animals, and are called **nekton**.

• **Plankton**. Microscopic aquatic animals and plants, vast numbers of which drift in lakes and seas, normally near the surface (plant plankton is **phytoplankton**, and animal plankton is **zooplankton**). Plankton is the food of many fishes and whales and is thus vital to the ecological balance (**food chains***) of the sea.

• **Littoral**. Living at the bottom of a lake or the sea near the shore, e.g. crabs and seaweed.

• **Benthos**. All **abyssal**, **demersal** and **littoral** plants and animals, i.e. all those which live in, on or near the bottom of lakes or seas.

Index

The page numbers listed in the index are of three different types. Those printed in bold type (e.g. **79**) indicate in each case where the main definition of a word (or words) can be found. Those in lighter type (e.g. 82) refer to supplementary entries (if there is no bold page number, the entries are of equal importance). Page numbers printed in italics (e.g. *34*) indicate pages where a word (or words) can be found as a small print label to a picture.

If a page number is followed by a word in brackets, it means that the indexed word can be found inside the text of the definition indicated. If it is followed by (**I**), the indexed word can be found in the introductory text on the page given.

Bracketed singulars and plurals are given where relevant after indexed words. In a small number of cases, the singular and plural of a word have separate entries (where they appear as separate entries in the book). In these cases, the word "see" is used to link the entries. The main use of the word "see", however, is to indicate synonyms. Oblique strokes (/) also have this function, used when words fall together alphabetically.

Abdomen, *36* (**Segmentation**), 66 (**Alimentary canal**)
Abomasum, 43 (**Rumen**)
Abscisic acid, 21 (**Abscission layer**)
Abscission layer, 21
Abyssal, 114
Accessory foods, 100 (**I**)
Accommodation, 84 (**Lens**)
Acellular, 10 (**I**)
Achene, 34
Aclitellata, 112 (**Annelida**)
Acrania, see **Cephalochordata**
ACTH, 106
Actin, 54 (**Striated muscle**)
Actinomorphy, 36 (**Radial symmetry**)
Actinopoda, 113 (Note 1)
Actinozoa, see **Anthozoa**
Active transport, 99
Adaptation(s),
  Evolutionary, see
    Adaptive radiation
  Protective, 9 (**Adaptive radiation**)
Adaptive radiation, 9
Adenine, 96
Adenohypophysis, see
  Anterior lobe
Adenoids, see **Pharyngeal tonsil**
Adenosine, 105 (**ADP**)
Adenosine diphosphate,
  see **ADP**
Adenosine triphosphate,
  see **ATP**
ADH, 106
Adipose tissue,
  82 (**Subcutaneous layer**)
ADP, 105
Adrenal glands, 69, *107*
Adrenalin/Adrenin, 106
Adrenocorticotropic hormone/
  Adrenocorticotropin,
  see **ACTH**
Adventitious roots, 17
Aerial parts (plants), 16
Aerial roots, 17
Aerobic respiration, 104
Aestivation, 9 (**Dormancy**)
Afferent, 78
Afferent arteriole,
  73 (**Glomerulus**)
Afferent neurons, see
  Sensory neurons
Afferent system, 78-79
  Somatic, 79
  Visceral, 79
Agglutinins, 59 (**Antibodies**)
Agnatha, 113 (Note 9)

Agonist, 54 (**Antagonistic pairs**)
Air bladder, see **Swim bladder**
Albumen, *48*
Aldosterone, 106
Algae (sing. **alga**), 110
Alimentary canal/tract, 66
Allantois, *48*
Alleles/Allelomorphs, 97 (**Genes**)
Alternation of generations, 93
Alula, see **Bastard wing**
Alveoli (sing. **alveolus**), 71
Amino acids, 100 (**Proteins**), 101, 108, 109
Amnion, *48, 91*
Amniota/Amniotes 113 (Note 11)
Amniotic fluid, *48* (**Amnion**), *91*
Amniotic sac, *48* (**Amnion**), *91*
Amoeba, *40*
Amphibia/Amphibians,
  45 (**External gills**), 46 (**Lateral lines, Tympanal organs**),
  49 (**Metamorphosis**),
  113 (**Chordata**)
Amphineura, 112 (**Mollusca**)
Ampulla, 87 (**Semicircular ducts**)
Ampulla of Vater, *69*
Amylases, 108 (**I**)
Anabolism, 102
Anadromous, 8
Anaerobic respiration, 104
Anal canal, *66, 67* (**Large intestine**)
Anal fin, 41 (**Median fins**)
Anal sphincter, 67 (**Large intestine**)
Anamniota, 113 (Note 11)
Anaphase,
  (meiosis), **95**
  (mitosis), 13
Androecium, *29*
Androgens, 88 (**Testes**), 106, 107 (**LH**)
Aneurin, see **Thiamine**
Angiospermae/Angiosperms,
  111 (Charts 1 and 2)
Animal Kingdom, 112-113
Animal starch, see **Glycogen**
Annelida/Annelids, 112
Annual rings, 18, *19*
Annuals, 8
Annulata, see **Annelida**
Anopla, 112 (**Nemertea**)
Antagonist, 54 (**Antagonistic pairs**)
Antagonistic hormones, 106
Antagonistic pairs (muscles), 54
Antennae (sing. **antenna**), 46
Anterior cavity (eyes),
  84 (**Aqueous humour**)

Anterior lobe (pituitary gland), 69
Anther, 28 (**Stamens**), *29*
Antheridium, *93*
Anthocerotae, 111 (Chart 1)
Anthophyta, 111 (Chart 2)
Anthozoa, 112 (**Coelenterata**)
Antibodies, 59
Anti-diuretic hormone, see **ADH**
Antigen(s), 59
  Rhesus, 59 (**Rhesus factor**)
Antigen-antibody complex,
  59 (**Antibodies**)
Anti-toxins, 59 (**Antibodies**)
Anus, *66, 67* (**Large intestine**)
Anvil (ears), see **Incus**
Aorta, *61, 62, 63*
Aortic valve, 63 (**Semilunar valves**)
Apatite, 56 (**Enamel**)
Apex (leaves), *20*
Apical meristem, 16 (**Meristem**)
Appendage, 36
Appendix, *66, 67*
Aqueous humour, *84*
Arachnida/Arachnids,
  112 (**Arthropoda**)
Arachnoid, *75* (**Meninges**)
Archegonium, *93*
Arterial system, 60 (**Arteries**)
Arteriole(s), 60 (**Arteries**)
  Afferent, 73 (**Glomerulus**)
  Efferent, 73 (**Glomerulus**)
Artery(ies), 60, 63
  Brachial, *61*
  Brachiocephalic, *62*
  Celiac, *61*
  Common carotid, *62*
  Common iliac, *61*
  Femoral, *61*
  Gastric, *61*
  Gonadal, *61*
  Hepatic, *61*
  Inferior mesenteric, *61*
  Pulmonary, *62, 63* (**Pulmonary trunk**)
  Renal, *61, 72* (**Kidneys**)
  Splenic, *61*
  Subclavian, *61, 62*
  Superior mesenteric, *61*
Arthropoda/Arthropods,
  37 (**Haemocoel**), *42, 43*,
  44 (**Spiracle, Tracheae**),
  45 (**Malpighian tubules**),
  46 (**Palps, Telson**),
  47 (**Compound eyes**),
  49 (**Larva**), 112, 113 (Notes 4 and 5)
Articular cartilage,
  53 (**Cartilage**)

Articular processes,
 Inferior, *50*
 Superior, *50*
Articulations, see Joints
Artificial propagation, 35
Aschelminthes, 112
Ascorbic acid, see Vitamin C
Asexual reproduction, 92
Aspidogastrea/Aspidobothrea/
 Aspidocotylea,
 112 (Platyhelminthes)
Association area(s), 74 (Brain), 75
 Auditory, 75
 Visual, 75
Association neurons, 77
Asteroidea, 113 (Echinodermata)
Astral rays/Asters, *13*
Atlas, 50 (Vertebrae), *51*
ATP, 99 (Active transport),
 104 (Aerobic respiration), 105
Atria (sing. atrium), 62
Atrioventricular valves, 63
Auditory association area, 75
Auditory ossicles, see
 Ear ossicles
Auditory tube, see
 Eustachian tube
Auricle(s),
 (ears), see Pinnae
 (heart), see Atria
Autografting, 35 (Grafting)
Autonomic actions,
 81 (Involuntary actions)
Autonomic ganglia, *81*
Autonomic nervous system,
 75 (Hypothalamus), 80
Autosomes,
 97 (Sex chromosomes)
Autotrophic, 6 (Food web)
Auxins, 23 (Growth hormones)
Aves, 113 (Chordata, Note 11)
AV valves, see
 Atrioventricular valves
Axil, 16 (Axillary bud)
Axillary bud, 16
Axis, 50 (Vertebrae), *51*
Axon, 76

Baby teeth, see Deciduous teeth
Bacillariophyta, 110
Backbone, see Vertebral column
Bacteria (sing. bacterium), see
 Schizophyta
 Denitrifying, 7
 Nitrate, 7
 Nitrifying, 7
 Nitrogen-fixing, 7 (Nitrogen
 fixation)
Baleen, see Whalebone
Ball-and-socket joints, 52
Barbels, *46*
Barbs, 39 (Feathers)
Barbules, 39 (Feathers)
Bark, 19 (Phellem)
Basal metabolic rate,
 102 (Metabolic rate)
Basal rosette, 22
Bastard wing, *41*
Batrachia/Batrachians, see
 Amphibia
Bell flower, 31
Benthos, 114
Berry, 34
Biceps, *54*
Bicuspids, see Premolars
Bicuspid valve,
 63 (Atrioventricular valves)

Biennials, 8
Bilateral symmetry, 36
Bile, 68 (Liver), 107 (CCK), 108
Bile acids, 108 (Bile)
Bile salts, 108 (Bile)
Binary fission, 12 (Cell division)
Biomes, 4
Biosphere, 4
Biotic factors, 4 (I)
Biotin, 109 (Vitamin B complex)
Bipinnate, 22
Bivalents, 94 (Prophase)
Bivalvia/Bivalves, see
 Lamellibranchiata
Bladder, 72, *73, 88*
 Air, see Swim bladder
 Gall, 69, 107 (CCK)
 Swim, 41
 Urinary, see Bladder
Blastocyst, 93 (Embryo)
Blending, see
 Incomplete dominance
Blind spot, 85
Blood, 58-59
Blood cells,
 Red, 58
 White, 58
Blood groups, 59,
 97 (Codominance)
Blood sinuses, 88 (Penis)
Blood vessels, 60 (I)
BMR, see Basal metabolic rate
Body (vertebrae), see Centrum
Bole, *19*
Bolus, 66 (Oesophagus)
Bone(s), 50-51
 Coracoid, *41*
 Cranial, 50 (Cranium)
 Facial, 50 (Cranium)
Bone (tissue), 52-53
 Compact, *52, 53* (Bone)
 Spongy, *52, 53* (Bone)
Bone marrow, 53
Bony fish, 113 (Note 10)
Bony labyrinth, 86 (Inner ear)
Book lungs, see Lung books
Bowman's capsule, *72, 73*
Brachial arteries, *61*
Brachial veins, *61*
Brachiocephalic artery, *62*
Brachiocephalic veins, *62*
Bract, 21
Brain, 74, *75,* 78, 80, 81
Brain stem, 75
Branchiae (sing. branchia),
 see Gills
Branchial, 45
Breastbone, see Sternum
Breathing, 71
Bronchi (sing. bronchus), *70,* 71
 Primary, *70,* 71 (Bronchi)
 Secondary, *70,* 71 (Bronchi)
 Tertiary, *70,* 71 (Bronchi)
Bronchial, 71
Bronchioles, *70,* 71
 Terminal, 71 (Bronchioles)
Bryophyta, 110
Buccal cavity, see Oral cavity
Bud(s),
 Axillary/Lateral, 16
 (plants), 16
 Primary, 33 (Plumule)
 Secondary, see Axillary bud
 Terminal, 16
Budding,
 (artificial propagation), 35
 (asexual reproduction), see
 Gemmation

Bulb,
 (hairs), *83*
 (plants), 34
Bulbourethral glands, see
 Cowper's glands

Caecum, 43, *66,* 67 (Large
 intestine)
Calcarea, 112 (Porifera)
Calciferol, see Vitamin D
Calcitonin, see TCT
Calories, 103
Calyx, 28 (Sepals)
Cambium, *14, 15,* 18 (Vascular
 cylinder), *19*
 Cork, see Phellogen
Canines (teeth), 57
Capillaries, 61, 64 (Tissue fluid)
 Lymph, 65 (Lymph vessels)
Capillary action, 24
Carapace, 38
Carbohydrates, 100, 108, 109
Carbon cycle, 7
Carboxypeptidase,
 108 (Pancreatic juice)
Cardiac, 63
Cardiac cycle, 62-63
Cardiac muscle, 55
Cardiac muscle (tissue), 55
Cardiac sphincter, *66, 67*
Cardiovascular system, 62 (I)
Carnassial teeth, 42
Carnivores, 6 (Secondary
 consumers)
Carotene, 27 (Pigments), *83,*
 109 (Vitamin A)
Carpals, *51, 52*
Carpel, *28,* 29
Carpus, 51 (Carpals)
Caryopsis, see Grain
Casein, 108 (Gastric juice)
Castes, 114 (Social)
Catabolism, 102
Catadromous, 8 (Anadromous)
Catalysts, 103 (Enzymes)
Catalytic proteins,
 100 (Proteins), 103 (Enzymes)
Caterpillar, *49* (Larva)
Caudal, 41
Caudal fin, 41 (Median fins)
Caudate, 41 (Caudal)
CCK, 106
Celiac artery, *61*
Cell(s), 10-13, 94-95
 Blood, 58
 Companion, 14 (Phloem)
 Daughter, 12 (Cell division)
 Egg, 30 (Ovules), 93 (Gametes),
 95 (Gamete production,
 female)
 Flame, 45 (Nephridia)
 Germ, see Gametes
 Guard, 21
 Interstitial, *88,* 107 (Androgens)
 Olfactory, 79 (Nose)
 Palisade, 20 (Palisade layer)
 Parent, 12 (Cell division)
 Passage, 15 (Endodermis)
 Schwann, 76 (Nerve fibres)
 Spongy, 20 (Spongy layer)
 Target, 106 (Hormones)
 Thread, see Cnidoblasts

116

Cell body, 76, *77*
Cell division, 12-13, 94-95
Cell membrane, 10, *11,* 99
Cell sap, 10 (Vacuoles),
    25 (Turgor)
Cellular respiration, see
    Internal respiration
Cellulase, 101 (Roughage)
Cellulose, *10* (Cell wall),
    42 (Rumen), 101 (Roughage)
Cell wall, *10*
Cement/Cementum (teeth), 56
Central incisors, *57*
Central nervous system
    (humans), 74-75
Centrioles, **12,** 13, 94, 95
Centromeres, 13, 94
Centrosome, 12 (Centrioles)
Centrum, 50 (Vertebrae), *51*
Cephalaspidomorphi,
    113 (Chordata, Notes 9 and 10)
Cephalic, 75
Cephalic veins, *61*
Cephalochordata,
    113 (Chordata, Note 6)
Cephalopoda/Cephalopods,
    44 (Siphon), 112 (Mollusca)
Cephalothorax, *46*
Cerebellum, 74
Cerebral, 75
Cerebral cortex, 74 (Cerebrum)
Cerebral hemispheres,
    74 (Cerebrum)
Cerebrospinal fluid, *75*
Cerebrum, 74
Cerumen, 86 (Outer ear)
Ceruminous glands, 86 (Outer
    ear)
Cervical canal, *89*
Cervical vertebrae, *51*
Cervix,
    (teeth), see **Neck**
    (uterus), 89
Cestoda, see **Cestoidea**
Cestoidaria,
    112 (Platyhelminthes)
Cestoidea,
    112 (Platyhelminthes)
Chaetae (sing. chaeta),
    40 (Parapodia)
Chalaza (sing. chalaza),
    (animal eggs), *48*
    (flowering plants), 29 (Ovaries)
Characteristics of life, 8 (I)
Chelae (sing. chela), *46*
Chelicerae (sing. chelicera),
    112 (Chelicerata)
Chelicerata/Chelicerates,
    112 (Arthropoda)
Chiasmata (sing. chiasma),
    94 (Crossing over)
Chilopoda, 112 (Arthropoda),
    113 (Note 5)
Chitin, 38 (Cuticle)
Chlorophyll, 27 (Chloroplasts,
    Pigments)
Chlorophyta, 110
Chloroplasts, 12 (Plastids),
    21 (Guard cells), 27
Cholecystokinin, see **CCK**
Chondrichthyes, see
    Elasmobranchiomorphi
Chondriosomes, see
    Mitochondria
Chordata/Chordates, 113
Chorion, *91*
Chorionic villi, *91*
Choroid/Choroid coat, *84*

Chromatids, 13, 94, 95
Chromatin, 10 (Nucleus),
    13 (Interphase),
    94 (Prophase)
Chromosomes, 10 (Nucleus),
    12 (Mitosis), 13, 94, 95, **96,** 97, 98
    Daughter, 13 (Anaphase)
    Homologous, 12 (Mitosis), 94,
        95, 96 (Chromosomes),
        98 (Law of segregation)
    Sex, 97, 98 (Sex linkage)
    X, 97 (Sex chromosomes),
        98 (Sex linkage)
    Y, 97 (Sex chromosomes),
        98 (Sex linkage)
Chrysalis, *49* (Pupa)
Chrysophyta, 110
Chyme, 67 (Stomach)
Chymotrypsin,
    108 (Pancreatic juice)
Chymotrypsinogen,
    108 (Note 2)
Cilia (sing. cilium), 40
Ciliary body, *84*
Ciliophora/Ciliata, 112 (Protozoa)
Circulatory system (humans),
    60-61
Cirri (sing. cirrus),
    42 (Filter-feeding)
Classes, 110 (I)
Classical taxonomy, 110 (I)
Classification, 110 (I)
Clavicle, *51*
Cleavage, 93 (Embryo)
Cleavage furrow,
    13 (Cytokinesis)
Cleidoic eggs, 48 (Eggs)
Climatic factors, 4 (I)
Climax community,
    5 (Ecological succession)
Clitellata, 112 (Annelida)
Clitoris, 89 (Vulva)
Cloaca, *43*
Cloacal aperture/vent, *43*
Clot, 59 (Clotting)
Clotting, 59
Clubmosses, see **Lycopodiales**
Cnidaria, see **Coelenterata**
Cnidoblasts, 42
CNS, see
    Central nervous system
Coagulation, see **Clotting**
Cobalamin, see **Cyanocobalamin**
Coccygeal vertebrae,
    51 (Coccyx)
Coccyx, *51*
Cochlea, 86
Cochlear duct, *86, 87*
Cocoon, *49* (Pupa)
Codominance, 97
Coelenterata/Coelenterates,
    42 (Cnidoblasts),
    47 (Tentacles), 112
Coelom, 37
Co-enzymes, 103 (Enzymes),
    109 (Vitamin B complex,
    Vitamin C)
Coitus, see **Copulation**
Coleoptile, 33
Collagen, 52 (Connective
    tissue), 109 (Vitamin C)
Collarbone, see **Clavicle**
Collecting duct/tubule, 73
Collenchyma, 15 (Cortex)
Colon, *66, 67* (Large intestine)
Colonial, 114
Commensalism,
    114 (Commensals)

Commensals, 114
Common bile duct, *68, 69* (Gall
    bladder)
Common carotid arteries, *62*
Common hepatic duct,
    68 (Liver)
Common iliac arteries, *61*
Common iliac veins, *61*
Community, 5
    Climax, 5 (Ecological
        succession)
    Pioneer, *5*
    Successional, *5*
Compact bone, *52, 53* (Bone)
Companion cells, 14 (Phloem)
Compensation points, 26
Complete metamorphosis, 49
Composite flower,
    see **Flowerhead**
Compound eyes, 47
Compound leaves, 20 (I), 22
Cones,
    (conifers), 111 (Coniferales)
    (eyes), 85 (Retina)
Coniferales/Coniferophyta,
    111 (Charts 1 and 2)
Coniferous forest (biome), 4
Conifers, see **Coniferales**
Conjunctiva, *84*
Connecting neurons,
    see **Association neurons**
Connective tissue, 52
Consumers,
    Primary/First order, 6
    Secondary/Second order, 6
    Tertiary/Third order, 6
Contour feathers, 39 (Feathers)
Contractile vacuoles, *40, 45*
Convoluted tubule(s),
    Distal, 73 (Uriniferous tubules)
    Proximal, 73 (Uriniferous
        tubules)
Copulation, 91
Coracoid bones, *41*
Cork, see **Phellem**
Cork cambium, see **Phellogen**
Corm, 35
Cornea, *84*
Cornified layer, see
    Stratum corneum
Corolla, 28 (Petals)
Corpus callosum, 74 (Cerebrum)
Corpuscles,
    Malpighian, see
        Renal corpuscles
    Meissner's, 82
    Pacinian, 83
    Red, see **Red blood cells**
    Renal, 72, *73*
    White, see **White blood cells**
Corpus luteum, 90 (Menstrual
    cycle), 107 (LH, Lactogenic
    hormone, Oestrogen)
Cortex,
    (adrenal glands), 69
    Cerebral, 74 (Cerebrum)
    (kidneys), *72*
    (plants), 15
    Renal, see **Cortex** (kidneys)
    Secondary, 19 (Phelloderm)
Corti,
    Organ of, *86, 87* (Cochlear duct)
Cortisol, see **Hydrocortisone**
Cortisone, 106
Costal cartilage, 50 (Rib cage)
Cotyledon, 33
Coverts, *39*
Cowper's glands, *88*

Cranial bones, 50 (Cranium)
Cranial nerves, 74 (Brain)
Cranial reflexes, 81 (Reflex actions)
Craniata, 113 (Chordata, Notes 7-11)
Craniate, 113 (Note 7)
Craniates, see Craniata
Cranium, 50, 51
Crinoidea, 113 (Echinodermata)
Cristae (sing. crista), 12 (Mitochondria)
Critical length, 23 (Photoperiodism)
Crop (birds, etc.), 43
Crossing over (chromosomes), 94
Cross pollination, 31
Crown (teeth), 56
Crustacea/Crustaceans, 45 (Internal gills), 46 (Antennae), 112 (Arthropoda)
Crypts of Lieberkühn, see Intestinal glands
Ctenophora, 112
Cud, 43 (Rumen)
Cupulae (sing. cupula), 87 (Semicircular ducts)
Curds, 108 (Gastric juice)
Cusp, 57 (Canines, Premolars, Molars)
Cuspids, see Canines
Cuticle, (animals), 38 (plants), 15
Cutin, 15 (Cuticle)
Cutis, see Skin
Cutting, 35
Cyanocobalamin, 109 (Vitamin B complex)
Cyanophyta, 110
Cycadales/Cycadophyta, 111 (Charts 1 and 2)
Cystic duct, 68, 69 (Gall bladder)
Cytokinesis, 13, 95 (Telophase)
Cytokinins, 23 (Growth hormones)
Cytoplasm, 10
Cytosine, 96

Darwinism, 9 (Adaptive radiation)
Daughter cells, 12 (Cell division)
Daughter chromosomes, 13 (Anaphase)
Daughter nuclei, 13 (Telophase), 94 (Meiosis)
Day-neutral plants, 23 (Photoperiodism)
Decay, 7
Deciduous, 8
Deciduous dentition, 56 (I)
Deciduous forest (biome), 4
Deciduous teeth, 56 (I)
Decomposers, 7
Decomposition reactions, 102 (Catabolism)
Decussate, 22
Defaecation, 67 (Large intestine)
Dehiscent, 32
Demersal, 114
Demospongiae, 112 (Porifera)
Dendrites, 76
Dendron, 76 (Dendrites)
Denitrifying bacteria, 7
Dens, see Dentes
Dentes (sing. dens), (teeth), 56 (I) (vertebrae), 50, 51

Denticles, 38
Dentine, 56
Dentition, 56 (I)
   Deciduous, 56 (I)
   Permanent, 56 (I)
Deoxygenated, 62 (Atria)
Deoxyribonucleic acid, see DNA
Deoxyribose, 96
Dermal papillae (sing. papilla), 82
Dermis, 82, 83
Desert (biome), 4
Detritus feeders, 114
Dextrin, 108 (Saliva)
Dextrose, see Glucose
Diaphragm, 70, 71
Diaphysis, 52
Diastases, see Amylases
Diastema (pl. diastemata), 42
Diastole phase, 63 (Cardiac cycle)
Diatoms, see Bacillariophyta
Dicotyledonae/Dicotyledons, 33 (Cotyledon), 111 (Chart 1)
Dictyosome, see Golgi complex
Didelphia, see Metatheria
Diencephalon, 75
Differentiation, 93 (Embryo)
Diffusion, 99
Digenoidea/Digenea, 112 (Platyhelminthes), 113 (Note 3)
Digestion, 66 (I)
Digestive enzymes, 103 (Enzymes), 108
Digestive glands, 68, 108
Digestive juices, 68 (Digestive glands), 108
Digestive system (humans), 66-67
Digitigrade, 40
Digits, 51
Dioecious, 28 (I)
Dipeptides, 109
Diploid number, 12 (Mitosis), 96 (Chromosomes)
Diplopoda, 112 (Arthropoda), 113 (Note 5)
Disaccharides, 109
Disc(s), Invertebral, 50 (Vertebrae), 51
Disc florets, 31
Dispersal/Dissemination, 32
Distal, 73
Distal convoluted tubule, 73 (Uriniferous tubules)
Divisions, 110 (I)
DNA, 10 (Nucleus), 96 (Nucleic acids)
Dog teeth, see Canines
Dominant, 97 (Genes), 98
Dormancy, 9
Dorsal, 41
Dorsal fin, 41 (Median fins)
Dorsal root, 74 (Spinal cord), 75
Double helix, 96 (Nucleic acids)
Down feathers, 39
Drupe, 34
Duct(s), 68 (Exocrine glands)
   Cochlear, 86, 87
   Collecting, 73
   Common bile, 68, 69 (Gall bladder)
   Common hepatic, 68 (Liver)
   Cystic, 68, 69 (Gall bladder)
   Hepatic, 68
   Lachrymal, 85 (Lachrymal glands)
   Nasolachrymal, 85 (Lachrymal glands)

Pancreatic, 68 (Pancreas)
Right lymphatic, 64, 65 (Lymph vessels)
Semicircular, 86, 87
Sperm, 88
Stensen's, 68
Sweat, 83 (Sweat glands)
Thoracic, 64, 65 (Lymph vessels)
Wharton's, 68
Ductless glands, see Endocrine glands
Duct of Wirsung, see Pancreatic duct
Duodenum, 66, 67 (Small intestine), 68
Dura mater, 75 (Meninges)

Ear(s), 86-87
   External, see Outer ear
   Inner/Internal, 86, 87
   Middle, 86
   Outer, 86
Ear canal, 86 (Outer ear)
Eardrum, 86
Early wood, see Spring wood
Ear ossicles, 86 (Middle ear)
Ecdysis, 49 (Larva)
Echinodera, see Kinorhyncha
Echinodermata/Echinoderms, 37 (Coelom), 113
Echinoidea, 113 (Echinodermata)
Ecological niche, 5
Ecological succession, 5
Ecology, 4 (I)
Ecosystem, 5, 6
Ectoplasm, 40
Edaphic factors, 4 (I)
Effectors, 77 (Motor neurons), 80 (I)
Efferent, 80
Efferent arteriole, 73 (Glomerulus)
Efferent neurons, see Motor neurons
Efferent system, 80-81
   Somatic, 80
   Visceral, see Autonomic nervous system
Egg(s), 48
   Cleidoic, 48 (Eggs)
Egg cell, 30 (Ovules), 93 (Gametes), 95 (Gamete production, female)
Ejaculation, 88 (Sperm duct), 91 (Copulation)
Elasmobranchiomorphi/ Elasmobranchs, 38 (Denticles), 113 (Chordata, Note 10)
Elastin, 52 (Connective tissue)
Elytra (sing. elytron), 38
Embryo, 32 (I), 48, 91 (Fertilization), 93
Embryophyta/Embryophytes, 110, 111 (Chart 2)
Embryo sac, 30 (Ovules), 95 (Gamete production, female)
Emulsification, 108 (Bile)
Enamel (teeth), 56
Endocardium, 62 (I)
Endocarp, 34 (I)
Endocrine glands, 69
Endodermis, 15
Endolymph, 86 (Inner ear)
Endometrium, 89 (Uterus), 90 (Menstrual cycle)

118

Endoneurium, *78*
Endoplasm, *40*
Endoplasmic reticulum, 11
Endopteryogotes, 49 (Complete metamorphosis)
Endoskeleton, 38 (I)
Endosperm, 30 (Fertilization), 33
Endothelium, 60 (I)
Energy level, see Trophic level
Enopla, 112 (Nemertea)
Enteric canal, see Alimentary canal
Enterocrinin, 106
Enterokinase, 108 (Intestinal juice)
Entire (leaves), 22
Environment, 4 (I)
Internal, 105 (Homeostasis)
Enzymes, 68 (Digestive glands), 103, 108
Digestive, 103 (Enzymes), 108
Respiratory, 103 (Enzymes)
Ephemeral, 8
Epicarp, 34 (I)
Epidermis,
(humans), 82, *83*
(plants), 15
Epididymis (pl. epididymides), *88*
Epigeal, 33
Epiglottis, 66 (Pharynx), *70*
Epigynous flower, 29
Epimysium, *54*
Epinephrin, see Adrenalin
Epineurium, *78*
Epiphytes, 114
Epithelium, 82 (Epidermis)
Equisetales, 111 (Chart 1)
ER, see Endoplasmic reticulum
Rough, 11 (Endoplasmic reticulum)
Smooth, 11 (Endoplasmic reticulum)
Erectile tissue, 88 (Penis), 89 (Vulva)
Erythrocytes, see Red blood cells
Eucestoda, see Cestoidea
Euglenophyta, 110
Eukaryotic, 111 (Note 1)
Eumycophyta/Eumycota, 110
Eustachian tube, *86*
Eutheria, 113 (Prototheria)
Evergreen, 8
Evolutionary adaptation, see Adaptive radiation
Excretion, 45, 72 (I)
Exhalant siphon, 44 (Siphon)
Exhalation, see Expiration
Exocrine glands, 68
Exodermis, 17 (Piliferous layer)
Exopteryogotes, 49 (Incomplete metamorphosis)
Exoskeleton, 38 (I)
Expiration, 71
Extensors, 55 (Skeletal muscles)
External auditory canal, see Ear canal
External ear, see Outer ear
External fertilization, 48 (Oviparous)
External gills, 45
External jugular veins, *62*
External respiration, 70 (I)
External urinary sphincter, 72 (Bladder), *73*
Extrinsic eye muscles, 85
Eye(s), 84-85
Compound, 47
Eyeball, 84 (I)

Eye muscles,
Extrinsic, 85
Intrinsic, *84* (Ciliary body)
Eye teeth, see Canines

Facet,
(bones), *51*
(compound eyes), *47*
Facial bones, 50 (Cranium)
Faeces, 67 (Large intestine)
Fallopian tubes, *89*, *91* (Fertilization)
False fruit, 34 (I)
False ribs, 50 (Rib cage)
Families, 110 (I)
Fascicles,
(muscles), 54 (Striated muscle)
(nerves), *78*
Fats, 67 (Small intestine), 65 (Lymph), 100, 101, 108
Fatty acids, 100 (Fats), 108 (I, Pancreatic juice)
Feather(s), 39
Contour, 39 (Feathers)
Down, 39
Flight, see Remiges
Primary, 39 (Remiges)
Secondary, 39 (Remiges)
Feather follicles, 39
Feedback, 105 (Homeostasis)
Negative, 105 (Homeostasis)
Femoral arteries, *61*
Femoral veins, *61*
Femur, *51, 52, 53*
Fenestra ovalis, see Oval window
Fenestra rotunda, see Round window
Ferns, see Filicales
Fertilization, 92 (Sexual reproduction)
(animals), 48
External, 48 (Oviparous)
(flowering plants), 30
(humans), 91
Internal, 48 (Viviparous)
Fibres, 14 (Xylem)
Muscle, 54 (Striated muscle)
Nerve, 76
Spindle, 13 (Metaphase)
Fibrils, 54 (Striated muscle)
Fibrin, 59 (Clotting)
Fibrinogen, 59 (Clotting)
Fibrous roots, 17
Fibula, *51, 53*
Filament(s),
Gill, 45 (Internal gills)
(muscles), 54 (Striated muscle)
(plants), 28 (Stamens)
Filicales, 111 (Chart 1)
Filter-feeding, 42
Fimbriae, *89*
Fin(s), 41
Anal, 41 (Median fins)
Caudal, 41 (Median fins)
Dorsal, 41 (Median fins)
Median, 41
Paired, 41
Pectoral, 41 (Paired fins)
Pelvic, 41 (Paired fins)
Ventral, *41*
First meiotic division, 94 (Meiosis)
First order consumers, see Primary consumers
First order sensory neuron, *78, 81*
First polar body, 95 (Gamete production, female)
Fixed joints, 52 (I)

Fixed macrophages, 58 (White blood cells)
Flagella (sing, flagellum), 40
Flagellata, see Mastigophora
Flagellate, 40 (Flagella)
Flame cells, 45 (Nephridia)
Flexion, 55 (Skeletal muscles)
Flexors, 55 (Skeletal muscles)
Flight feathers, see Remiges
Floating ribs, 50 (Rib cage)
Florets, 31 (Flowerhead)
Disc, 31
Ray, 31
Florigen, 23 (Photoperiodism)
Flower(s), 28-29
Bell, 31
Composite, see Flowerhead
Epigynous, 29
Hypogynous, 29
Lipped, 31
Pea, 31
Perigynous, 29
Spurred, 31
Flowerhead, 31
Foetus, 91 (Pregnancy)
Foliage, 20 (I)
Folic acid, 109 (Vitamin B complex)
Follicle(s),
Feather, 39
Graafian, 89 (Ovarian follicles), 90 (Menstrual cycle)
Hair, 82
Ovarian, 89, 107 (FSH, LH, Oestrogen)
Follicle-stimulating hormone, see FSH
Food chains, 6 (Food web)
Food vacuole, *40*
Food web, 6
Foramen (pl. foramina),
Invertebral, *51*
Vertebral, 50 (Vertebrae)
Foreskin, *88*
Fossil fuels, 7
Fovea/Fovea centralis, 85 (Macula lutea)
Fronds, 111 (Filicales)
Fructose, 108 (Intestinal juice), 109 (Monosaccharides)
Fruit, 34
False, 34 (I)
Key, see Samara
True, 34 (I)
FSH, 106
FSHRF/FSH releasing factor, 106 (Regulating factors)
Fungi (sing. fungus), 92, 110 (Eumycophyta), 111 (Note 3)
Funicle, 29 (Ovaries)
Fusion, 92 (Sexual reproduction)

Galactose, 108 (Intestinal juice), 109 (Monosaccharides)
Gall bladder, 69, 107 (CCK)
Gametes, 93, 94, 95
Gametophyte, 93 (Alternation of generations)
Ganglia (sing. ganglion), *78*
Autonomic, *81*
Gastric artery, *61*
Gastric glands, 68 (Digestive glands), 108 (Gastric juice)
Gastric juice, 107 (Gastrin), 108
Gastric lipase, 108 (Gastric juice)
Gastric vein, *61*
Gastrin, 107

119

Gastroesophageal sphincter,
see **Cardiac sphincter**
Gastrointestinal tract, see
Alimentary canal
Gastropoda/Gastropods,
112 (**Mollusca**)
Gastrotricha,
112 (**Aschelminthes**)
Gause's principle, 5 (**Ecological
niche**)
Gemmation, 92
Genera, 110 (**I**)
Generative nucleus, 30 (**Pollen**)
Genes, 97
Sex-linked, 98 (**Sex linkage**)
Genetics, 96 (**I**)
Genital organs/Genitalia, 88 (**I**)
Genotypes, *97*
Geotropism, 23
Germ cells, see **Gametes**
Germination, 32
Gestation, see **Pregnancy**
Gestation period, 91 (**Pregnancy**)
Gibberellins, 23 (**Growth
hormones**)
Gill(s), 45
External, 45
Internal, 45
Gill bar/arch, 45 (**Internal gills**)
Gill filaments, 45 (**Internal gills**)
Gill lamellae (sing. lamella),
45 (**Internal gills**)
Gill rakers, *45*
Gill slits, 45 (**Internal gills**)
Gingiva, see **Gum**
Ginkgoales/Ginkgophyta,
111 (**Charts 1 and 2**)
Gizzard, 43
Gland(s), 68-69
Adrenal, 69, 107
Bulbourethral, see
Cowper's glands
Ceruminous, 86 (**Outer ear**)
Cowper's, *88*
Digestive, 68, 108
Endocrine/Ductless, 69
Exocrine, 68
Gastric, 68 (**Digestive glands**),
108 (**Gastric juice**)
Intestinal, 68 (**Digestive
glands**), 108 (**Intestinal juice**)
Lachrymal, 85
Lymph, see **Lymph nodes**
Mammary, *90*, 107 (**Oestrogen**)
Mucous, 67 (**Mucous
membrane**)
Parathyroid, 69, 107 (**PTH**)
Parotid, *68*
Pineal, 69
Pituitary, 69, *75*,
106 (**Hormones**), 107
Prostate, *88*
Salivary, 68 (**Digestive glands**),
108 (**Saliva**)
Sebaceous, 82
Silk, *37*
Sublingual, *68*
Submandibular/
Submaxillary, *68*
Suprarenal, see
Adrenal glands
Sweat/Sudoriferous, 83
Tear, see **Lachrymal glands**
Thymus, 65
Thyroid, 69, 107 (**TSH**,
Thyroxin, TCT)
Uropygial, *39* (**Uropygium**)
Glans, *88*
120 Glia, see **Neuroglia**

Gliding joints, 52
Glomerular filtrate,
72 (**Glomerular filtration**)
Glomerular filtration, 72
Glomerulus, *72*, 73
Glottis, 70 (**Larynx**)
Glucagon, 106
Glucose, 100 (**Carbohydrates**),
101, 104 (**Anaerobic
respiration**), 108 (**Intestinal
juice**), 109 (**Monosaccharides**)
Glycerol, 100 (**Fats**), 108 (**I,
Pancreatic juice**)
Glycogen, 101, 108 (**Saliva**),
109 (**Polysaccharides**)
Glycolysis, 104 (**Anaerobic
respiration**)
Gnathostomata, 113 (**Note 9**)
Gnetales/Gnetophyta,
111 (**Charts 1 and 2**)
Golgi complex/apparatus/body, 11
Gonadal arteries, *61*
Gonadal veins, *61*
Gonads, 88 (**I**)
Gordiacea, see **Nematomorpha**
Graafian follicle, 89 (**Ovarian
follicles**), 90 (**Menstrual
cycle**)
Grafting, 35
Grain, 34
Granular layer, see
Stratum granulosum
Grassland (biome), 4
Temperate, 4 (**Biomes**)
Great saphenous veins, *61*
Grey matter, 75 (**Neuroglia**)
Gristle, see **Cartilage**
Growing point (roots), 16, *17*
Growth hormone(s),
Human, see **STH**
(plants), 23
Growth regulators, see
Growth hormones (plants)
Grub, *49* (**Larva**)
Guanine, 96
Guard cells, 21
Gullet, see **Oesophagus**
Gum, 56 (**I**)
Gustatory pore, *79*
Gustatory sensations,
79 (**Tongue**)
Gut, see **Alimentary canal**
Guttation, 25
Gymnospermae/Gymnosperms,
111 (**Charts 1 and 2**)
Gynaecium, 29

Habitat, 5
Haemocoel, 37
Haemoglobin, 58 (**Red blood
cells**)
Haemopoiesis, 58 (**I**)
Hair erector muscles, 82
Hair follicles, 82
Hair plexuses, 83
Halophytes, 114
Haltères, *47*
Hammer, see **Malleus**
Haploid number, 94 (**Meiosis**),
98 (**I**)
Haptotropism, 23
Hard palate, *79*
Haustra (sing. haustrum), *66*
Haversian canals, 53 (**Bone**)
Heart, *60*, 62-63
Heartwood, 14 (**Xylem**), 19
Heat-losing centre,
105 (**Homeostasis**)

Heat-promoting centre,
105 (**Homeostasis**)
Heliotropism, 23 (**Phototropism**)
Henlé,
Loop of, 73 (**Uriniferous
tubules**)
Hepaticae, 111 (**Chart 1**)
Hepatic artery, *61*
Hepatic ducts, *68*
Hepatic portal vein, *61*,
68 (**Liver**)
Hepatic vein, *61*
Herbaceous, 8
Herbaceous perennials,
8 (**Perennials**)
Herbivores, 6 (**Primary
consumers**)
Hermaphrodite, 28 (**I**),
49 (**Spermatheca**)
Heterografting, 35 (**Grafting**)
Heterozygous, *97*
HGH, see **STH**
Hibernation, 9 (**Dormancy**)
Higher animal, 36 (**I**)
Hilum,
(lungs), 71 (**Bronchi**)
(seeds), 33
Hinge joints, 52
Hip girdle, see **Pelvis**
Histones, 96 (**Chromosomes**)
Holdfast, 110 (**Phaeophyta**)
Homeostasis,
75 (**Hypothalamus**), 105,
106 (**Hormones**)
Homiothermic,
105 (**Homeostasis**)
Homografting, 35 (**Grafting**)
Homologous chromosomes,
12 (**Mitosis**), 94, 95,
96 (**Chromosomes**), 98 (**Law
of segregation**)
Homozygous, *97*
Honey guides, 28 (**Nectaries**)
Hormone(s), 69 (**Endocrine
glands**), 106-107
Adrenocorticotropic, see
ACTH
Antagonistic, 106
Anti-diuretic, see **ADH**
Follicle-stimulating, see **FSH**
Growth (plants), 23
Human growth, see **STH**
Interstitial cell stimulating,
see **LH**
Lactogenic, 106
Luteinizing, see **LH**
Parathyroid, see **PTH**
Sex, 69 (**Pineal gland**),
106 (**Oestrogen,
Progesterone, Androgens**)
Somatotropic, see **STH**
Thyroid-stimulating, see **TSH**
Tropic, 69 (**Pituitary gland**)
Hornworts, see **Anthocerotae**
Horny layer, see
Stratum corneum
Horsetails, see **Equisetales**
Hosts, 114 (**Parasites**)
Human growth hormone, see
STH
Humerus, *51*, *54*
Humour,
Aqueous, *84*
Vitreous, *84*
Hydathodes, 25 (**Guttation**)
Hydrochloric acid, 108 (**Gastric
juice**)
Hydrocortisone, 106
Hydrophytes, 114

Hydrostatic skeleton, 37 (Body cavities)
Hydrotropism, 23
Hymen, 89
Hypertonic, 99
Hyphae, 110 (Eumycophyta)
Hypogeal, 32
Hypogynous flower, 29
Hyponome, 44 (Siphon), 47
Hypopharynx, 43
Hypophysis, see Pituitary gland
Hypothalamus, 75,
    105 (Homeostasis),
    106 (Hormones),
    107 (Oxytocin, ADH)
Hypotonic, 99

ICSH, see LH
Ileum, 66, 67 (Small intestine)
Ilium, 51 (Pelvis)
Imago, 49
Impacted, 57 (Wisdom teeth)
Implantation, 91 (Fertilization)
Incisor(s), 56, 57
    Central, 57
    Lateral, 57
Incomplete dominance (genes), 97
Incomplete metamorphosis, 49
Incus, 86 (Middle ear)
Indehiscent, 32
Independent assortment,
    Law of, 98
Inferior (ovary), 29 (Epigynous flower)
Inferior articular processes, 50
Inferior mesenteric artery, 61
Inferior mesenteric vein, 61
Inferior vena cava, 61, 62, 63
Inflorescence, 31
Infraclasses, 110 (I)
Infundibulum, 89
Ingestion, 66 (I)
Inhalant siphon, 37 (Mantle siphon), 44 (Siphon)
Inhalation, see Inspiration
Inheritance, 96 (I)
Inhibiting factors,
    106 (Regulating factors)
Inner ear, 86, 87
Inner labia, see Labia minora
Insecta, 112 (Arthropoda)
Insectivores, 114
Insects, see Insecta
Inspiration, 71
Insulin, 105 (Homeostasis), 106
Integumentary system, 82 (I)
Integuments, 30 (Ovule), 33 (Testa)
Intercellular fluid, see Tissue fluid
Intercostal muscles, 71 (Inspiration)
Internal ear, see Inner ear
Internal environment, 105 (Homeostasis)
Internal fertilization, 48 (Viviparous)
Internal gills, 45
Internal jugular veins, 62
Internal respiration, 27 (Photosynthesis), 70 (I), 104
Internal urinary sphincter, 72 (Bladder), 73
Interneurons, see Association neurons
Internode, 16
Internuncial neurons, see Association neurons

Interphase, 13, 95 (Telophase)
Interstitial cells, 88, 107 (Androgens)
Interstitial cell stimulating hormone, see LH
Interstitial fluid, see Tissue fluid
Intervillous spaces, 91
Intestinal glands, 68 (Digestive glands), 108 (Intestinal juice)
Intestinal juice, 107 (Enterocrinin), 108
Intestine,
    Large, 66, 67
    Small, 66, 67
Intrinsic eye muscles, 84 (Ciliary body)
Invertase, see Sucrase
Invertebral discs, 50 (Vertebrae), 51
Invertebral foramen, 51
Invertebrates, 46 (Statocysts), 47 (Setae), 49 (Spermatheca, Metamorphosis), 113 (Note 8)
Involuntary actions, 81
Involuntary muscles, 54 (I), 55 (Cardiac muscle, Visceral muscles)
Iris, 84
Irritability, see Sensitivity
Ischium, 51 (Pelvis)
Islets of Langerhans, 68 (Pancreas)
Isotonic, 99
Ivory, see Dentine

Jejunum, 66, 67 (Small intestine)
Joints, 52-53
    Ball-and-socket, 52
    Cartilaginous, 53 (Cartilage)
    Fixed, 52 (I)
    Gliding, 52
    Hinge, 52
    Pivot, 50
    Plane/Sliding, see Gliding joints
    Synovial, 53 (Synovial sac)
Jugular veins,
    External, 62
    Internal, 62

Karyokinesis, 12 (Cell division)
Karyolymph, see Nucleoplasm
Keel,
    (animals), 41 (Pectoralis muscles)
    (plants), 31 (Pea flower)
Keratin, 39 (Feathers), 82 (Stratum corneum, Hair follicles)
Kernel, see Grain
Key fruit, see Samara
Kidneys, 61, 72
Kilocalories, 103 (Calories)
Kilojoules, 103 (Calories)
Kingdoms, 110 (I)
Kinorhyncha, 112 (Aschelminthes)
Kneecap, see Patella
Krill, 42 (Filter-feeding)

Labia (sing. labium),
    (humans), 89 (Vulva)
    Inner, see Labia minora
    (insects), 43
    Outer, see Labia majora
Labia majora, 89
Labia minora, 89

Labium, see Labia
Labour, 91 (Pregnancy)
Labrum, 43
Lachrymal canals, 85 (Lachrymal glands)
Lachrymal ducts, 85 (Lachrymal glands)
Lachrymal glands, 85
Lactase, 108 (Intestinal juice)
Lacteals, 65 (Lymph vessels), 67 (Small intestine)
Lactic acid, 104 (Oxygen debt)
Lactogenic hormone, 106
Lactose, 108 (Intestinal juice), 109 (Disaccharides)
Lacunae (sing. lacuna), 52 (Bone), 53
Lamella, see Lamellae
Lamellae (sing. lamella), (bone), 53
    Gill, 45 (Internal gills)
    Middle, 13 (Cytokinesis)
Lamellibranchiata/ Lamellibranchs, 112 (Mollusca)
Lamina, 20 (I)
Langerhans,
    Islets of, 68 (Pancreas)
Large intestine, 66, 67
Larva (pl. larvae), 49
Larynx, 47 (Syrinx), 70
Lateral, 16
Lateral bud, see Axillary bud
Lateral incisors, 57
Lateral lines, 46
Lateral roots, 17 (Tap root)
Late wood, see Summer wood
Law of independent assortment, 98
Law of segregation, 98
Leaflets, 20 (I), 22 (I)
Leaf scar, 21 (Abscission layer)
Leaf trace, 21
Leaves, 20-22
    Compound, 20 (I), 22
    Scale, 34 (Bulb)
    Simple, 20 (I)
Lecithin, 109 (Vitamin B complex)
Legume, 34
Leguminous plants, 7 (Nitrogen fixation)
Lens (eyes), 84
Lenticels, 19
Leucocytes, see White blood cells
Leucoplasts, 12 (Plastids)
LH, 106
LHRF/LH releasing factor, 106 (Regulating factors)
Lichens, 114 (Symbionts)
Lieberkühn,
    Crypts of, see Intestinal glands
Life cycle, 8 (I)
Ligament(s), 52
    Ovarian, 89
    Periodontal, 56 (Root)
    Suspensory, 84 (Lens)
Lignin, 15 (Vessels)
Lingual, 79
Lingual flower, 31
Lingual tonsil, 65 (Tonsils)
Lipases, 108 (I)
Lipped flower, 31
Lithophytes, 114
Littoral, 114
Liver, 61, 66 (I), 68
Liverworts, see Hepaticae
Lobed (leaves), 22
Lobe(s),
    Anterior (pituitary gland), 69

121

Lobe(s) (cont'd)
(leaves), 22 (Lobed)
(liver), 68, 69
Posterior (pituitary gland), 69
Locus, 97
Long-day plants,
23 (Photoperiodism)
Loop of Henle,
73 (Uriniferous tubules)
Lower animal, 36 (I)
Lower motor neuron, 80, 81
Lumbar, 51 (Lumbar vertebrae)
Lumbar vertebrae, 51
Lung books, 44
Lungs, 61, 70
Luteinizing hormone/
Luteotropin, see LH
Lycopodiales/Lycophyta,
111 (Charts 1 and 2)
Lymph, 65
Lymphatic(s), 65 (Lymph
vessels)
Lymphatic organs, see
Lymphoid organs
Lymphatic system (humans), 65
Lymphatic tissue, see
Lymphoid tissue
Lymphatic vessels, see
Lymph vessels
Lymph capillaries, 65 (Lymph
vessels)
Lymph glands, see
Lymph nodes
Lymph nodes, 65
Lymphocytes, 58 (White blood
cells), 65 (Lymphoid organs)
Lymphoid organs, 65
Lymphoid tissue, 65 (Lymphoid
organs)
Lymph vessels, 65
Lysosomes, 11

Macrohabitat, 4 (Biomes)
Macrophages, 58 (White blood
cells)
Fixed, 58 (White blood cells)
Wandering, 58 (White blood
cells)
Macula (pl. maculae),
87 (Saccule)
Macula lutea, 85
Maggot, 49 (Larva)
Male nuclei, 30 (I, Pollen),
93 (Gametes), 95 (Gamete
production, male)
Malleus, 86 (Middle ear)
Malpighian corpuscles, see
Renal corpuscles
Malpighian layer, see
Stratum basale
Malpighian tubules,
37 (Haemocoel), 45
Maltase, 108 (Intestinal juice)
Maltose, 108 (Pancreatic juice)
Mammalia/Mammals,
41 (Pectoralis muscles),
43 (Rumen), 47 (Vibrissae),
113 (Chordata, Note 11)
Mammary glands, 90,
107 (Oestrogen)
Mandible(s),
(arthropods), 43
(birds), 39
(humans), 50, 51
Mantle,
(birds), 39
(snails, etc), 37 (Mantle cavity)
Mantle cavity, 37

Mantle siphon, 37
Maquis, 4
Margin, 20, 22
Marrow,
Bone, 53
Red, 53 (Bone marrow)
Yellow, 53 (Bone marrow)
Marrow cavities, see
Medullary cavities
Marsupiala/Marsupials, see
Metatheria
Marsupium, 113 (Metatheria)
Mastigophora, 112 (Protozoa)
Matrix, 52 (Connective tissue)
Maxillae (sing. maxilla),
(arthropods), 43
(humans), 50 (Cranium)
Median/Medial, 41
Median fins, 41
Medulla,
(adrenal glands), 69
(brain), 75
(kidneys), 72
(plants), see Pith
Renal, see Medulla (kidneys)
Medulla oblongata, see
Medulla (brain)
Medullary cavities, 53 (Bone
marrow)
Medullary pyramids, see
Renal pyramids
Meiosis, 94
Meiotic division,
First, 94 (Meiosis)
Second, 94 (Meiosis), 95
Meissner's corpuscles, 82
Melanin, 83
Membranous labyrinth,
86 (Inner ear)
Menaquinone, see Vitamin K
Mendel's laws, 98
Meninges (sing. meninx), 75
Menopause, 90 (Menstrual cycle)
Menstrual cycle, 90, 107 (FSH,
Oestrogen)
Menstruation, 90 (Menstrual
cycle)
Meristem, 16
Apical, 16 (Meristem)
Merostomata, 112 (Arthropoda)
Mesencephalon, see Midbrain
Mesenteric artery,
Inferior, 61
Superior, 61
Mesenteric vein,
Inferior, 61
Superior, 61
Mesenteries, 66 (Alimentary
canal)
Mesocarp, 34 (I)
Mesophyll, 20 (Spongy layer)
Mesophytes, 114
Mesozoa, 113 (Note 2)
Messenger RNA, 11 (Ribosomes)
Metabolic rate, 102
Basal, 102 (Metabolic rate)
Metabolism, 102
Metacarpals, 51
Metacarpus, 51 (Metacarpals)
Metameres, 36 (Segmentation)
Metameric segmentation/
Metamerism,
36 (Segmentation)
Metamorphosis, 49
Complete, 49
Incomplete, 49
Metaphase,
(meiosis), 94
(mitosis), 13

Metatarsals, 51
Metatarsus, 51 (Metatarsals)
Metatheria, 113 (Prototheria)
Metazoa, 112
Microhabitat, 5 (Habitat)
Micropyle, 30 (Ovules), 33
Microspora, 112 (Protozoa)
Microtubules, 12 (Centrioles)
Micturition, see Urination
Midbrain, 74, 75
Middle ear, 86
Middle lamella, 13 (Cytokinesis)
Midrib, 20 (Veins)
Midriff, see Diaphragm
Migration, 9
Milk teeth, see Deciduous teeth
Mimic, 9 (Mimicry)
Mimicry, 9
Minerals, 101
Mitochondria, 11, 12,
104 (Aerobic respiration)
Mitosis, 12
Mitral valve, 63 (Atrioventricular
valves)
Mixed nerves, 78 (Nerves)
Model, 9 (Mimicry)
Molars, 42 (Carnassial teeth), 57
Mollusca/Molluscs,
37 (Haemocoel, Mantle
cavity), 42 (Radula),
45 (Internal gills, Nephridia),
47 (Tentacles), 112
Monera, 111 (Note 1)
Monocotyledonae/
Monocotyledons,
33 (Cotyledon), 111 (Chart 1)
Monocytes, 58 (White blood
cells)
Monoecious, 28 (I)
Monogenoidea/Monogenea,
112 (Platyhelminthes),
113 (Note 3)
Monoplacophora,
112 (Mollusca)
Monosaccharides, 109
Monotremata, 113 (Prototheria)
Morula, 93 (Embryo)
Mosaic image, 47 (Compound
eye)
Mosses, 93, 111 (Musci)
Motor areas, 74 (Brain), 75
Motor end-plate, 55
Motor nerves, 78 (Nerves)
Motor neuron(s), 77, 80 (Efferent
system)
Lower, 80, 81
Postganglionic, 81
Preganglionic, 81
Upper, 80, 81
Motor root, see Ventral root
mRNA, see Messenger RNA
Mucosa, see Mucous membrane
Mucous glands, 67 (Mucous
membrane)
Mucous membrane, 67
Mucus, 67 (Mucous membrane)
Multicellular, 10 (I)
Musci, 111 (Chart 1)
Muscle(s), 54-55
Cardiac, 55
Extrinsic eye, 85
Hair erector, 82
Intercostal, 71 (Inspiration)
Intrinsic eye, 84 (Ciliary body)
Involuntary, 54 (I), 55 (Cardiac
muscle, Visceral muscles)
Oblique, 85
Pectoralis, 41
Rectus, 85

Muscle(s) (cont'd)
  Skeletal, 55, 80
  Visceral, 55
  Voluntary, 54 (I), 55 (Skeletal
    muscles)
Muscle (tissue), 54
  Cardiac, 55
  Smooth, 55
  Striated/Striped, 54
  Visceral, see Smooth muscle
Muscle fibres, 54 (Striated muscle)
Muscle spindle, 55
Mycelium, 92,
  110 (Eumycophyta)
Myelin, 75 (Neuroglia),
  76 (Nerve fibres)
Myofibrils, see Fibrils
Myofilaments, see
  Filaments (muscles)
Myosin, 54 (Striated muscle)
Myriapoda/Myriapods,
  36 (Segmentation),
  46 (Antennae), 113 (Note 5)
Myxini, 113 (Chordata, Notes 7, 9
  and 10)
Myxomycophyta/Myxomycota, 110

Nasal, 79
Nasal cavities, 66 (Pharynx),
  79 (Nose)
Nasolachrymal duct,
  85 (Lachrymal glands)
Natural selection,
  9 (Adaptive radiation)
Neck (teeth), 56
Nectar, 28 (Nectaries)
Nectaries, 28
Needles, 111 (Coniferales)
Negative feedback,
  105 (Homeostasis)
Negative tropism, 23 (I)
Nekton, 114 (Pelagic)
Nematocyst, 42 (Cnidoblasts)
Nematoda, 112 (Aschelminthes)
Nematomorpha,
  112 (Aschelminthes)
Nemertea, 112
Nephridia, 37 (Coelom), 45
Nephridiopore, 37,
  45 (Nephridia)
Nephrons, 72
Nerve(s), 78
  Cranial, 74 (Brain)
  Mixed, 78 (Nerves)
  Motor, 78 (Nerves)
  Optic, 84, 85
  Sensory, 78 (Nerves)
  Spinal, 74 (Spinal cord)
Nerve fibres, 76
Nervous system,
  Autonomic,
    75 (Hypothalamus), 80
  Central (humans), 74-75
  Peripheral, 76 (I), 78 (I)
Neural canal, 50 (Vertebrae)
Neural pathways, 78, 80, 81
Neural spine, see
  Spinous process
Neuroglia, 75
Neurohypophysis, see
  Posterior lobe
Neuron(s), 76 (I)
  Afferent, see Sensory neurons
  Association/Connecting, 77
  Efferent, see Motor neurons
  First order sensory, 78, 81
  Internuncial, see
    Association neurons

Lower motor, 80, 81
Motor, 77, 80 (Efferent system)
  Postganglionic motor, 81
  Preganglionic motor, 81
  Relay, see
    Association neurons
  Second order sensory, 78
  Sensory, 77, 78 (Afferent system)
  Third order sensory, 78
  Upper motor, 80, 81
Neurotransmitters,
  77 (Synapses),
  109 (Vitamin B complex)
Niacin, 109 (Vitamin B complex)
Niche,
  Ecological, 5
Nicotinamide/Nicotinic acid, see
  Niacin
Nitrate bacteria, 7
Nitrates, 7
Nitrifying bacteria, 7
Nitrites, 7
Nitrogen base, 96
Nitrogen cycle, 7
Nitrogen fixation, 7
Nitrogen-fixing bacteria,
  7 (Nitrogen fixation)
Nitrogenous, 73 (Urea)
Nocturnal, 114
Node(s),
  Lymph, 65
  (plants), 16
Node of Ranvier, 76
Nodules,
  Root, 7 (Nitrogen fixation)
Noradrenalin/Norepinephrin, 106
Nose, 79
Notochord, 113 (Chordata)
Nuclear membrane, 10 (Nucleus)
Nuclei, see Nucleus
Nucleic acids, 96
Nucleoli, 11, 12
Nucleoplasm, 10 (Nucleus)
Nucleotides, 96 (Nucleic acids)
Nucleus (pl. nuclei), 10,
  12 (Mitosis), 94 (Meiosis),
  96 (Chromosomes)
  Daughter, 13 (Telophase),
    94 (Meiosis)
  Generative, 30 (Pollen)
  Male, 30 (I, Pollen)
    93 (Gametes), 95 (Gamete
    production, male)
  Tube, 30 (Pollination)
Nuda, 112 (Ctenophora)
Nut, 34
Nutrients, 100 (I)
Nymph, 49

Oblique muscles, 85
Oddi,
  Sphincter of, 69, 107 (CCK)
Odontoid process, see
  Dens (vertebrae)
Oesophagus, 66, 67
Oestrogen, 106, 107 (FSH, LH)
Olfactory bulb, 79
Olfactory cells, 79 (Nose)
Olfactory hairs, 79 (Nose)
Olfactory sensations, 79 (Nose)
Omasum, 43 (Rumen)
Ommatidia (sing. ommatidium),
  47 (Compound eye)
Omnivores, 6
Onychophora, 112 (Arthropoda),
  113 (Note 4)
Ootid, 95 (Gamete production,
  female)

Operculum,
  (fish), 45 (Internal gills)
  (snails, etc), 37
Ophiuroidea,
  113 (Echinodermata)
Opposing pairs, see
  Antagonistic pairs
Opposite (leaves), 22
Optic, 85
Optic disc, see Blind spot
Optic nerve, 84, 85
Oral cavity, 66 (Pharynx), 79
Oral groove, 40
Orbit, 50, 84 (I), 85
Orders, 110 (I)
Organ, 10 (I)
Organelles, 11-12
Organism, 10 (I)
Organ of Corti, 86, 87 (Cochlear
  duct)
Osmosis, 99
Osmotic pressure, 99 (Osmosis)
Osseous tissue, see Bone
Ossicles,
  Ear/Auditory, 86 (Middle ear)
Ossification, 53 (Cartilage)
Osteichthyes, 38 (Scales),
  41 (Swim bladder),
  113 (Chordata, Note 10)
Osteoblasts, 52 (Periosteum)
Osteocytes, 52 (Bone), 53
Osteogenesis, see Ossification
Otoliths, 87 (Saccule)
Outer ear, 86
Outer labia, see Labia majora
Ova (sing. ovum), 48,
  89 (Ovaries), 90 (Menstrual
  cycle), 93 (Gametes),
  95 (Gamete production,
  female), 107 (FSH)
Oval window (ears), 86
Ovarian cycle, 90 (Menstrual
  cycle)
Ovarian follicles, 89, 107 (FSH,
  LH, Oestrogen)
Ovarian ligaments, 89
Ovaries,
  (humans), 89, 107 (Oestrogen)
  (plants), 29
Oviduct, 49
Oviparous, 48
Ovipositor, 49
Ovulation, 89 (Fallopian tubes),
  90 (Menstrual cycle), 107 (LH)
Ovules, 29 (Ovaries), 30
Oxidation, 104 (Aerobic
  respiration)
Oxygenated, 62 (Atria)
Oxygen debt, 104
Oxytocin, 106

Pacinian corpuscles, 83
Pain receptors, 83
Paired fins, 41
Palate,
  Hard, 79
  Soft, 66 (Pharynx), 79
Palatine tonsils, 65 (Tonsils)
Palisade cells, 20 (Palisade layer)
Palisade layer, 20
Palmate, 22
Palps, 46
Pancreas, 68, 69
Pancreatic amylase,
  108 (Pancreatic juice)
Pancreatic duct, 68 (Pancreas)
Pancreatic juice, 68 (Pancreas),
  106 (Secretin/PZ), 108

Pancreatic lipase, 108 (Pancreatic juice)
Pancreatic vein, *61*
Pancreozymin, see PZ
Pantothenic acid, 109 (Vitamin B complex)
Papillae (sing. papilla), *79*
Dermal, *82*
Paramecium, *40, 45*
Parapodia (sing. parapodium), 40
Parasites, 114
Parasympathetic division, 80
Parathormone/Parathyrin, see PTH
Parathyroid glands, 69, 107 (PTH)
Parathyroid hormone, see PTH
Parazoa, 112
Parenchyma, 15 (Cortex)
Parent cell, 12 (Cell division)
Parotid glands, *68*
Parturition, 91 (Pregnancy)
Passage cells, 15 (Endodermis)
Patella, *51, 52, 53*
Pathogenic, 110 (Schizophyta)
Pauropoda, 112 (Arthropoda), 113 (Note 5)
Pea flower, 31
Pectoral fins, 41 (Paired fins)
Pectoralis major, 41 (Pectoralis muscles)
Pectoralis minor, 41 (Pectoralis muscles)
Pectoralis muscles, 41
Pedicles, *50*
Peduncle, 28 (Receptacle)
Pelagic, 114
Pelecypoda, see Lamellibranchiata
Pelvic fins, 41 (Paired fins)
Pelvic girdle, see Pelvis (skeleton)
Pelvis, (kidneys), *72*
Renal, see Pelvis (kidneys)
(skeleton), *51*
Penis, 88, 91 (Copulation)
Pepsin, 108 (Gastric juice)
Pepsinogen, 108 (Note 2)
Peptidases, see Proteinases
Peptide links, 100 (Proteins), 108 (I)
Perennials, 8
Herbaceous, 8 (Perennials)
Woody, 8 (Perennials)
Perfoliate, 22
Perianth, *28*
Pericardial cavity, 62 (I)
Pericardial fluid, 62 (I)
Pericardial sac, 62 (I)
Pericardium, 62 (I)
Pericarp, 34 (I)
Periderm, 19 (New outer tissue)
Perigynous flower, 29
Perikaryon, see Cell body
Perilymph, 86 (Inner ear)
Perimysium, *54*
Perineurium, *78*
Periodontal ligament, 56 (Root)
Periosteum, 52
Peripheral nervous system, 76 (I), 78 (I)
Peristalsis, 67
Peritoneum, 37 (Coelom), 66 (Alimentary canal)
Perivisceral cavity, 37 (Body cavities)
Permanent dentition, 56 (I)
Permanent teeth, 56 (I)
Petals, 28
Wing, 31 (Pea flower)

Petiole, *20*
Phaeophyta, 110
Phagocytosis, 40 (Pseudopodium)
Phalanges (sing. phalanx), *51*
Pharyngeal tonsil, 65 (Tonsils)
Pharynx, 66
Phellem, 19
Phellogem, 19
Phenotypes, *97*
Pheromone, 47
Phloem, 14, *15,* 18 (Secondary thickening), *19*
Primary, *14* (Primary tissue)
Secondary, 18 (Secondary thickening)
Phosphate groups, 96, 105 (ADP)
Photoperiodism, 23
Photoperiods, 23 (Photoperiodism)
Photoreceptors, 85 (Retina)
Photosynthesis, 26-27
Phototropism, 23
Phycocyanin, 110 (Cyanophyta)
Phyla (sing. phylum), 110 (I)
Phylloquinone, see Vitamin K
Phytohormones, 106 (Hormones)
Phytoplankton, 114 (Plankton)
Pia mater, *75* (Meninges)
Pigments, 27
Piliferous layer, *16, 17*
Pineal gland/body, 69
Pinion, *39*
Pinna, see Pinnae
Pinnae (sing. pinna), (ears), *86* (Outer ear)
(leaves), *22* (Pinnate)
Pinnate, 22
Pinocytosis, 99
Pioneer community, *5*
Pisces, 113 (Note 10)
Pistil, see Carpel
Pistillate, 28 (I)
Pith, 15
Pituitary gland/body, 69, *75,* 106 (Hormones), 107
Pivot joint, 50 (Vertebrae)
Placenta, (humans), *91,* 107 (Oestrogen)
(plants), 29 (Ovaries)
Placentalia/Placental mammals, see Eutheria
Placoid scales, see Denticles
Plane joints, see Gliding joints
Plankton, 42 (Filter-feeding), 45 (Gill rakers), 114
Plantigrade, 41
Plant Kingdom, 110-111
Plasma, 58
Plasmalemma/Plasma membrane, see Cell membrane
Plasmolysis, 25
Plastids, *10,* 12
Platelets, 58
Platyhelminthes, 112, 113 (Notes 2 and 3)
Pleura, 70
Pleural cavity, 70 (Pleura)
Pleural fluid, 70 (Pleura)
Pleural membrane, see Pleura
Pleural sac, 70 (Pleura)
Plexuses, Hair/Root hair, 83
Plumage, 39 (Feathers)
Plumule(s), (birds), see Down feathers
(plants), 33

Pod, see Legume
Poikilothermic, 105 (Homeostasis)
Polar body, First, 95 (Gamete production, female)
Second, 95 (Gamete production, female)
Pollen, 28 (Stamens), 30, 95 (Gamete production, male)
Pollen sacs, 28 (Stamens)
Pollen tube, 30 (Pollination)
Pollination, 30
Cross, 31
Self, 31
Polypeptides, 100 (Proteins), 109
Polysaccharides, 109
Pome, 34
Pons/Pons Varolii, 74, *75*
Pore, *83*
Gustatory, *79*
Porifera, 112 (Parazoa)
Positive tropism, 23 (I)
Posterior cavity, *84* (Vitreous humour)
Posterior lobe (pituitary gland), 69
Postganglionic motor neuron, *81*
PR, see Lactogenic hormone
Predators, 114
Preganglionic motor neuron, *81*
Pregnancy, 91
Premolars, 42 (Carnassial teeth), ∮
Preoptic area, 105 (Homeostasis)
Prepuce, see Foreskin
Prey, 114 (Predators)
Priapulida, 112 (Aschelminthes)
Prides, 114 (Social)
Primaries, see Primary feathers
Primary auditory area, 75
Primary bronchi, *70, 71* (Bronchi)
Primary bud, 33 (Plumule)
Primary consumers, 6
Primary feathers, 39 (Remiges)
Primary gustatory area, 75
Primary olfactory area, 75
Primary phloem, *14* (Primary tissue)
Primary root, 17 (Tap root), 33 (Radicle)
Primary sex characters, 90 (Puberty)
Primary tissue, *14*
Primary visual area, 75
Primary xylem, *14* (Primary tissue)
Prime mover, see Agonist
Proboscis, *42,* 112 (Nemertea)
Procarboxypeptidase, 108 (Note 2)
Process(es), 50 (Vertebrae)
Inferior articular, *50*
Odontoid, see Dens (vertebrae)
Spinous, *50*
Superior articular, *50*
Transverse, *50*
Producers, 6
Progesterone, 90 (Menstrual cycle), 106, 107 (LH)
Prokaryota, 111 (Note 1)
Prokaryotic, 111 (Note 1)
Prolactin, see Lactogenic hormone
Propagation, Artificial, 35
Vegetative, see Vegetative reproduction
Prophase, (meiosis), **94**
(mitosis), **13**
Prop roots, 17
Prostate gland, 88

Protective adaptations,
9 (Adaptive radiation)
Proteinases, 108 (I)
Proteins, 100, 101, 108, 109
Catalytic, 100 (Proteins),
103 (Enzymes)
Structural, 100 (Proteins)
Prothrombin, 59 (Clotting),
109 (Vitamin K)
Protista, 111 (Note 2)
Protochordata/Protochordates,
113 (Note 6)
Protonema, 93
Protonephridia, 45 (Nephridia)
Protoplasm, 10
Prototheria, 113 (Chordata)
Protozoa, 111 (Note 2), 112
Proximal, 73
Proximal convoluted tubule,
73 (Uriniferous tubules)
Pseudopodium (pl.
pseudopodia), 40
Pseudotracheae, 42
Psilophyta/Psilotales,
111 (Charts 1 and 2)
Pteridophyta/Pteridophytes,
111 (Charts 1 and 2)
Pterophyta, 111 (Chart 2)
PTH, 106
Ptyalin, see Salivary amylase
Puberty, 90, 107 (Oestrogen,
Androgens)
Pubic hair, 90
Pubis, 51 (Pelvis)
Pudendum, see Vulva
Pulmonary, 63
Pulmonary arteries, 62,
63 (Pulmonary trunk)
Pulmonary trunk, 62, 63
Pulmonary valve, 63 (Semilunar
valves)
Pulmonary veins, 62, 63
Pulp, 56 (Pulp cavity)
Pulp cavity, 56
Pupa (pl. pupae), 49
Pupil, 84 (Iris)
Pycnogonida, 112 (Arthropoda)
Pyloric sphincter/valve/Pylorus,
66, 67
Pyramid(s),
Renal/Medullary, 72 (Medulla)
Pyramid of biomass, 6
Pyramid of numbers, 6
Pyridoxine, 109 (Vitamin B
complex)
Pyrrophyta, 110
Pyruvic acid, 104 (Anaerobic
respiration)
PZ, 106

Rachis, see Shaft (birds)
Radial symmetry, 36
Radiation,
Adaptive, 9
Radicle, 33
Radius, 51, 54
Radula, 42
Ranvier,
Node of, 76
Raptors, 114 (Predators)
Ray(s), 41 (Fins)
Ray florets, 31
Receptacle, 28
Receptors, 77 (Sensory
neurons), 79
Pain, 83
Recessive, 97 (Genes), 98 (Sex
linkage)

Rectrices (sing. rectrix), 39
Rectum, 66, 67 (Large intestine)
Rectus muscles, 85
Red blood cells/corpuscles, 58
Red marrow, 53 (Bone marrow)
Reduction division, see
First meiotic division
Reflex(es),
Cranial, 81 (Reflex actions)
Spinal, 81 (Reflex actions)
Reflex actions, 81
Reflex arc, 81 (Reflex actions)
Refraction, 84 (Lens)
Regulating factors, 106
Relay neurons, see
Association neurons
Releasing factor(s),
106 (Regulating factors),
FSH, see FSHRF
LH, see LHRF
Remiges (sing. remix), 39
Renal, 72
Renal arteries, 61, 72 (Kidneys)
Renal corpuscles, 72, 73
Renal cortex, see
Cortex (kidneys)
Renal medulla, see
Medulla (kidneys)
Renal pelvis, see Pelvis (kidneys)
Renal pyramids, 72 (Medulla)
Renal tubules, see
Uriniferous tubules
Renal veins, 61, 72 (Kidneys)
Rennin, 108 (Gastric juice)
Reproduction, 92-95
(animals), 48-49
Asexual, 92
(flowering plants), 28-31
(humans), 88-91
Sexual, 92
Vegetative, 34
Reproductive system (humans),
88-89
Reptilia/Reptiles, 38 (Scales),
48 (Eggs), 113 (Chordata,
Note 11)
Respiration,
Aerobic, 104
Anaerobic, 104
(animals), 44-45
Cellular, see
Internal respiration
External, 70 (I)
(humans), 70-71
Internal, 27 (Photosynthesis),
70 (I), 104
(plants), 26 (Compensation
points), 27 (Photosynthesis)
Tissue, see Internal respiration
Respiratory centre,
71 (Breathing), 75 (Medulla)
Respiratory enzymes,
103 (Enzymes)
Respiratory system (humans),
70-71
Reticulum, 43 (Rumen)
Endoplasmic, 11
Retina, 85
Retinol, see Vitamin A
Rhabdom, 47 (Compound eye)
Rhesus antigen, 59 (Rhesus
factor)
Rhesus factor, 59
Rhesus negative, 59 (Rhesus
factor)
Rhesus positive, 59 (Rhesus
factor)
Rh factor, see Rhesus factor
Rhizoids, 110 (Bryophyta)

Rhizome, 35
Rhizopoda, 113 (Note 1)
Rhodophyta, 110
Rhodopsin, 109 (Vitamin A)
Rhynchocoela, see Nemertea
Rib(s), 50 (Rib cage), 51
False, 50 (Rib cage)
Floating, 50 (Rib cage)
Rib cage, 50, 51
Riboflavin, 109 (Vitamin B
complex)
Ribonucleic acid, see RNA
Ribose, 96
Ribosomal RNA, 11 (Ribosomes)
Ribosomes, 11
Right lymphatic duct, 64,
65 (Lymph vessels)
RNA, 11 (Ribosomes),
96 (Nucleic acids)
Messenger, 11 (Ribosomes)
Ribosomal, 11 (Ribosomes)
Transfer, 11 (Ribosomes)
Rods, 85 (Retina)
Root(s)
Adventitious, 17
Aerial, 17
Dorsal, 74 (Spinal cord)
Fibrous, 17
(hairs), 83
Lateral, 17 (Tap root)
Motor, see Ventral root
(plants), 16-17
Primary, 17 (Tap root),
33 (Radicle)
Prop, 17
Secondary, see Lateral roots
Sensory, see Dorsal root
Tap, 17
(teeth), 56
Ventral, 74 (Spinal cord)
Root canals, 56 (Pulp cavity)
Root cap, 16, 17
Root hair(s), 16, 17
Root hair plexuses, see
Hair plexuses
Root nodules, 7 (Nitrogen
fixation)
Root pressure, 24
Rosette, 22
Basal, 22
Rotifera/Rotatoria,
112 (Aschelminthes)
Roughage, 101
Rough ER, 11 (Endoplasmic
reticulum)
Round window (ears), 86
Rugae (sing. ruga), 67 (Stomach),
69 (Gall bladder),
72 (Bladder), 73
Rumen, 43
Ruminants, 43
Rumination, 43
Runner, see Stolon

Saccharase, 108 (Intestinal juice)
Saccule/Sacculus, 86, 87
Sacral vertebrae, 51
Sacrum, 51 (Sacral vertebrae)
Saliva, 108
Salivary amylase, 108 (Saliva)
Salivary glands, 68 (Digestive
glands), 108 (Saliva)
Samara, 34 (Achene)
Saprophytes, 114
Sapwood, 19
Sarcodina, 112 (Protozoa),
113 (Note 1)
Sarcolemma, 54

125

Savannah (biome), 4
Scala tympani, *86*
Scala vestibuli, *86*
Scale(s),
  (animals), 38
  (conifers), 111 (Coniferales)
  Placoid, see Denticles
Scale leaves, 34 (Bulb)
Scaphopoda, 112 (Mollusca)
Scapula, *51, 54*
Scavengers, 114
Schizophyta/Schizomycophyta, 110
Schwann cells, 76 (Nerve fibres)
Scion, 35 (Grafting)
Sclera, *84*
Sclerites, 38 (Cuticle)
Sclerospongiae, 112 (Porifera)
Sclerotic coat, see Sclera
Sclerotin, 38 (Cuticle)
Scrotum, 88 (Testes)
Scuta (sing. scute or scutum), 38
Scutella (sing. scutellum), *39*
Scyphozoa, 112 (Coelenterata)
Sebaceous glands, 82
Sebum, 82 (Sebaceous glands)
Secondaries, see
  Secondary feathers
Secondary bronchi, *70,
  71* (Bronchi)
Secondary bud, see Axillary bud
Secondary consumers, 6
Secondary cortex,
  19 (Phelloderm)
Secondary feathers,
  39 (Remiges)
Secondary phloem,
  18 (Secondary thickening)
Secondary roots, see Lateral roots
Secondary sex characters,
  90 (Puberty),
  107 (Oestrogen, Androgens)
Secondary thickening, 18
Secondary tissue, 18 (I)
Secondary xylem, 18 (Secondary
  thickening)
Second meiotic division,
  94 (Meiosis), 95
Second order consumers, see
  Secondary consumers
Second order sensory neuron, 78
Second polar body, 95 (Gamete
  production, female)
Secretin, 106
Sedentary, 114
Seed-leaf, see Cotyledon
Seedling, 32 (Germination)
Seeds, 32-33
Segmentation, 36
  Metameric, 36 (Segmentation)
Segments, 36 (Segmentation)
Segregation,
  Law of, 98
Selectively-permeable, see
  Semipermeable
Self pollination, 31
Semen, 91 (Copulation)
Semicircular canals, *86, 87*
Semicircular ducts, *86, 87*
Semilunar valves, 63
Seminal fluid, 91 (Copulation)
Seminal vesicles, *88*
Seminiferous tubules,
  88 (Testes)
Semipermeable, *99*
Sense organs, 79
Sensitivity,
  (animals), 46-47
  (humans), 78 (I)
  (plants), 23

Sensory areas, 74 (Brain), 75
Sensory nerves, 78 (Nerves)
Sensory neuron(s), 77,
  78 (Afferent system)
  First order, *78, 81*
  Second order, *78*
  Third order, *78*
Sensory root, see Dorsal root
Sepals, 28
Serrate, 22
Serum, 59
Sessile, *20*, 114
Seta, see Setae
Setae (sing. seta),
  (animals), 47
  (simple plants),
  93 (Sporophyte),
  110 (Bryophyta)
Sex characters,
  Primary, 90 (Puberty)
  Secondary, 90 (Puberty),
  107 (Oestrogen, Androgens)
Sex chromosomes, 97, 98 (Sex
  linkage)
Sex hormones, 69 (Pineal gland),
  106 (Oestrogen,
  Progesterone, Androgens)
Sex linkage, 98
Sex-linked genes, 98 (Sex linkage)
Sexual intercourse, see
  Copulation
Sexual reproduction, 92
  (animals), 48 (I)
  (flowering plants), 30 (I)
  (humans), 90-91
Shaft,
  (feathers), *39*
  (bones), see Diaphysis
  (hairs), *83*
Shinbone, see Tibia
Shoot, 16
Short-day plants,
  23 (Photoperiodism)
Shoulderblade, see Scapula
Sieve plates, 15 (Sieve tubes)
Sieve tubes, 15
Silk gland, *37*
Simple leaves, 20 (I)
Sinews, see Tendons
Sinus(es), *79*
  Blood, 88 (Penis)
Siphon, 44
  Exhalant, 44 (Siphon)
  Inhalant, *37* (Mantle siphon),
  44 (Siphon)
  Mantle, *37*
Siphonopoda, see Cephalopoda
Skeletal muscles, 55, 80
Skeleton, 50-51
  Hydrostatic, 37 (Body cavities)
Skin, 38 (I), 82-83
Skull, see Cranium
Sliding joints, see Gliding joints
Slime moulds, see
  Myxomycophyta
Small intestine, 66, 67
Smooth ER, 11 (Endoplasmic
  reticulum)
Smooth muscle, 55
Social, 114
Soft palate, 66 (Pharynx), *79*
Solenocytes, see Flame cells
Solute, 99 (I)
Solutions, 99 (I)
Solvent, 99 (I)

Somatic afferent system, 79
Somatic efferent system, 80
Somatotropic hormone/
  Somatotropin, see STH

Specialization, 9 (Adaptive
  radiation)
Species, 110 (I)
Sperm, 48, 88 (Testes),
  91 (Copulation),
  93 (Gametes), 95 (I),
  107 (FSH)
Spermatheca, 49
Spermatids, 95 (Gamete
  production, male)
Spermatophyta/
  Spermatophytes, 111 (Charts
  1 and 2)
Spermatozoa (sing.
  spermatozoon), see Sperm
Spermatozooids, see Sperm
Sperm ducts, *88*
Sphenophyta. 111 (Chart 2)
Sphincter, 66
  Anal, 67 (Large intestine)
  Cardiac, 66, 67
  External urinary, 72 (Bladder), *73*
  Gastroesophageal, see
  Cardiac sphincter
  Internal urinary, 72 (Bladder), *73*
  Pyloric, 66, 67
Sphincter of Oddi, *69*, 107 (CCK)
Spinal canal, see Neural canal
Spinal column, see
  Vertebral column
Spinal cord, 74
Spinal nerves, 74 (Spinal cord)
Spinal reflexes, 81 (Reflex
  actions)
Spindle, 13 (Metaphase),
  94 (Metaphase)
  Muscle, 55
Spindle fibres, 13 (Metaphase)
Spine,
  (humans), see Vertebral column
  Neural, see Spinous process
  (plants), 21
Spinous process, *50*
Spiracle, 44
Spiral (leaves), 22
Spleen, 65
Splenic artery, *61*
Splenic vein, *61*
Spongy bone, *52, 53* (Bone)
Spongy cells, 20 (Spongy layer)
Spongy layer, 20
Sporangium, *92, 93*
Spores, 92 (Sporulation)
Sporophyte, *93* (Alternation of
  generations)
Sporozoa, 112 (Protozoa)
Sporulation, 92
Spring wood, 18 (Annual rings)
Spurred flower, 31
Spurs, 31 (Spurred flower)
Stamens, 28
Staminate, 28 (I)
Standard, 31 (Pea flower)
Stapes, 86 (Middle ear)
Starch, 101, 108 (Saliva),
  109 (Polysaccharides)
  Animal, see Glycogen
Statocysts, 46
Statoliths, 46 (Statocysts)
Stem(s),
  Brain, 75
  (plants), 16
Stensen's duct, *68*
Sternum, *41, 51*
STH, 106
Stigma, see Stigmata
Stigmata (sing. stigma),
  (animals), 44 (Spiracle)
  (flowers), 29, 30 (Pollination)

Stipule, 21
Stirrup, see Stapes
Stock, 35 (Grafting)
Stolon, 35
Stomach, 66, 67
Stomata (sing. stoma), 21
Strata, 82 (Epidermis)
Stratum basale, 82 (Stratum germinativum)
Stratum corneum, 82
Stratum germinativum, 82
Stratum granulosum, 82
Stratum spinosum, 82 (Stratum germinativum)
Striated, 54 (Striated muscle)
Striated muscle, 54
Stridulation, 47
Striped muscle, see Striated muscle
Structural proteins, 100 (Proteins)
Style (flowers), 29
Sub-classes, 110 (I)
Subclavian arteries, 61, 62
Subclavian veins, 61, 62, 65 (Lymph vessels)
Subcutaneous, 83 (Subcutaneous layer)
Subcutaneous layer, 82, 83
Suberin, 19 (Phellem)
Suberization, 19 (Phellem)
Sub-kingdoms, 110 (I)
Sublingual glands, 68
Submandibular glands/ Submaxillary glands, 68
Sub-phyla, 110 (I)
Succession, Ecological, 5
Successional community, 5
Succus entericus, see Intestinal juice
Sucrase, 108 (Intestinal juice)
Sucrose, 108 (Intestinal juice), 109 (Disaccharides)
Sudoriferous glands, see Sweat glands
Summer wood, 18 (Annual rings)
Superficial fascia, see Subcutaneous layer
Superior (ovary), 29 (Hypogynous flower, Perigynous flower)
Superior articular processes, 50
Superior mesenteric artery, 61
Superior mesenteric vein, 61
Superior vena cava, 62, 63
Suprarenal glands, see Adrenal glands
Suspensory ligament, 84 (Lens)
Sutures, 50 (Cranium)
Sweat, 83 (Sweat glands)
Sweat duct, 83 (Sweat glands)
Sweat glands, 83
Swim bladder, 41
Symbionts, 114
Symbiosis, 114 (Symbionts)
Symbiotes, see Symbionts
Sympathetic division, 80
Symphyla, 112 (Arthropoda), 113 (Note 5)
Synapses, 77
Synaptic cleft, 77 (Synapses)
Synaptic knob, 77
Synovial capsule, see Synovial sac
Synovial fluid, 53 (Synovial sac)
Synovial joints, 53 (Synovial sac)
Synovial membrane, 53 (Synovial sac)
Synovial sac, 53

Synthesis reactions, 102 (Anabolism)
Syrinx (pl. syringes), 47
System, 10 (I)
Systole phase, 63 (Cardiac cycle)

Tactile, 78
Tagma (pl. tagmata), 36 (Segmentation)
Tannin, 27 (Pigments)
Tap root, 17
Target cells, 106 (Hormones)
Target organs, 106 (Hormones)
Tarsals, 51
Tarsus, 51 (Tarsals)
Taste buds, 79 (Tongue)
Taxonomy, 110 (I)
Classical, 110 (I)
TCT, 106
Tear glands, see Lachrymal glands
Tectorial membrane, 86, 87 (Cochlear duct)
Teeth, 56-57.
Baby, see Deciduous teeth
Carnassial, 42
Deciduous, 56 (I)
Dog/Eye, see Canines
Milk, see Deciduous teeth
Permanent, 56 (I)
Wisdom, 57
Telophase, (meiosis), 95
(mitosis), 13
Telson, 46
Temperate grassland, 4 (Biomes)
Tendons, 53
Tendril, 21
Tentacles, 42 (Cnidoblasts), 47
Tentaculata, 112 (Ctenophora)
Terminal bronchioles, 71 (Bronchioles)
Terminal bud, 16
Ternate, 22
Territorial, 114
Territory, 114 (Territorial)
Tertiary bronchi, 70, 71 (Bronchi)
Tertiary consumers, 6
Testa, 33
Testes (sing. testis)/Testicles, 88, 90
Testosterone, 106 (Androgens)
Tetrad, 94 (Prophase)
Thalamus, 75
Thallophyta, 110
Thallus, 110 (Algae)
Theria, 113 (Prototheria)
Thiamine, 109 (Vitamin B complex)
Thighbone, see Femur
Thigmotropism, see Haptotropism
Third order consumers, see Tertiary consumers
Third order sensory neuron, 78
Thoracic duct, 64, 65 (Lymph vessels)
Thoracic vertebrae, 51
Thorax, 36 (Segmentation), 50 (Rib cage)
Thread cells, see Cnidoblasts
Thrombin, 59 (Clotting)
Thrombocytes, see Platelets
Thromboplastin, 59 (Clotting)
Thymine, 96
Thymus gland, 65
Thyrocalcitonin, see TCT
Thyroid gland, 69, 107 (TSH, Thyroxin, TCT)

Thyroid-stimulating hormone/ Thyrotropin, see TSH
Thyroxin, 106, 107 (TSH)
Tibia, 51, 52, 53
Tissue(s), 10 (I)
Tissue fluid, 64
Tissue respiration, see Internal respiration
Tocopherol, see Vitamin E
Tongue, 65, 79
Tonsil(s), 65
Lingual, 65 (Tonsils)
Palatine, 65 (Tonsils)
Pharyngeal, 65 (Tonsils)
Trabeculae (sing. trabecula), 52, 53 (Bone)
Trace elements, 101 (Minerals)
Trachea, see Tracheae
Tracheae (sing. trachea), (animals), 44
(humans), 70
(plants), see Vessels
Tracheoles, 44 (Tracheae)
Tracheophyta/Tracheophytes, 111 (Charts 1 and 2)
Trait, 97 (Genes)
Transfer RNA, 11 (Ribosomes)
Translocation, 24 (I)
Transpiration, 24
Transpiration stream, 24
Transverse processes, 50
Trematoda/Trematodes, 113 (Note 3)
Triaxonida, see Hexactinellida
Triceps, 54
Tricuspid valve, 63 (Atrioventricular valves)
Trifoliate, 22
tRNA, see Transfer RNA
Trophic level, 6
Tropic hormones, 69 (Pituitary gland)
Tropical forest (biome), 4
Tropism, 23 (I)
Negative, 23 (I)
Positive, 23 (I)
True fruit, 34 (I)
Trypsin, 108 (Pancreatic juice)
Trypsinogen, 108 (Note 2)
TSH, 106
Tube feet, 36
Tube nucleus, 30 (Pollination)
Tuber, 35
Tubular reabsorption, 73
Tubular secretion, 73
Tundra (biome), 4
Tunicata, see Urochordata
Turbellaria, 112 (Platyhelminthes)
Turgid, 25 (Turgor)
Turgor, 25
Turgor pressure, 25 (Turgor)
Tympanal organs/Tympani (sing. tympanum), 46
Tympanic canal, see Scala tympani
Tympanic cavity, see Middle ear
Tympanic membrane, see Eardrum

Ulna, 51, 54
Umbellifer, 31
Umbels, 31 (Umbellifer)
Umbilical cord, 91
Unguligrade, 41
Unicellular, 10 (I)
Uniramia, 112 (Arthropoda)
Univalves, 112 (Gastropoda)

Upper motor neuron, *80, 81*
Uracil, **96**
Urea, **73**
Ureters, **72**, *73, 88*
Urethra, *72, 73, 88, 91*
Urethral orifice, *73, 89*
Urinary bladder, see **Bladder**
Urinary sphincter,
  External, **72 (Bladder)**, *73*
  Internal, **72 (Bladder)**, *73*
Urinary system (humans), **72-73**
Urination, **73 (Urethra)**
Urine, **73**
Uriniferous tubules, **73**,
  107 **(ADH, Aldosterone)**
Urochordata, **113 (Chordata,**
  Note 6)
Uropygial gland, *39* **(Uropygium)**
Uropygium, *39*
Uterine tubes, see
  Fallopian tubes
Uterus, **89, 90 (Menstrual cycle),**
  107 (LH, Oxytocin,
  Oestrogen)
Utricle/Utriculus, *86, 87*

Vacuole(s), **10**, *11,*
  99 **(Pinocytosis)**
  Contractile, **40, 45**
  Food, *40*
Vagina, **89**, *91* **(Copulation)**
Vaginal orifice, *89*
Valve(s),
  Aortic, **63 (Semilunar valves)**
  Atrioventricular/AV, **63**
  Bicuspid, **63 (Atrioventricular**
    valves)
  Mitral, **63 (Atrioventricular**
    valves)
  Pulmonary, **63 (Semilunar**
    valves)
  Pyloric, see **Pyloric sphincter**
  Semilunar, **63**
  Tricuspid, **63 (Atrioventricular**
    valves)
Vane, *39*
Vascular bundles, **14 (Vascular**
  tissue)
Vascular cylinder, **18**
Vascular plants, **14-15**
Vascular system, see
  Circulatory system
Vascular tissue, **14**
Vas deferens (pl. **vasa**
  deferentia), see **Sperm ducts**
Vasopressin, see **ADH**
Vater,
  Ampulla of, *69*
Vegetative reproduction/
  propagation, **34**
Vein(s),
  (blood vessels), **60**
  Brachial, *61*
  Brachiocephalic, *62*
  Cephalic, *61*
  Common iliac, *61*
  External jugular, *62*
  Femoral, *61*
  Gastric, *61*
  Gonadal, *61*
  Great saphenous, *61*
  Hepatic, *61*
  Hepatic portal, *61, 68* **(Liver)**
  Inferior mesenteric, *61*
  Internal jugular, *62*
  (leaves), *20*
  Pancreatic, *61*
  Pulmonary, *62, 63*

Renal, *61, 72* **(Kidneys)**
Splenic, *61*
Subclavian, *61, 62, 65* **(Lymph**
  vessels)
Superior mesenteric, *61*
Vena cava (pl. **vena cavae**),
  Inferior, *61, 62, 63*
  Superior, *62, 63*
Venation, *20*
Venous system, **60 (Veins)**
Ventilation, **70 (I)**
Ventral, **41**
Ventral fin, *41*
Ventral root, **74 (Spinal cord)**
Ventricles,
  (brain), *75*
  (heart), **62**
Venules, **60 (Veins)**
Vertebrae (sing. **vertebra**), **50**, *51, 74*
  Cervical, *51*
  Coccygeal, *51* **(Coccyx)**
  Lumbar, *51*
  Sacral, *51*
  Thoracic, *51*
Vertebral canal, see **Neural canal**
Vertebral column, **50**, *51*
Vertebral foramen,
  50 (Vertebrae)
Vertebrata/Vertebrates,
  37 (Coelom),
  49 (Spermatheca),
  113 (Craniata, Notes 7 and 8)
Vessels,
  Blood, **60 (I)**
  Lymph, **65**
  Lymphatic, see **Lymph vessels**
  (plants), **15**
Vestibular canal, see
  Scala vestibuli
Vestibule, *86*
Vestigial, **67 (Appendix)**
Vibrissae (sing. **vibrissa**), *47*
Villi (sing. **villus**), **67 (Small**
  intestine)
  Chorionic, *91*
Viscera, **50 (I)**
Visceral afferent system, **79**
Visceral efferent system, see
  Autonomic nervous system
Visceral muscle (tissue), see
  Smooth muscle
Visceral muscles, **55**
Visual, **85**
Visual association area, **75**
Vitamin(s), **101, 109**
Vitamin A, **109**
Vitamin B complex, **109**
Vitamin C, **109**
Vitamin D, **82 (I), 109**
Vitamin E, **109**
Vitamin H, see **Biotin**
Vitamin K, **109**
Vitreous humour, *84*
Viviparous, **48**
Vocal cords, **70 (Larynx)**
Volkmann's canals, *53*
Voluntary actions, **80**
Voluntary muscles, **54 (I),**
  55 (Skeletal muscles)
Vulva, **89**

Wall pressure, **25 (Turgor)**
Wandering macrophages,
  58 (White blood cells)
Whalebone, **42 (Filter-feeding)**
Wharton's duct, *68*
Whiskers, see **Vibrissae**
White blood cells/corpuscles, **58**

White matter, **75 (Neuroglia)**
Whorl, see **Rosette**
Wilting, **25**
Windpipe, see **Trachea** (humans
Wing petals, **31 (Pea flower)**
Wirsung,
  Duct of, see **Pancreatic duct**
Wisdom teeth, **57**
Womb, see **Uterus**
Wood, **18 (Secondary thickening**
  Spring/Early, **18 (Annual rings**
  Summer/Late, **18 (Annual**
    rings)
Woody perennials,
  8 (Perennials)
Woody plant, **18 (I)**

Xanthophyll, **27 (Pigments),**
  110 (Xanthophyta)
Xanthophyta, **110**
X chromosomes, **97 (Sex**
  chromosomes), 98 (Sex
  linkage)
Xerophytes, **114**
Xylem, **14**, *15,* **18 (Secondary**
  thickening), *19, 24*
  Primary, *14* **(Primary tissue)**
  Secondary, **18 (Secondary**
    thickening)

Y chromosomes, **97 (Sex**
  chromosomes), 98 (Sex
  linkage)
Yellow marrow, **53 (Bone**
  marrow)
Yellowspot, see **Macula lutea**
Yolk, *48*
Yolk sac, *48* **(Yolk)**

Zona pellucida, **91 (Fertilization)**
Zone of elongation, **16**, *17*
Zooplankton, **114 (Plankton)**
Zygomorphy, **36 (Bilateral**
  symmetry)
Zygote, **30 (Fertilization),**
  91 (Fertilization), 93